Sun Valley Court

Sun Valley Court

Jane E. Griffioen

RESOURCE *Publications* • Eugene, Oregon

SUN VALLEY COURT

Resource Publications
An Imprint of Wipf and Stock Publishers
199 W. 8th Ave., Suite 3
Eugene, OR 97401

www.wipfandstock.com

PAPERBACK ISBN: 979-8-3852-4932-9
HARDCOVER ISBN: 979-8-3852-4933-6
EBOOK ISBN: 979-8-3852-4934-3
VERSION NUMBER 08/18/25

In the Best Interest of the Children

"... the wind, which bends the palms
and from time to time
tore the proudest trees out by the root,
the ones that do not bow their heads ..."

ISABELLA ALLENDE
SUM OF OUR DAYS

I know why moms run away to California. Pack a bag. Withdraw seven or eight hundred from the savings. Leave a note so no one suspects foul play.

After housecleaning in the spring, the kids go with me to drop off used clothes at the women's shelter downtown. A supervisor answers the door, never the ladies. They're in hiding. Hiding from drunks, or addicts, or men who steal the grocery money or beat them or their children. Hiding from their husbands.

That wasn't the kind of protection I needed.

One

An April afternoon warmed to the 70s. I opened all the windows upstairs before the school bus dropped Sam and Meike at the corner.

A breeze toyed with the pink canopy that matched the ruffled chiffon quilt spread over Meike's bed. She pulled out the bottom drawer of her white bureau, the kind with a mirror attached and rosettes painted on little ceramic pieces under the knobs.

Meike balanced on one bare foot, then the other. "Dad said I should just keep some PJs there."

"Well," I shrugged. "I suppose you can keep a pair there for now."

She rummaged in the drawer and found a pair of faded navy shorts. "Can I wear these?"

"That's fine, but you'll need overalls for tomorrow. And your sweatshirt." Folding both, I put them in her backpack along with PJs and three Care Bear undies. "We'll leave your Sunday dress on the hanger so it doesn't get wrinkled." I buttoned her little white cardigan over the top of the dress.

Meike pulled a Detroit Tiger shirt over her ponytail and adjusted the waistband of her knit shorts. Seven years ago when she was born, her hair had been dark brown like her dad's. The fluff of soft baby hair stuck up all over her little head until settling down into a loose, natural wave around her first birthday. By the time she was two, it grew out as blonde as Sam's and mine.

"Why don't you pick a few books from your shelf to bring while I see if your brother's ready."

A fever we get in Michigan at any hint of springtime had also caught Sam. Dressed in his shorts and t-shirt, he tied his tennis shoe, a foot up on his bunk-sized bed.

I reached out and messed his hair. "All set, pal?"

"What time's Dad coming?"

"Around six he said."

The very first weekend Walt took the kids, he came early. At my insistence, he stayed on the rug in the hallway while I finished gathering their things. He picked up Sam and Meike on Tuesdays as well. Weekend or weekday, when they were gone with their dad, emptiness echoed in my head, exploding through bedrooms, stairway, basement—invisible shrapnel piercing me like landmines under the carpeting.

"I want to take some Legos to Dad's." Sam opened the closet next to the Lego village he had constructed. He eyed the half-dozen jumbo tubs. We had separated reds into one, yellows in another, whites and blacks in another. One of the quart tubs held wheels and axles, another windows, another Lego people, another just clear pieces. "He said we could buy the helicopter set tonight."

"Oh." I pointed to the fresh laundered pile on his bed. "Let's put another pair of socks in here. And your jeans. We'll be back to cold weather tomorrow."

"We're going for pizza after we drop Odie at Dad's apartment."

Odie is the charcoal-gray schnauzer-poodle, our pet since we left the farm in 1985 and moved here. Sam and Mike helped pick him out of the litter when he was a puppy. He goes where they go.

Our two-story house was half a mile from school where Sam was in fourth grade and Meike in second. Walt rented his apartment just blocks from school in the other direction. Three weeks ago we sat around the kitchen table with chocolate-chip cookies and milk. I knew Walt planned to tell them. We had agreed on that part. We hadn't agreed on what to say.

"Tomorrow I'm moving away for a while," he started. "Not far. I have a little place that's close by Russell and Jody's on Coleman. It's your place, too."

Sitting on her knees in the oak dining chair, Meike set her cookie on her plate, got up and climbed on my lap. I rubbed her neck with my fingers while her clunky rubber tennis shoe bonked softly on the table leg. Her head rested on my chest.

"Why?" Sam asked. "Why are you going there? Why not live here?"

"It's not because of you guys. That's the first thing you should know." Walt ran a hand over his hair, avoided our eyes and looked out the window to the backyard. "Your mom and I just need a time-out."

They watched him with a confused look.

"And we're not getting what people call 'a divorce.' You don't need to worry about that," he said. "We're just going to be separate for a little while."

That's what he told them. And that's what he had told me.

Sam filled a tub of Legos halfway and snapped on the cover. He set it on the bed next to his backpack and his copy of *Big Red.* "Wanna shoot baskets 'til Dad comes?"

"Sure," I said. "Meike and I will be down in a minute."

The panging rhythm of the basketball Sam dribbled outside sounded up through Meike's window. I fit the books she'd chosen into her backpack and set it at the end of the hallway. After I hung her Sunday dress over the banister, we went out the front door. Odie watched through the screen.

An attached two-stall garage held the backboard and basketball hoop, the concrete driveway nearly as wide as it was deep. When he purchased his '75 Corvette, Walt built a third stall onto the garage and extended the concrete another eight feet along the north side to park the camper out of sight.

We're at the end of the cul-de-sac, so there are five driveways within the two-thirds circle. Our next-door neighbor on the north, Ike, drives a '63 Corvette. He took Sam, three years old at the time, for his first ride the spring we moved in, after Sam asked Ike's permission to "check the wheels."

Next door to the south, Doug and Judy Lynch live with their four children. They drive a van.

Sam's best friend, Matt VanderWilp, lives two more houses down. Matt's dad drives an old beat-up Camaro the entire neighborhood hears whenever he goes anyplace or comes home.

It is impossible for me to shoot baskets without a replay of that first afternoon after Walt left running through my head. Ike pulled into his yard that day and parked his Corvette in his driveway. "Almost!" he called as Sam's shot ricocheted off the rim. Minutes later, the van turned in next door. "Hey there!" We waved as Doug pushed aside the bicycle blocking his garage. Not five minutes more and the Camaro rumbled up the street. Matt's dad revved the engine a few times at the curb like he always did when he came home for the night.

That's when it must have hit Sam.

The picture is stuck in my head forever. Sam's face when he stopped dribbling, his arms gone limp, his heart in smithereens like a ceramic basketball all over the driveway.

Meike and I chased Sam until finally I slapped the ball, swiped it, and gave it to Meike. In two seconds, Sam stole it back and made a basket. When I rolled the ball to Meike again, she spread her legs apart and tossed it underhanded with an oomph. It landed on the roof, caught behind the backboard. Meike giggled behind her hands.

I tried to reach the ball with the handle of the push broom. "Guess we need the ladder," I told the kids.

The ladder hung from one of those stainless steel hooks coated in red plastic on the wall of the garage. Setting it to the left of the backboard, I climbed two steps with no intention of going higher. Using the broom handle, I poked from different angles but failed to move the ball one single inch. I handed the broom down just as Walt pulled in.

"Having a little trouble?" he laughed and climbed out of the pickup.

"Daddy!" Meike grabbed his leg like she was two years old again.

He hugged her back. "Hi ya, Meikie." He put an arm around Sam's shoulder. "Hi, bud."

Walt climbed the ladder and reached the ball without needing the broom. He dropped the ball through the basket. "Ready guys?"

"Gotta get my stuff," Sam said. He made a dash for the house, his sister close behind.

They missed their dad. I understood that. But even a little eagerness hurt.

I clipped the leash on Odie's collar and he yipped at the front door in anticipation.

One by one, I kissed the top of their heads while we hugged goodbye. I struggled to hold off my tears. I don't want the kids feeling lousy or responsible.

Sam took the end of Odie's leash, and Meike followed. I handed Walt the Lego tub and Meike's Sunday dress. He put the hanger on the window hook and the tub in the back seat next to Sam and Odie. Meike took the front.

The neighbors must notice, but it doesn't matter to me. I always stand in the driveway until the pickup reaches the end of the street and turns the corner out of sight. At least Sam and Meike can see me if they're watching.

Walt backed up slowly, braked, and rolled down his window. "Start taking the lithium yet?"

"None of your business," I answered.

Two

Meike's violin case and music stood forgotten in the corner of the den. I should have sent it with her. Three days without practice was not good. Walt would come back for it if I called, but I hesitated to interfere once the weekend started.

I sank into the oversized Barcalounger the kids and I gave Walt on Father's Day.

It would take some time before the tears stopped. I wasn't afraid of that.

Sometimes I allowed myself to manage the vacuum cleaner, load the dishwasher, or throw in a pile of laundry while tears ran down my face. If the kids were in school, I let this go on while I worked. If they were gone overnight with their dad, I just sat with it.

A murkiness huddled around me and lingered. I wasn't afraid of that either.

Daylight slid away, and the sky glowed pink before the room turned dim and the yard invisible. I watched the process, looking hard into it without moving until darkness laid a chill on me. I got up to check if all the doors were locked, put the classical music station softly on the radio, and grabbed the woven blanket from the couch.

Meike had her own bedroom at the apartment and Sam shared Walt's. Sam told me Walt slept on the couch and Odie wandered back and forth, finally settling with Sam. They kept the bedroom doors open and Meike called Odie up on her bed in the mornings, like at home.

When I released the wooden handle of the recliner, the footrest popped up. In daylight, the chair gave me a view through the sliding glass door to the backyard that fanned out in a wide, green lawn, and into the vacant field of grasses and wild saplings behind us, still untouched by development.

Spreading the blanket across my jeans, I pulled it over my arms. A couple of Dvorak's Slavonic Dances played. The tempo is fast, then slow, fast, then slow, alternating between the major and minor key—gay, then yearning. I pictured the women with headscarves, skipping to the ballad in the street with men. Everyone promenades, joyful for a minute, until they turn and remember how cold it is in the house and that Janko is dead and what little bread there is.

At nine o'clock, I heated a mug of water for tea and considered Walt's long-time expectation of a home-cooked meal on the table at six each day. These days, he often takes the kids out to eat or orders in a pizza.

With a handful of raisins and nuts, I brought my tea into the den and put the three-way lamp on low. The station switched to jazz. I sipped and listened. That had to be the local guy, Jim Palmer, doing the drum solo. My brother, Gerrit, and I had listened to a couple sets live at Doctor John's Tuesday night.

The radio announcer said something about Segovia, and I heard a Spanish guitar.

I ate a bowl of cereal with half of a banana sliced on it around eleven, wondering if the kids would have their HoneyNut Cheerios in the morning. Matt would call at the door for Sam, and I'd have to tell him he's at his dad's. Stacy would come around for Meike, and soon the whole neighborhood would know.

I set the bowl to soak in the sink, checked the door again, and went upstairs to brush my teeth and wash my face.

Kneeling properly, I prayed at the side of the bed like I have Sam and Meike do. I don't have a problem with lowliness before God. But I don't let Walt see me that humble.

I climbed in bed, my eyes wet and soon, the pillow damp. I knew God could keep Sam and Meike safe, but I didn't know if Walt would.

~

In the morning, I made myself go for a run. Regular exercise helps lessen bipolar's intensity, so I try to maintain a routine of fifteen miles a week. I've been jogging for years but lately slowed to an eleven-minute mile because lithium carbonate soaks up a good deal of my energy.

I zipped my sweatshirt, threw the hood up, pulled the sleeves over my bare hands and started out. I set my pace before the first block ended. Catching the rhythm of my footfall, I began to summarize to myself the sequence that led to my decision on lithium.

All through the past September and October during the hours when Sam and Meike were in school, I had spent my time writing the first draft of a manuscript I already hoped for years to publish.

During November, when the kids were in school, I often spent mornings at St. John's Lutheran Church, where I attended lately. The pastor had given me permission to use the grand piano in the sanctuary. I carried my favorite music pieces from home in a shoulder bag and played for hours at a time. After about three weeks of this schedule, the pastor kindly asked one morning if perhaps I should visit my doctor.

The first week of December, while speaking with Dr. Jennings, I let him in on my plan to sing a love song to Walt at his annual company Christmas party. Instead, Jennings prescribed complete bed rest. Not because I couldn't sing. I'd already rehearsed with a Manhattan Transfer cover group that played weekends at the prestigious downtown lounge where Walt had reserved the balcony for the evening party. The pianist remarked, "Lovely," and said he would call me on stage at the beginning of the second set.

But Jennings made me promise to stay away from the party. "I want to save you the embarrassment if Walt reacts unkindly," he explained.

During those weeks of bed rest, Walt's sister-in-law, Nancy, and a friend, Cindy, took turns arriving at our house a half an hour or so before Sam and Meike got home from school. They stayed until Walt got home from work. Until the week of Christmas, I "rested in bed" scribbling notes in a spiral notebook and playing quiet, soothing music from the cassette player on the nightstand. Sam and Meike came in our bedroom and filled me in on their day at school every afternoon. In the evenings we had bedtime story there, and afterward Walt tucked them in.

Once the holidays were over, I agreed to one of those eight-week plans where a person is officially admitted to the hospital but still went home each night. From nine to five Monday through Friday, I participated in the program. Mid-January, two weeks into the program, Dr. Jennings wrote out a discharge slip with the words "treatment not needed," and handed me a copy, which I politely folded and carried in my purse for the next five years.

Dr. Jennings recommended I meet with him each week for one-on-one therapy. At our first appointment, he introduced me to what DSM classified as Bipolar II. He suggested I consider taking lithium, the first time any reference to medication was ever made to me.

I hesitated.

Not six days later, Walt threatened to leave if I didn't start the lithium.

Dr. Jennings insisted that Walt was overreacting. "This is your decision, Jane," Jennings told me during our next appointment. "A choice you have. It's obvious to me the bipolar has receded. Sam and Meike are doing fine. They've started the second semester." He sat up straighter as if anyone could sit any straighter, and crossed his legs. "On the other hand, if another episode occurred, well . . . it takes a good week or so for the medication to take effect."

Jennings recognized my reluctance. "It's a natural chemical found in the earth," he said. "The effects of lithium are gradual. We don't know if an episode will reoccur but . . . give it some thought. The idea of lithium maintenance takes most people a while to get used to." He wrote a prescription and I kept it.

When I decided to begin lithium toward the end of January, I didn't tell anyone. I wanted to see if Walt could notice, and I wanted to make sure my taking it wasn't just to keep him around.

And now it was Sunday morning in April. The air was calm but nippy on my legs. Without any clouds, the sky expanded into an illustrious backdrop for spring. So many greens. Lawns and shrubbery, forsythia—a tinge of yellow remaining—treetops in celery-colored leaves, pollen brushed all over the asphalt.

The neighborhood was quiet, most people gone to church. With Sunday service already started, no one would notice me, but I took off in another direction anyway. Sam and Meike were inside the church.

Without me. I knew all too well what that salt-in-the-wound felt like and knew there would be nothing Christian about what I'd be thinking as I jogged by.

The first weekend Sam and Meike were with their dad, back in March, I started reading William Manchester's *The Last Lion: 1874-1932.* This morning after my run and a long hot shower, I decided to wait with *1932-1940* and instead, chose *Theology in Conflict*, by Gustaf Wingren from my bookshelf. Eighty some pages in, Gerrit called to invite me for dinner.

My brother, Gerrit, and his wife, Laura, live in town about twenty minutes from our place. After I'd been diagnosed with bipolar, Dr. Jennings thought a monitor of sorts might be a good idea. Since I no longer trusted Walt's judgment, Gerrit volunteered.

"Of course, you have to come around now and then," Gerrit teased.

The pug barked as I knocked on the front door of my brother's house and walked in. "Hey, Frank, no need to bark. It's me." I bent over and scruffed up the top of his head while he snorted in my other hand. The aroma of simmering beef roast came my way, summoning a memory of Sunday dinner on London Street, the neighborhood where Gerrit and I grew up.

"Hello," Laura greeted. "Don't mind Frank." She laughed, pushing him away with her foot so I could maneuver through the entryway.

"Come on in," Gerrit said from the living room.

We don't shake hands or hug or anything, but lately look each other in the eye for a few seconds until I nod once that I'm okay.

Laura is the only adult in the family smaller than I am, but then, she's an in-law. The fitness of her petite frame attests to faithful workouts. "Glass of wine?"

"Sure. Smells good in here. Can I help?"

"I pretty much have things under control. Why don't you and Gerrit have a seat and relax? Frank, get out of the way."

"Red okay?" Gerrit asked taking three stemmed glasses from the oak wine rack. He held the bottom of his cardigan with one hand to keep it from dragging in the sink.

Although people often assume the opposite, Gerrit is three years younger than I am. With his stocky build and thinning hair, he looks like our uncles on my mother's side. Gerrit teaches theology at a private college in town. I had audited a few night classes in Gerrit's department before Sam and Meike were born. Although Walt's father is a minister, Walt never appreciated my interest in systematic theology. I guess that for Walt, wives weren't supposed to seem smarter than their husbands.

Gerrit left Laura's wine on the counter and carried ours into the living room. He set a glass on a coaster on the end table next to the couch, where I made myself comfortable. Frank plunked down over my feet.

"Kids all right?"

"They seem to be." I picked up my glass and held it by the stem to admire the ruby tones. "And at school earlier this week I talked with their teachers again. They don't notice any difference in Sam or Meike. Well, Sam's teacher said he's a little quieter, but top of the class as usual. Meike doesn't talk any less and still gets her A's."

Gerrit chose "Rhapsody in Blue" from the CD tower and settled into the Sleepy Hollow, crossing his ankles on the ottoman. One of the things I appreciate about Gerrit and Laura is that they're not chatty people. For a few minutes, Gerrit and I quietly sipped our wine listening to Gershwin. And Frank snoring.

Laura announced dinner, and we sat down to whipped potatoes and gravy, beef roast, and fresh asparagus in the dining room. Nosing his way under the old-mission style table, Frank settled on his haunches against my leg. Gerrit opened a Cabernet of some kind and tended our glasses.

"How's school, Gerrit?" I asked after everyone had tasted everything.

"Four more weeks." He rolled his eyes. "Then I'll be up to my ass in papers."

"And grumpy as all get out." Laura laughed as she fluffed her potatoes on her plate.

I sliced the tender asparagus with my fork. "I'm thinking of auditing a class again."

Gerrit wiped his mouth with his napkin, then swallowed some wine. "You should think about taking them for real like you've always wanted. Register. Pay tuition. Get credit."

"I don't know about that."

"Why not, Janie?" Laura asked. "You'd be good at it."

Elbows on the table, I stared at my plate and shrugged. "Heck. I'm thirty-nine years old. Two kids." I lifted my glass and then set it back on the tablecloth. "Walt would have a fit."

Gerrit scratched his head and smirked. "Ummmm . . . so what?"

Three

Four tries and the mower still wouldn't start. I tugged until my arm hurt and I was out of breath. After waiting a few minutes, I yanked the pull again. The engine almost caught, but the gas fumes made me think the engine was flooded.

"Damn thing," I said under my breath, and went inside for a glass of iced tea.

Two more attempts and the engine fired up. After adjusting the idle, I charged into the backyard and maneuvered back and forth across the grass with long swipes for about a half an hour. I mowed my way along the south side of the house, then tackled the front, keeping my eye out for the school bus.

There are eleven houses on our suburban street, Sun Valley Court, with twelve teenagers and eighteen children under the age of ten. Thirteen attend a private elementary school, including Sam and Meike. The other five arrive home fifty minutes later on a different route. Scheduling complications separate the group, not their religious differences, and though the boys like to keep a distance from the girls, the youngsters pretty much play well together.

Caution lights flashing, the bus stopped at the other end of the cul-de-sac and let out a good dozen kids. I cut the mower engine. Odie began to whimper and yip through the screen door.

Sam reminded me as soon as we entered the kitchen. "Nineteen more days until summer vacation."

"That's less than three weeks." I was looking forward to it as much as the kids.

Meike crouched on the kitchen floor next to her backpack and rubbed Odie's belly. "Then we can sleep in every morning," she told the dog while lifting one of his ears and talking into it like the two of them were making plans together.

I opened a box of granola bars and set them on the counter. "What's new at school?"

"The groundbreaking's tomorrow after lunch," Sam said. He pulled a yellow slip from his pack and handed me a note. "We won't have math, and when the program's over, we can go home."

"Can I have Nestle's Quik?" Meike asked. She got the tin from the spin-around and dug in the drawer for a spoon while I poured two glasses of milk. Examining the granola bars, she tore the wrapper off one and jumped up on the counter.

"Dad's coming for the program," Sam said. "He said he's cutting holes for the anchors when they start the new building."

"Wow," I said, trying to sound impressed. "That's cool."

"Can I ride home with him?"

I raised my eyebrows and shrugged. "Sure. I guess. As long as he brings you right back."

"Me too," Meike said.

I made an effort not to sound reluctant. "Oo-kaay." I boosted her down, already dreading the whole ordeal at school tomorrow.

Sam brought his empty glass to the sink. "I'm going to Matt's. We're riding bikes to the creek."

"You guys be careful down there." I don't know why I said that. Only a few blocks away, the creek never ran more than ankle deep except in the very early spring when it might reach six or seven inches. "What's your plan, Meike? I have to finish the lawn."

"I'm helping you, Mom."

We put Odie on the leash and sat on the stoop petting him between the ears. "You stay here with Odie. When I'm done cutting, you can help me sweep."

Still warm, the motor started easily, and it took less than ten minutes to finish. Meike waited with Odie's leash in one hand and her snack in the other. When I finished, we wrapped the end of a chain around the post of the porch, clipped it to the leash, and let Odie roam through the lawn. Meike grabbed the straw broom and the kids' old plastic snow shovel we use to scoop the clippings.

She dragged the broom across the cement behind her, not accomplishing anything. I heard a heavy sigh as she tried to push it along instead, brushing it left, brushing it right. She let go and the broom fell on the grass. "Mom! It won't work!"

"The grass is still a little heavy because it's damp." I picked up the broom and made hard short sweeps on the walk, exaggerating the swing of my rear-end to get a laugh. "It's okay to brush it right back up into the grass." I bumped my hip against hers on purpose and handed the broom back.

She didn't seem to think it was funny. Determined, she held the broom firmly and tried to copy me, but the clippings only scattered further around the sidewalk.

"I can't!" The broom handle smacked on the cement and she ran for the house.

"Meike!" I called.

Odie barked and the screen door slammed.

I let her go.

Before long, I could hear her crying through the window of her bedroom upstairs. I stopped, listened, and resisted the urge to go inside and calm her.

After a long minute, her sobbing grew to a sort of howling, and I had to remind myself that she could use some venting without interference. Scooping up the pile of grass in the driveway, I slid it into the five-gallon bucket. Minutes later, muffled sounds came from the window. I could not resist any longer.

She was on her bed, on her tummy, her face in the pillow. I could see the slight spasms in her shoulders as she breathed, sniffling in and out.

"Meike," I said quietly. When I leaned over her and gently put my hand on her back, she turned and faced away from me. But she nudged over a few inches. I sat down next to her. "It's all right."

I stroked her hair, circling it around her ear with my index finger. "It's all right," I repeated. Turning over, she sat up and when she reached her arms out to me, I saw the bleeding scratches and a bite mark.

"Oh, Meike," I whispered. I pulled her on my lap and there we sat rocking.

~

I arrived at school on time to stop in each of their rooms during lunch to make sure they knew I was there for the program.

Mrs. Gelderlewis summoned me from her desk when I knocked on the door frame. "Please. Come in."

A bag of potato chips in his hand, Sam met me at the circle of desks students had formed for lunch hour. "Hi, Mom. Want to see the rock collections?"

The fourth-graders had been assigned groups accumulating their minerals, crystals, metals, and gems in various displays. Together, Sam and I scanned all of them. Rachael, the only girl in his group, had donated a purple strip of linen to set off the stones.

"Your layout's my favorite."

He walked me to the hall.

"I'll watch for you in the program, Sam." I knew better than to even come close to any physical display of affection in front of his classmates. "See you back home."

The second-grade room was noisy with lunchtime chatter. When Meike turned around and noticed me, she ran over and wrapped her arms around my hips, beaming at her classmates.

"This is my Mom," she said, as if her friends wouldn't recognize me from last week, as if I hadn't been there before helping at hot lunch, a field trip, or Mrs. Boerma's birthday surprise. As if I was never president of Mother's Club.

The bell rang. I went out with the girls and turned jump rope on the playground until, from the corner of my eye, I spied Walt in his truck looking for a parking spot. Meike hadn't noticed him, but I handed her my end of the rope. "I'm going to use the bathroom and find a good seat for the program." She grabbed my arm, so I squeezed her up against me for a second and told her, "See you in a while, honey," before she skipped back to her friends.

From the last row, I can wave at the kids without disturbing folks behind me. Meike's class ushered in. Her eyes expectant and searching, she soon acknowledged me with a smile. When Sam nodded at me, I squinted, pulling up my nose at him and smiled goofy.

Following a short speech by the president of the board, everyone filed outside to the vacant field behind the school. The teachers passed out hand-sized garden spades to each student, and, after Dwight Sytsma, the school principal, said a short prayer, the children bent over and pushed their shovels into the ground. We all clapped and that was the end of the ceremony.

I hoped to get back to my car without having to acknowledge anyone. Since Walt left home, I knew people here watched me, talked about me. It wasn't paranoia. I had heard enough conversations about other folks at PTA meetings and pancake breakfasts over the years to understand this community's inclination to gossip.

This was Walt's territory. He had attended the school since he was twelve, when his parents sold their farm in Minnesota and moved to Michigan. Many parents of Sam and Meike's classmates were old classmates of Walt's, and though by now we were well acquainted, in my mind I considered most of them his friends, not mine. This was the burbs. I'd grown up in the city. Walt used to tell people he "rescued me from the ghetto."

I found my keys and had my hand on the ignition when Jesse knocked on the car window. I rolled it three quarters down. "Hey there."

Jesse had stopped in the day before yesterday, after her photography session. When she and I first met at church a few years ago, we'd hit it off discovering neither of us cared so much about cooking and cleaning as we did about reading and writing and good music.

"How ya doing, Janie?"

"Not bad," I told my friend. "Especially now the program's over."

"At least it wasn't too drawn out. The kids with Walt?"

"For now, but they're coming right back and I need to beat them home."

"Art wants you to call and set up a time for the two of you to meet."

I shook my head and frowned. "I don't know about that." By "Art," Jesse meant the Reverend Arthur Byker, our pastor. Jessie's the part-time secretary, so the two of them spend a good deal of time making schedules and putting the church bulletin together.

"Well, think about it."

I looked through the rear view mirror. "Okay, Jesse, Thanks, but I need to go."

She winked and pulled away. "I'll give you a holler on Friday."

I drove straight home, and, realizing Walt would probably stand around for a while chatting after the program, went inside to make a cup of coffee.

When the truck pulled in, Odie and I met them at the door.

"Meike and Sam, go on in and put your things away," Walt said in the garage. "I have to talk to Mom alone for a minute."

He seemed expectant, like I might invite him in, but I stepped outside and closed the door behind me.

"Nice program, huh?"

"It was all right. What's on your mind?"

Walt ran a hand over the top of his hair and shuffled his feet, but looked at me straight on. "I went to see a lawyer today."

"Oh?"

"I'm filing for a divorce."

Back in January when Dr. Jennings suggested I was bipolar, Walt got his hands on a book by Patty Duke. Ever since, he thought himself an expert on the subject. No shopping binges, no jumping off roofs, no slitting my wrist in the bathroom, but Walt continued his plan to move out anyway.

And yet his announcement about filing hit me like a punch in the stomach.

"I'm not surprised," I said.

He might be threatening, trying to intimidate, waiting for me to say something like, "Oh, please, Walt. Don't do this. I'll do whatever it takes." Though I let him know my opinions, over the twenty years we have been married, Walt's become used to my eventual compliance.

I pressed the top of the door handle. "A divorce isn't my idea."

"Janie, you know there's no other way."

The aluminum door clicked shut again without my going inside. "No, I don't know that." I glared at Walt. "We went to counseling twice. Then you quit. You and your attitude that everything's my problem. I'm the one screwed up, not you. You even refuse to talk with Dr. Jennings."

"You tricked him into that discharge."

"Oh. And you know better?"

"You've got him wrapped around your little finger."

"I think you're afraid he'd tell you you're overreacting."

He sighed and shook his head. "I could've talked with my lawyer sooner." Walt had a knack for condescension that even my father, who wears a hearing aid, picks up on. "But I just couldn't do that when you were sick."

"Really?" Wrapping my arms across my chest, I clenched my hands underneath them. "Well, don't do me any more favors."

"Do you have a lawyer yet?"

"No, I don't have a lawyer yet. Why would I have a lawyer already?"

"I have to send the papers somewhere. You going to use that Dekker guy?"

"I said I hadn't thought that far."

"Oh, get real, Janie. I mean business here."

"I suppose you do," I decided and reached for the door. "Good night."

Four

Reverend Byker called the next day, inviting me to come and talk with him. I agreed to see him in his office the following morning, thinking it wise that somebody in this community hear my side of the story. That, and my conscience kept suggesting maybe our marriage was supposed to be some kind of cross to bear, like Jesus. Maybe I should renounce myself for Walt's sake or for the kids. I've heard ministers preach such a thing.

The morning brought me another perspective.

I zipped Sam and Meike's lunchboxes inside their backpacks like every morning, hugged them goodbye, and watched at the door as they waited for their bus at the end of the cul-de-sac.

When I pulled into the church parking lot an hour later, Reverend Byker met me at the door.

Only in his thirties, Reverend Byker has a boyish look about him—not much taller than I am, brown and wavy hair combed forward and cut straight across the forehead. Sheepish grin. On Sundays, I would see him holding his tie at the top, wiggling his neck around inside the collar like his mother made the knot too tight. Taking the call as pastor to our church in early summer, he and his wife, along with their four daughters and a son still in diapers, had moved into the parsonage just before school started last fall. The congregation has hundreds of members, a million of which are kids, likely one of the reasons the Bykers packed up the whole bunch and left the east side of the state to join us.

He offered me a chair and a cup of coffee before sitting down behind his desk.

"Are you comfortable with us starting in a word of prayer?"

"Um . . ." I cleared my throat. "Tell you the truth, I'd be real uncomfortable with that. I'm sort of a . . . you know . . . private person. Pray in the closet. That kind of thing."

"Jesse mentioned you weren't the prayer chain type."

He was grinning and I managed a smile myself.

A faint sound of organ music came down the hall from the sanctuary. Someone practicing "Beautiful Savior," and it made me relax a bit more.

"Walt was here last week," Reverend Byker said, more seriously now. "I asked him not to do anything until you and I talked, but he seemed bent on going through with it."

"Well, thank you for that, Reverend Byker."

"Please. Call me Art."

"Okay. You're right, though, he's already filed for the divorce."

It was the first time I said it, first time I told anyone, and at first it sounded sad and embarrassing. Then even sadder.

I looked down at my lap and watched the little drops fall, spotting my jeans. My face still wet, I lifted my head, pulled my mouth in a firm line and focused on Reverend Byker. He rolled his lower lip and nodded with what I took to be understanding. I sighed heavily and picked up my coffee.

"It's hard, huh?" he asked.

I laughed with a quick snort. "I'm okay," I finally said. "I'm okay."

"And the divorce, it's all right with you?"

"No . . . no, of course not . . . and . . . ." I swallowed the lump coming up in my throat again. "It really sucks for Sam and Meike."

"Yes. It does."

"But . . . it occurred to me this morning, watching them leave for school." And now I just had to say it. "Why in the world would I want to be married to anyone who doesn't want to be married to me?"

~

Meike's violin teacher was married to Richard Dekker, the man I wanted as my attorney. Walt hadn't been real keen on Meike taking up the violin in second grade, given the school didn't have an orchestra. Too out of the norm. So Meike and I had always made Monday girls' night out, going to her music lesson first, followed by supper at Blimpie or her favorite, Taco Bell.

Meike's teacher, Kristine, gave private instructions from her house located inside the city limits, about a fifteen-minute drive from our place. I always sit in on the lessons, something Kristine suggested to the relief of little Meike since that very first night. Richard would sometimes tap on the door before entering the room and say, "Excuse me, dear, but . . ." and relay an important message or ask a question about their kids' supper. His respectful manner always impressed me.

And there was another reason for my choice. Richard's father came from the same blue-collar old neighborhood where I grew up. The ghetto Walt claims he rescued me from. Although I didn't know his father well, I remember Richard's grandfather, long legs and ears like Dumbo, trekking past our house on London Street every afternoon with his lunch bucket after the Kelvinator factory let out.

Today, in the prestigious downtown law firm for the first time, I began to worry I was out of my league. The receptionist, wearing her black business suit, pearls and heels, was congenial enough. But Queen Anne chairs upholstered in dark forest green and burgundy stripes and the deep mahogany end tables with antique brass lamps shedding just enough light to read by, reminded me of an old library at the University of Michigan. Or a smoking room for men who signed "Esquire" behind their names.

That day in May, promptly at one p.m., Richard ushered me into a large conference room and indicated a chair at the long mahogany table. He waited until I settled in before taking a seat across from me. He was a lot taller than I remembered, six-foot-four or five I guessed. There wasn't much space between his dark, bushy eyebrows. At least his demeanor wasn't intimidating. The nonchalant way he laid a yellow legal pad on the table, in addition to the panned view of the city through the tenth-floor windows behind him, bumped my apprehension down a couple of notches.

He tugged at his earlobe and then pulled a slender pen out of the inside pocket of his suit jacket and patiently rotated the end. His hands were huge. So were his ears.

Someone knocked quietly. "Yes," Richard said. An assistant entered with a file folder. "Thank you." She left without a word, softly closing the door behind her. He pushed one of twenty buttons on the desk phone to hold the calls.

"This is the document from the office of Sy Hofstra, Walt's attorney." Reaching across the table, Richard set the document right-side-up in front of me. INTENT OF DIVORCE. After I scanned the front page, he turned the pages for me upside down, one by one, and with his pen pointed to paragraphs sectioned off in underlined capital letters.

"Sy tells me Sam and Meike are with you and that you and Walt have made visitation arrangements that are satisfactory for now."

I nodded.

"The court will issue an official order to verify the temporary arrangement," he explained.

"I see."

Setting the document aside, he folded his hands on the legal pad. "I want to ask a few questions, make a few notes, let you ask questions. But before that, there are a few things I want to mention."

"That's fine." I crossed my legs under my ankle-length cotton skirt and sat back.

Richard pinched one of his earlobes. "My fee is one-ten an hour."

I nodded again, having done some homework on legal counsel beforehand.

He waited before saying more, blinking his eyes slowly. "You're welcome to call me any time here at the office. A secretary screens my calls. If I'm not available, she'll let you know when I can get back to you."

"Okay," I said.

"Everything here will be professional and confidential. We won't talk shop if we happen to run into each other at the grocery." Richard smiled and added kindly, "Or at a violin recital."

"I understand."

"Also, please keep in mind, I am not a therapist."

I tried to sound amiable. "I already have a therapist. He's a professional as well."

For the next half hour, I relayed general information, prompted by Richard's questions. "We were married in 1973, nineteen years ago. We have two children, Sam, who's ten, born in 1982, and Meike, who'll be nine in two months, born in '83. Walt is from Minnesota, a little rural town, and moved to Michigan with his parents when he was thirteen. I've lived around here all my life."

I made a meandering outline of our assets and Richard took notes. "We have a house with a little over two years left on the mortgage. We own a small cottage on Selkirk Lake. There's a Four Winns inboard, a Bass Buggy, paddleboat." I took a breath and thought for a minute. "Last year, we built a spankin' new house next to Crystal Springs. Never moved in. Haven't sold it."

While Richard scratched on the legal pad, I looked through the window behind him. I could see the Federal Building across the street. When I was a little girl, my mother would take me downtown on the city bus and we'd go to Steketee's basement for a new blouse and knee socks in the fall before school started. After high school graduation, I worked in the office of a jewelry store on Monroe Avenue and later at the Michigan National Bank next door.

"Okay. What else?" Richard asked, bringing my attention around.

"There's W&M. We own it. It's a cement-cutting business we started up with a partner back when Sam was a baby. It does pretty well. We also have a printing company. No partner. Sonora Printing. Walt's brother runs it for us." Richard just nodded, so I went on. "A few years ago, Walt started a cement-pumping business. There's three or four—I forget—large trucks, big like fire trucks, with huge lifts and pumps. I remember Walt more or less announcing his plan for the pumping company. One day he said to me, 'I'm a millionaire now, you know.' Not 'we are' or anything."

Richard chuckled and I saw him underline 1 Million in his notes.

"Anyway, he told me it would be a good investment and that I should just trust him on this one. Which I pretty much did. Let's see. There are new buildings he had built for each of these. Also some vacant industrial property"

"We'll have to get a look at the books. Think he'll cooperate?"

"I don't know."

"We can get a court order if we need to. You might want to consider hiring your own accountant."

We stopped at 2:30. I like to get home before Sam and Meike.

Five

My brothers, Gerrit and Jerry, made reservations for six small cabins set in a crescent shape along Silver Lake, two and a half hours north of town. Initially, I thought I might have to pass on the June vacation with my parents and siblings, until Walt surprised me and agreed to give up his visit with the kids that week.

"Or I could drive up on Tuesday night and see them for a while," he'd suggested.

"Nooo. I don't think so," I said. Just like him to imagine he could show up without my family stoning him to death.

Sam, Meike and I rented our own cabin on one end, next to Jerry, his wife Lynn and their three boys. Gerrit, Laura and their daughter shared the center cabin with my mother and father. My sisters and their husbands occupied the other three. All my sisters' children were married with kids of their own who planned to make day trips up to visit.

The week was one of those wonderful warm spells Michigan can have now and then before summer officially begins. I slept with the windows open to the night air and sounds. Meike would have shared the bedroom with me, but when she learned Sam was sleeping on the screened-in porch, she convinced him to let her throw her sleeping bag on a cot opposite his.

The first morning, I woke to noises in the kitchenette. It was daylight. Six-thirty. Even with the bedroom door closed, I could hear someone rummaging through silverware and dishes and Meike say, "Shhh. Don't wake Mom up."

I rolled over to snooze some more, thinking how nice it was of them to get their own breakfast and let me sleep a bit longer on my birthday. I drifted in and out a while until a light rap on the bedroom door made me open one eye. "Yup," I said, stretching under the sheet.

"Surprise!" Meike said as she burst in and jumped on the bed.

Behind her, Sam toted a tray we had used for lemonade glasses the night before, his face bright as sunrise. "Happy Birthday!"

As I sat up, Meike started to arrange the bed pillows behind me and plopped another one on my lap. She patted the pillow flat. With a bow, Sam placed the tray on top.

"What's this?" I asked, eyeing three buttered pancakes with maple syrup. "Yum!" A paper napkin was folded neatly in half, covered by a knife and a fork. In one corner of the tray, a stoneware mug held a cup of coffee, and in the other, two dandelions were stuck in a glass of water.

"Go ahead. Try it," Sam said and sat down on the other side of me.

I nodded and winked at Meike. "Let me have a sip of this coffee first." With the cup to my face, I breathed in, slow and deep, like it was the most pleasing aroma on earth. It was the instant stuff, not hot enough, but I pretended anyway, sipping carefully. "Aaaaah." With formality, I tucked the tip of the napkin into the neck of my nightshirt, cut the pancake easily with the fork and took a bite. "Delicious." I ate while looking back and forth at Sam and Meike. "How did you know when to flip them?"

Sam started waving his arm and flapping his hand around in the air. "When the smoke detector started going off."

I stopped chewing. "The smoke detector went off?"

"Just started beeping."

I looked at Meike, but she just sat there squirming, trying to pull off an innocent, blank face. My snicker was the give-away. The three of us laughed until I could feel the pancakes in my stomach expanding. "This is great, you guys," I said. "Thank you. I sure am lucky."

"We got a present, too," Sam announced.

"I'll get it!" Meike came back two seconds later with a package, gift-wrapped in black and aqua paper with a silver ribbon and bow. She plopped down and handed it to me.

"It's too pretty to open," I teased as I fondled the ribbon.

"Open it," Sam said, his voice impatient.

"Yeah," Meike added. "Come on, Mom."

I slid off the ribbon, slipped it over Meike's head and, without ripping the paper, loosened the cellophane tape. Inside a sheet of tissue paper, a black t-shirt had been carefully folded. I held it up and read the slanted, messy script across the front. "*I got this shirt when I turned 40. I hate this shirt.*"

"I love it," I said.

"The lady at the Hallmark store wrapped it," Meike said.

"Dad thought you'd like it." As soon as he said it, Sam's face turned scarlet.

I put a finger under his chin. "I *still* love it," I said.

His smile told me he'd caught what I was trying to say. I blinked away tears, so near the surface these days.

My family doesn't make a big deal out of mealtime when we're on these vacations. The only time we eat together is on Sunday after church and on the last night when we have a pie-iron smorgasbord at the campfire. But that day, while Lynn and I were having morning coffee at the picnic table, she said, "We're thinking about all of us grilling hamburgers together tonight."

Meike sat on the bench between my legs fiddling with her American Girl doll, waiting for me to finish braiding her hair.

"Okay with me." I pulled a cloth-wrapped elastic band from my wrist and wound it around the ponytail shaping in my hands. "There you go, Peanut."

Part of the fun for Sam and Meike this week was hanging around with their cousins. There was plenty of room within the semi-circle for catch, kickball, a game of Monopoly, or just hanging out. Of course, everybody could keep their eye on everybody else, but that was okay for a week. Anyone who wanted privacy would just retreat inside their cabin since we had an unspoken rule that no one entered another cabin without invitation. Or at least knocking first.

"Where's Marty?" Meike asked, referring to her favorite cousin.

"The boys are playing championship Rummy with Grandpa." Lynn pointed to my parent's cabin.

"Here, Mom." Meike handed me the doll and skipped away toward the card game.

The late morning sun peeked over the tallest branches of the oak trees and the back of my new t-shirt soaked it in. "I think I'll go and read for a while. Thanks for coffee."

"It's your birthday," Lynn said. "You should take the whole day off."

I set up my chair in the sun, pulled my tennis shoes and socks off with my feet and opened my book. About a half hour into it, I looked up to see Meike running over, sweatshirt tied around her waist.

"Grandma and I are going to take a walk down the path," she said catching her breath.

I glanced over her shoulder and saw my mother—checkered shirt, "pedal-pushers," as she called them, visor hat and all. She did a full-arm wave which I returned. Meike ran back and I watched them head down the gravel road hand in hand.

Our camera was on the counter, just inside the door, and I grabbed it on time to zoom in and catch a shot of the two of them at the edge of the woods. When Sam and Meike and I haul out our photos from this vacation, it would make a good memory. By that time, maybe I wouldn't be ashamed I was the only one without a husband all week. By then, it might not hurt that Walt didn't see Sam beat Uncle Jerry at the go-cart track yesterday. Maybe it won't rip me up to remember Gerrit helping Meike turn her marshmallow stick instead of her own dad, or Sam's sad face in the campfire light.

Stepping backward through the grass, I took a panoramic of the cabins before focusing in on Sam and his cousins playing cards with their grandpa. When the Rummy game dispersed, the boys set out with Jerry for a climb in the sand dunes. My father strolled over and set a lawn chair next to mine in the grass.

"How's it going, Skeezix?" he asked after a deep breath.

"Not bad. Have a sit-down."

Six years ago, my father was diagnosed with emphysema, not surprising given the decades he spent in smokehouses curing hams for a living and his smoking Camel straights since the time they were invented. Now instead of cigarettes, he carried an inhaler in his pocket wherever he went and, after his eightieth birthday last summer, keeps a green portable tank of oxygen in his bedroom.

When he sat, an inch of his bony white leg stuck out between his trousers and the top of the dark socks that didn't go with his canvas shoes.

Up until this year, my parents had admired Walt. Polite, strong, masculine, a hard worker brought up in the same denomination as the church we were raised in—a church that taught divorce was not an option. My mother and father weren't naïve. They knew few marriages were ideal, including their own, but a husband and a wife vow before God to stay together in sickness and in health, for better or for worse. The wife submits to the husband. They remain together 'til death doth them part.

My father removed the red *petje* he wore and set the cap on his lap. Together, we looked out over the glimmer on the water to the dunes piled up behind.

"Your minister needs to have a good long talk with Walt," he said.

Rather than being upset with my father, I reminded myself how my parents were struggling with the whole situation. "Walt's talked with him before," I explained.

"He needs some sense knocked into his head."

My father would be the type to look Walt up one day at work and give him a good bawling out. I closed my eyes, slowly shaking my head, and let my father hear the defeat in my voice. "It won't make any difference."

For a moment we were quiet. To identify anyone on the dunes from here was impossible, but I scouted for Jerry and the boys anyway.

My father uncrossed his legs and turned his entire skinny body toward me, making me look his way. "Do you think there's another woman?" he asked.

Richard Dekker had asked me that. He claims ninety-five percent of the time it's what things end up being all about.

"No, Dad. I don't think there's another woman."

Six

My family isn't in the habit of making a big deal out of birthdays. We mail cards to each other, that's about it. That night we grouped our charcoal grills together and pushed the picnic tables in a line. I wore my new t-shirt. My mother and Meike arranged a bouquet of wild phlox in a peanut butter jar and set it on the middle table. After my father said a prayer, we sat down to hamburgers, potato salad, and pork and beans.

When we finished the picnic feast, Lynn asked who wanted coffee. "I got the big pot on inside," she said and made for her kitchen. But instead of the coffee pot, she came out carrying a sheet cake topped with lavish frosting and a candle in the shape of a large 40. Everyone started singing "Happy Birthday to you . . . ." While the kids scooted in close to me, their Grandpa swiped my camera and took a picture.

~

During the week we were at the lake, Walt had made plans to take Sam and Meike to Cedar Point in July. The kids and I returned early Saturday afternoon. Walt was having them overnight to finish off the weekend.

"We'll leave on Wednesday morning and come back Sunday night," Walt said in front of Sam and Meike.

It seemed to me his plan detracted and diminished the past week. Our time at the lake had hardly finished and sunk in before on to the next thing. This whole Cedar Point thing smelled like competition to me.

From the garage, I watched Sam open the pickup door and let the dog jump in. Meike followed with her mini-duffle bag. We had already hugged and said good-bye, but she threw me a kiss from the truck window.

"Doug and Judy invited me," Walt explained. "We'll all drive out in the van."

Back when Walt still lived at home we'd go out for dinner every few months with our next door neighbors, Doug and Judy. Their daughter, Sarah, was Meike's friend, and their son, Jason, a year younger than Sam. Good neighbors, nice people, my kids' friends.

Like any sane mother would do, I agreed to the trip. Fair was fair.

When Walt pulled in on the morning of their trip, he parked the truck along the side of the house.

Sam chased out to meet him. "Dad's here!" he yelled.

"Meike, you ready?" I asked on my way upstairs to get her.

Sprawled across her bed, she checked through the double window were she could scope out the whole street. "Yoo-hoo!" she called down. The ends of her French braids brushed the screen.

"Okay. Give me an extra-long hug to last while you're gone." I reached over and lifted as she climbed me like a panda would.

"Go in and say goodbye to your mom," I heard Walt say.

"I'll miss you, Sam," I said when he came in the kitchen. We squeezed each other. I forced myself to add in a bouncy voice, "But Odie will keep me company."

The three of them crossed over the grass to the neighbors. I went for the Barcalounger in the den at the back of the house so all the excitement wasn't smeared in my face.

Five days in a row was the longest the kids would be away with Walt since the whole mess started. Dread has followed me around since the trip was first brought up, its shadow slipping over me sometimes. I might as well move over and share it with the Barcalounger.

Odie curled up on my lap. I thought I might fall back asleep since it was only 8:30. After half an hour, I gave up and turned on public radio. They were doing a fund raiser.

"Crap." I punched the power off.

Odie and I got comfortable again. I read my entire monthly theological journal by eleven o'clock, then went upstairs and took a shower. Wednesday afternoon meant my standing appointment with Dr. Jennings. If I didn't show up, I'd get charged anyway.

I used to have a woman therapist. Dorothy. She was part of the team that helped me through my first clinical depression at the end of the very long time when Walt and I tried to adopt a baby. The adoption process had been a drawn-out affair—over four years—that ended happily with a surprise pregnancy.

Dorothy and I hit it off right away. Nearly twenty years older than me, she had earned her doctorate in psychiatry back in the days when women usually had to choose between a career or a family. After Sam was born, Dorothy and I spent more hours talking books and music and theology than therapy.

Or maybe that's exactly what it was.

By the time Meike was born, I didn't see anyone professionally anymore. Now and then, Dorothy and I met for lunch. When Walt first insisted I enter the hospital last November, naturally I called Dorothy. "Janie," she told me, "you need to decide if you want me for a friend or for a therapist. We can't do both."

I chose friend.

Since then, Dorothy often invited me for tea. She introduced me to her roommate and encouraged me to join her book club. I invited Dorothy to my place and we shared a bottle of Cabernet Franc.

Meanwhile, I started with Dr. Jennings, a colleague of Dorothy's she recommended.

He and I did not hit it off so easily.

One of the forms to complete that first appointment was a diagram of a family tree. Dr. Jennings started filling in blanks while I watched.

"Father?" he asked.

"Gerrit."

"Age?"

"Eighty-one."

He didn't look up. "Grandparents?"

"You mean my father's parents?"

"Yes. And your grandmother's maiden name."

I gave Dr. Jennings the information. "How far back do we have to go?"

"That's far enough. Are your grandparents still alive?"

"No way. They died at different times when I was in junior high."

He noted it on the diagram. "Mother?"

"Pearl Vegter," I answered. "Seventy-six."

"Her parents?"

I hated giving this kind of information. In my opinion, family charts are over-rated. A few years ago, my niece was excused from a family tree assignment in high school because the task became so complicated. I exhaled impatiently before giving grandparent names on my mother's side.

Dr. Jennings continued. "Brothers? Sisters?"

"I have three sisters. No wait. There's Ada, the oldest. I don't always count her. We hardly see her. She's my half-sister." I should have just stuck with the three, but I never know for sure what to say.

"And how's that?" Dr. Jennings turned and looked at me.

I pulled my mouth to a disgusted frown. "My father was married before." Whenever I make an effort not to get all emotional, my voice turns shaky. "Look. Do we have to do this?"

Laying the pen down, Dr. Jennings folded his hands on the top of his desk. "We can finish it next time."

Next time, about a minute into our appointment, he started on the tree business again.

"So. Your father's first wife."

"I never knew her," I shrugged. "Her name was Leda. She died of some kidney disease, when Ada was five. They had a little boy, Gerrit Junior, my dad's first born. He died. A few weeks after he was born. Suffocated. They left a teddy bear in a plastic bag in the crib."

Dr. Jennings closed his eyes and winced, but I kept going. "I do know the kidney disease was really painful. My brother says she killed herself. Lost her will. I don't know. Maybe my father pulled the plug or something."

Dr. Jennings took a deep breath and blew it out loudly. He filled in some of the diagram while I looked out the window.

"Okay," he began again. "Let's see. Last time, you said your mother was born in the Netherlands?"

"Yeah. She was eight when her family came over." I never minded repeating the stories my mother told me about Ellis Island.

Dr. Jennings wanted to go somewhere else. "So, your mother and father married and she helped raise Ada."

"Well," I said slowly. "Not exactly." I shifted in my chair and crossed my arms tight to my chest. "Forget it."

"Go ahead. It might be good for you to tell me."

It might be none of his business.

I rested my forehead on three finger tips and crooked my neck sideways, sighing. Holding back, I thought for a very long minute. "Okay." There were plenty of families in the world far more screwed-up than mine. "Ada was in a foster home a lot. She and Marge didn't get along, I guess. Or she didn't get along with my mother. Or she didn't get along with my father."

"Who's Marge?"

I shook my head, stubborn, cutting my arms through the air. "I don't want to do this."

Dr. Jennings set the family tree to one side. "All right. Enough for this time."

The next appointment, he started out with the stinking sheet of paper with the family tree again.

"So, tell me about Marge. She's your sister?"

"When my mother was a teenager, she was raped. Some older, respectable guy she already knew from church. That was before she met my father. When they got married, Marge was four."

Dr. Jennings sighed. He rubbed his chin and took a long look at me before turning back to his paperwork. I hoped he was an artist of some sort because I doubted there was a branch on his sheet for that.

"Two other sisters, you said?" he asked next.

"Yup. Betty and Gert."

He put them on their lines. "Brothers?"

I hesitated.

"Do you have brothers?"

"Two. Well for a while, three. I mean, I don't always count him. He's really my nephew. For years, I thought he was my brother. Until . . ." I just quit talking. Tears ran from my eyes and down my face.

Dr. Jennings took the sheet of paper, opened the bottom drawer of his desk, threw the damn diagram in and closed the drawer. He looked at me and nodded once. "How are Sam and Meike doing?" he asked.

From then on, we got along fine.

Seven

I woke up Friday remembering there was still most of the weekend to go before Sam and Meike would be home. The imposing sunlight was only slightly distilled by sheers and Dutch lace on the window. Kicking off the sheet and pulling a t-shirt over my head, I went to the kitchen and started coffee before unlocking the door and sliding the screen open for Odie. I stepped on to the deck, squinting, expecting the sun to nudge my brain from its slump.

Around ten o'clock, Jessie called to invite me and the kids over for dinner. I reminded her this was Cedar Point weekend. She said she forgot but that I should come anyway. I tried to explain over the phone how an evening with someone else's children and not my own didn't sound like a good time. She wasn't offended and suggested we come the next weekend instead.

The best part of Friday was when I had an unexpected call at noon from Sam and Meike. Everyone was going to spend the afternoon at the hotel pool, they said. As it grew cooler toward dusk, they'd go to view the park from the Ferris wheel at night and watch the whirling blur of lights aboard the octopus ride.

Before we hung up, I knocked on the kitchen cupboard so the kids would hear Odie bark hello.

No doubt the kids initiated the call, but I gave Walt credit for being a sport and going through with it. Until I remembered Doug and Judy were there, and suspected Walt's cooperation had to do with impressing them.

In late afternoon I phoned Gerrit.

"You guys home tonight?" I asked.

"Yup. We're just hanging out. Coming over?"

"If that's all right."

"You're always welcome here, you know that. Want supper?"

"No, thanks." Inviting myself over was hard enough. Including a meal would have thrown self-worth overboard. "I'll be there around seven-thirty."

"Your call. See you then."

We shared a good amount of wine that night. Around midnight, Laura suggested I stay.

"Suppose I should," I admitted. "Odie's okay in his cage, but first thing in the morning, I'm gone."

"Suit yourself," Gerrit said, so I slept on the basement couch next to Frank the pug.

No one woke me in the morning, and it was ten-thirty before I heard anybody walking around above me.

"Coffee?" Laura asked as I came out of the bathroom.

"Sure. And then I gotta go." Holding the mug with two hands, I drank half of it and then headed for the door. "Thanks for having me. Bye, Frank."

"Any time," Gerrit called from the stoop.

I started my car and left.

I'd missed my jog on Saturday morning at Gerrit's and on Sunday decided to bag it too. I clicked on Sunday radio. "Pipe Dreams" and "Choral Traditions." Jesse called and said she'd signed me up that morning for a bike trip the church group was planning next month.

I sighed into the phone. "But I haven't decided I wanted to go for sure."

"Well, they wanted a count. Art said it would be easier to take your name off than to add it later."

"I guess. Has it occurred to you that only gives me three weeks to get in shape?"

"You'll manage," Jesse answered. "Hey, look, my potatoes are boiling over. Talk to you later."

I had started the second volume of *The Last Lion*, which covered Churchill from the time Roosevelt was elected president until 1940 when Churchill became Prime Minister. I found the book next to the Barcalounger and carried it out to the deck. A haze covered the full force of the sun while a nice breeze cut through the humidity. After about an hour, the breeze picked up and became annoying, lifting my pages as I tried to read. The haze turned toward a grayish over-cast and I thought I heard a rumble of thunder. Tipping the deck chairs forward and leaning them against the rail, I went in with Odie right behind.

The phone rang again and I swore out loud I wouldn't pick it up. But I did anyway.

"Did you know there's a tornado watch?" my mother informed me. "Our church is cancelled and Dad thought he heard yours, too."

"Oh, okay. But when the kids are gone, I go to St. John's, you know."

"That Lutheran place?"

"Ah-huh. They don't have an evening service."

"That's terrible. Why not?"

"Well, guess they do it right the first time."

"That's not funny. You know better." My mother paused. "The kids home yet?"

"Not 'til six or seven."

"Hope they're not on the road in the storm."

"Right," I said. "Well, thanks, Mom. I'll put the radio back on."

The thunderstorm ended out not a big deal.

When Odie barked a little before seven, I went outside to meet the kids. Walt set their stuff just inside the door while Sam and Meike hugged me, excited and talking over each other.

"I rode the Blue Streak yesterday," Sam was saying.

"We went to the pool again this morning," Meike said.

"Sounds like fun. Weren't you scared, Sam? You'll have to tell me more. Hungry?"

"We stopped at Wendy's just before Kalamazoo," Walt said. "Less than an hour ago." He picked up his duffle bag by the strap and hung it on his shoulder. "Say goodbye, guys."

Sometimes I wonder if Sam would say anything to have his dad hang around just a few minutes longer. But I picked up an innocent bragging in his voice, the eagerness, like the first time a boy goes deer hunting with his dad, to participate in Walt's version of manhood. "Hey, Mom. Dad's going to buy Mike's share of the company."

Tempting as it can be, I don't pump the kids for scoops on their dad. Still, I certainly took pleasure in seeing Walt squirm a second.

"What makes you say that, Sam?" Walt threw back, as if the statement was downright ridiculous. His dismissal slapped the pride right off Sam's face, and I winced because I could feel the sting.

"I heard you and Doug talking in the van," Sam answered as his chin hit his chest.

Walt looked at me and shrugged his shoulder. "He wants out."

"So, Sam's right," I answered, slipping my arm around Sam's.

Nor do I play holier than thou, especially in front of the kids, although not playing holier than thou could actually make me seem holier than thou. Odie yipped at the door and I suggested Sam and Meike say goodbye to their dad and go in.

I followed Walt to the pickup. "Can you do that without me? Buy him out?" I asked when the kids were out of range.

"Sure I can." He opened the driver's side door.

"Isn't my name still on everything?"

"That'll all be taken care of eventually."

"Richard Dekker is still waiting for your financial statement."

"I'm working on it." He got in and reached for the ignition.

I crossed my arms and stepped between the door of the truck and Walt. "I don't appreciate your talking business in front of the kids."

With a shrug he turned the key and I stepped back.

~

Since my eighth birthday, maybe before, I hadn't missed seeing a game at Tiger Stadium at least once a summer, and my brothers saw to it the tradition continued. Just before the All-Star break, Sam, Meike and I drove to Detroit with Gerrit and Jerry and their families for an afternoon contest against the Milwaukee Brewers.

A few days later, Walt said he managed three tickets to a Cubs game, which felt like another competitive reaction to me. When Sam and Meike left for Wrigley Field chatting on about Harry Caray, the seventh-inning stretch, and the pool at their hotel, I got an idea to just load the kids in the car when they returned and take off. We would leave for California. Get as far from Walt as possible.

The notion flashed, but common sense took over after a moment or two. Instead of packing our suitcases while the kids were in Chicago, I took Jesse up on an invitation to join her and Reverend Byker for lunch.

They were meeting at the Great Lakes Steak House to finalize plans for the bike trip. "Okay, I'll come for lunch," I said. "But I'm taking my own car. My brother's expecting me out that way later for dinner."

Inside the restaurant, the three of us took a small square table near the windows. As seemed typical, the air conditioning was set for employees, not the patrons, and I was glad I remembered my cardigan. After ordering sandwiches, we scribbled an outline of the bike trip for an insert in the church bulletin, including information about when we were leaving, transporting our bikes on a trailer, the address of the church where the group would sleep overnight, and the fifty-mile route around Mission Peninsula. Folding the notes in half, Jesse dropped them in her bag to type when they returned to the church office.

The college where Gerrit teaches is four blocks from the restaurant. I noticed him and a couple of his colleagues paying at the front register, and when I acknowledged him with a nod, he walked over.

"This is my brother, Gerrit. Gerrit, this is Jesse and Reverend Byker."

"That's Art, please," Reverend Byker said.

Gerrit's smile showed the dimples that run in our family. "I've had the pleasure to meet Jesse at Meike's violin concert once," he said with a polite nod her way. He offered his hand to Reverend Byker. "Pleased to meet you."

"Gerrit teaches at Calvin," I said. "Doctor of Theology." Gerrit shot me a dirty look.

"Seminary?" Reverend Byker asked him.

"Oh, no. Undergraduate only, thank you very much." He checked over his shoulder and motioned to his lunch mates. "Gotta get back. See you at six, Janie."

The three of us had agreed on separate tabs, and the waitress slipped one next to each of our plates.

Either Reverend Byker missed Gerrit's little aspersion on the ministry or didn't take it personally. "I gather that's why you know so much about theology, Janie," he said.

Amused, I shook my head. "You have to give me more credit than that. I grew up with it. Systematics is kind of a hobby of mine."

"Runs in the family, huh?"

"My father owns his own copy of Calvin's *Institutes*, Hoeksema's *Triple Knowledge*, lots of Berkhof and Kuyper stuff. He only went through sixth grade but can quote pretty much anything in the catechism. He reads journals, knows the details of the repudiation at the Synod of Dordrecht. About all we heard at the dinner table. That and baseball."

Reverend Byker crossed his arms and leaned back. "And Biblical theology?"

"That's there, too. But when I was a kid, my dad was the only father worried over the new minister making us memorize Bible verses. He thought we'd all become Evangelicals. Funny thing though, he's a literalist." I raised my thumb and index finger in the air with an eighth-inch gap between them. "He comes this close to being a Fundy himself. But he's too European, thank God."

Apparently we lost Jesse in the conversation somewhere. Good sport as she is, she jumped in. "Did you know Janie used to teach catechism?" she asked Reverend Byker.

"At Fourth?"

"Uh-huh," I said. "High school kids. For five years, now that I think of it."

"You've never mentioned that."

"I quit just before you came."

"Thanks a lot."

"That wasn't it. When Nyhoff did the grape juice thing, it was the last straw for me. I started going to St. John's Lutheran regularly, taking communion there. I figured the parents would have a fit."

"Our loss, I bet."

His comment embarrassed me and I switched the subject away from theology. "I don't think I told you, Jesse, but Gerrit talked to the

Dutch professor and he's letting me in his class. The registrar granted my late enrollment."

Jesse's excitement for me was unmistakable. "You're going to do it?"

"I have a high-school geometry requirement to fulfill, but the teacher at South's going to tutor me. I've never taken a foreign language, either, but they're waiving the prerequisite and letting me start from scratch."

"Don't you already know Dutch?" Jesse asked.

"Only a little Gronings," I said, but she seemed puzzled. "It's a dialect. Not official de Nederlands. Anyway, that and the frickin' geometry will be hard enough for an old lady like me. Non-traditional student is the nice way they say it on campus.

On my way to Gerrit's later that afternoon, I made a mental note to have my brother write down the address where our bike group was staying overnight. Just in case anything happened. Sam and Meike knew I was going on the trip. They'd been rooting for me during my workouts climbing steep hills on 92nd Street and pedaling long, gradual inclines along Hickory Road. If it happened Walt needed to get ahold of me that weekend, he'd have to go through Gerrit.

No obligations came attached to Gerrit and Laura's hospitality, and I drew on it nearly every weekend that Sam and Meike were with their dad. Gerrit and Laura had a knack of drawing me out of my broody quietness, but didn't push or intrude on my privacy. They didn't squirm if I cussed over Walt out loud. No one felt awkward if we discussed Sam and Meike and my voice cracked or my eyes teared up, even spilled over. They offered dinner. Wine. Great music to boot.

I pulled in front of Gerrit's and parked along the curb. Frank barked through the screen door. Like most pugs getting on in years, he doesn't see well, but as soon as I called "Hi, Frank" across the lawn, he recognized my voice and quieted.

Laura called "Com-on-in" from the kitchen. I gently nudged Frank away with my foot. "Hi, there," she said, looking up from grating Parmesan over a huge Caesar salad. "How's it going? Want a brew?"

The aroma of chicken grilling came through an open window. "Thanks. Maybe later. Don't want to interfere with my appetite. How can I help?"

"Get a time from Gerrit, would you? I'm going to slice a loaf of Semolina."

Vertical, six-foot cedar fenced in the backyard and kept Frank from getting lost. Daylilies and a lilac tree lined the south side of the small city lot, a one-stall garage butted against the north. Ancient maples camouflaged the neighbor on the next block, west. About a third of the deck off the house was shaded by a green canvas awning. Gerrit stood near the charcoal grill in the sun, Amstel in one hand, stainless tongs in the other.

"Hey," I said.

"Howdy." He pulled his mouth into an exaggerated wide grin, nose wrinkled and eyes squished, a private joke between us to sneer at all happy-face mentality at any opportunity. "What's happening?"

"Laura's wondering your ETE."

"Estimated time of eating is . . ." The chicken breast spattered as he turned them. "three minutes!" he hollered so Laura could hear. "Need a cold one?"

"No thanks. Was going to have a smoke, but I'll wait. Yum. This smells like summer festival at St. Adalbert's."

We sat around the dining room table. Frank got comfortable under my chair. Laura had cut the chicken in long, juicy strips and laid them over the jumbo salad.

"There's red. But you might want to give this Riesling a try," Gerrit said. "Great with the salad on a warm summer night."

He was correct about the white wine. Crisp, dry, just a hint of sweet. When we passed the Caesar a second time, we each took another splash of Riesling.

"Gerrit mentioned seeing you," Laura said.

I swiped my mouth with a napkin and nodded. "We were writing a plan for the bike trip."

"Sam and Meike going to ride?" she asked.

"Naw. There are some older kids going, but it's Walt's weekend. I'm not sure they could do the miles anyway. We leave that Friday night and come back Saturday night," I said. "Just so you know."

"You could come on Sunday," Gerrit said.

Sometimes my brother reads me just a little too well. "I'll be fine," I said, not as certain as I tried to sound. "And sorry, by the way, if I set you up there in the restaurant with Reverend Byker."

"Not a big deal," he answered. He lifted a section of tablecloth to check on Frank before shuffling his feet. "What I want to know is, where's this guy's wife?"

Eight

I preferred the eight o'clock service at St. John's and was home starting a second cup of coffee by nine-fifteen Sunday morning. I changed into my running shorts and t-shirt but waited to stretch and begin my jog until the neighborhood migration to church was over. From ten o'clock, when most services began until just after eleven when benedictions were announced, the streets would be vacant and my three-mile run no one else's business.

With a terrycloth sweatband around my ears, I secured the head phones, pushed play, and set off to Hayden's #104. Catching my wind, I settled into the symphony's stride.

I don't mind the heat. I actually relish the humidity of our Michigan dog days. It's when temperatures strain to reach 45 degrees in November that my motivation drops like tired leaves.

After the first mile and a half, which takes me fifteen minutes, I turned back in a homeward direction. The route through the suburban neighborhood was unseasonably green for August. Just before my last sprint up the cul-de-sac, I took advantage of the spray from a neighbor's underground sprinkling system that waters the sidewalk.

Before Sam and Meike returned home that evening, I'd have to fit in a climb up the 92nd Street hill on my bike, though the thought of *fitting in* anything, as if my day was full, seemed ridiculous. Last Wednesday when we met, Dr. Jennings commended me on tackling this bike trip. Pointing out my habit of isolation, he promoted the outing as a social opportunity. He knew he was pushing it. Just showing up regularly at Gerrit's was a stretch for me. If it weren't for Jesse's urging and her promised company, I would have removed my name from the outing altogether.

After a bowl of granola and a peach for lunch, I checked the air in my tires, pedaled up the hill, came back in just under an hour, then took a shower. The rest of the day, I holed up with Odie.

It would help if, somewhere during the weekend, Walt would brush through Meike's hair. A further complication is Meike's super sensitive scalp. She downright hates me when we brush out her hair on Sunday nights.

Never to bad-mouth Walt in the presence of Sam and Meike is one of the most difficult promises I've ever made to myself. The last thing they needed was an already bad situation dragged into competition. No child's heart is that limber. But as I raked my fingers through Meike's ponytail Sunday night, untangling the difference between sparing and honesty wasn't easy.

"Oouw!" she yelped a thousand times. She covered her eyes with clinched fists and sobbed.

"I know it hurts. I know it hurts," I repeated quietly instead of damning Walt.

When the chore was finished, I ran a fresh washcloth under cold water and patted Meike's face with it until we were friends again.

"Now go downstairs and ask Sam to set the ice cream on the counter to soften," I said. Behind the bathroom door, I took a minute to sit on the edge of the tub and swallow the venom in my throat.

We skipped violin practice for Meike, and also Sam's piano scales. "We'll do it in the morning," I told them as we ate our ice cream and licked fudge off our bowls with our tongues.

In two weeks, school would start, both for Sam and Meike and for me. Long lazy Monopoly games, experiments with homemade popsicles, and building Legos until late at night would all dwindle.

Late one afternoon, I stood at the end of the cul-de-sac with Matt's mom, Ruth. Ever since moving here six years ago, Sam considered Matt his best friend. Our coming from a twenty-acre hobby farm off a gravel road made the spanking new sidewalks a novelty, and Sam's big wheel was the first thing unloaded from the U-Haul on moving day. He took off immediately. Not ten minutes later, no introduction needed, Sam and Matt VanderWilp followed each other back and forth, back and forth, a racket of sturdy plastic wheels on the concrete grooving through the neighborhood. From then on the boys were tight.

That meant that Ruth and I were often in touch by quick phone calls or chats on the street and, over the years, she's become my friend. And not because I'm married to Walt. Ruth doesn't like Walt.

The two of us watched Matt's little sister, Stacy, push her Cabbage Patch baby in the stroller. Meike carried her doll wrapped in a receiving blanket and walked next to her.

"Wonder if the boys will be in the same room this year," Ruth said.

"I hope Sam gets Annette Bylsma, but I think he wants Wellinga," I said.

"Matt wants Wellinga."

"It'd be cool for them to have a guy. But I like Annette."

Ed's beat up Camaro turned in the street. In front of the Vander-Wilp house, he revved the engine three times, a signal he was home and for the boys to move the bikes that blocked the drive.

"Best time for the pool is about two," Ruth said. "See ya tomorrow."

"We'll be there. Send Sam home, will you?"

Of the thirty people who took the bike trip around Mission Peninsula, I was the oldest. Besides seven teenagers and two twelve-year-old boys, I was the only one without a spouse, except for Reverend Byker, who brought his daughter.

I was also the only female who scaled the steepest hill without stopping to rest, something that earned me a lot of pats on the back at the barbeque that night. After I told Sam and Meike about the feat, they were so impressed they bragged about it to Walt the next time he picked them up.

The day after Labor Day, we started school. Sam to fifth grade, Meike to third grade, and me to Dutch class in the morning three times a week, with geometry at the high school in the afternoon on Mondays and Thursdays.

In the evenings, the kids did their music lessons while I cleaned up supper. Afterward we used the kitchen table as a common area for homework. Meike labeled her leaf collection with magic marker, Sam sketched his maps of Central America. Afterward, they took turns drawing with my protractor and quizzed me with my flashcards—Dutch side toward me, English toward them.

They knew I didn't have all the answers, but at least saw me plug along beside them.

~

When I called Richard on Monday to set our next appointment, I said I hadn't contacted the accountant he recommended yet, but that the financial statement wasn't ready anyway.

"I have a message about it from Walt's attorney this morning," Richard said, "asking for two more weeks."

"It doesn't seem to be a priority for him. I guess he's too busy with buying Michael out."

"He's going to buy his partner out?"

"Yeah. He used to talk about it every once in a while. Guess now he's making work of it."

"Aaah . . . I'm beginning to see."

"See what?" I asked

Richard took a minute to answer, something I was getting used to. And liked. He didn't say much without thinking it out first. "He's probably toying with the value."

Nine

Richard Dekker ushered me into the conference room and explained he would join me momentarily. Having just finished studying Walt's financial statement that morning, he wanted to make an additional copy for me. I nodded and took a seat at the long polished mahogany table facing the view of downtown.

From time to time when I'd run into Richard at Meike's violin lessons, he'd been in his jeans and a t-shirt. Here at the office, he dressed in pressed tailored suits, subtle dark browns or grays. Never a sport coat. Never a knit collar. Like the professional atmosphere inside the law firm, his wardrobe suggested not just good taste, but trustworthiness. When he came in and sat down across from me, carefully soothing his tie over the front of his white shirt, the gesture had meticulous written all over it.

"I'd like your permission to send this to an outside accountant." Richard placed the copy of the financial document on my side of the table. "Are you still fine with Leonard Zwart?"

"Sure. And thanks for referring him. We met on Tuesday to look over the realtor's assessment on the Glendale Street house." I lifted the top few pages of Walt's financial statement. "But how will we know this is legit?"

Richard had admitted his general cynicism from day one. Now it was evident in his smirk. "Specifically, we won't." He thumbed the report quickly. "I suspect it's deflated, but Zwart can tell us if he thinks it's way out there. Do you know this accountant, Koening?"

"Guy from our church. Part of the Walt network."

Richard picked up his pen. "It would be stupid of them to cook it." Instead of making a note, he leaned forward. "We could get an order for records over the last few years, but my guess is Walt knows that. A thorough review like that would be expensive for him." From a neat stack next to his yellow legal pad, he lifted a single sheet of paper and frowned. "And a proposal to buy Michael out reinforces the figures, although I'd bet anyone the figures are hedged downward."

Frustrated, I took a deep breath and exhaled a short, impatient sigh. The intention wasn't to milk Walt for everything I could get. Checks payable to me in the same amount I had run the house with before Walt left arrived promptly in the mail twice a month, no questions asked. I paid all the expenses, even half of the kids' tuition—and still had a few bucks left over to do with as I wished.

We didn't have any personal debts other than thirty-two months left on the mortgage and a few hundred dollars on a Master Card. I knew the value of the houses, the one the kids and I live in and the one built and never lived in on Glendale Street, and I knew the cottage and lake property's worth. I used to do the cement-cutting accounts as well as bookkeeping and payroll for the printing company. After Sam and Meike were born, I kept informed of the day-to-day business of both places, but lost interest in details of Walt's further entrepreneurial adventures. Still, staring at the totals in front of me, I didn't think it possible to know an honest fair share or its future potential.

"What do you think?" I asked Richard.

"My job is to get you a fair settlement." He sat back and drew his hands to his mouth in a flat, prayer-like position, blinking slowly. "But my advice is we get Zwart's take on it. Then decide."

Since advice is what I paid him for, I agreed.

With that settled, Richard clicked his ball point and smiled just enough for me to notice. "Do your homework?"

I pulled the manila folder from under my purse then shifted my chair closer to the table.

Air conditioned environments chill me, and I wear a light cardigan indoors all summer long. Abruptly warm, I pushed my sweater sleeves up to my elbows, as if the most confident person in the building ready to get down to business.

Inside the folder was one lousy sheet of ruled paper. Three short lines of Walt's handwriting were scribbled across it in blue ink.

"I had him write it down," I told Richard. "Walt has this annoying habit of altering what he said earlier, or denying he said it in the first place. I asked him, just like you said. 'Why exactly is it you want a divorce?' And a few days later, there it was, supposedly in a nut shell."

I cleared my throat, sat up straight, and wiggled like getting ready for performance. "Number one: you want to be a Lutheran," I announced. "Number two: you want to write a book." I looked up to see if he was catching my charade. "Number three." I returned my eyes to the note as if I didn't know it by heart. "You want to go to college."

He didn't laugh. I lowered my voice and cut the drama. "He said no particular order." My eyes teared up and out of habit I blamed the lithium first instead of Walt's pathetic reasoning.

Richard pulled on one of his earlobes before speaking. "I like this guy less and less."

I had to look away.

The slant of the sun on the buildings appeared noticeably different than a couple of months ago during summer vacation, though our appointments had been the same time, the same days when Meike and Sam were with Walt. Staring at the brick façade outside the tenth-story windows, I shook my head. "Those aren't the real reasons."

I don't waste time chatting nor offer information Richard doesn't ask for. Even Dr. Jennings has to practically yank stuff out of me. By now, Richard had a sense for that and asked me straightforward.

"What's the real reason?"

I turned slowly and faced him. "My bipolar."

Only one of his bushy eyebrows shot up, and that, only for a second. "Oh?" He laid his ball point down on the legal pad and waited.

It's stupid thinking, but if there was a choice involved I'd pick some other chronic ailment. Asthma, migraines, thyroid disorder. Dr. Jennings encourages me to think of bipolar like one would think of diabetes or arthritis, implying there's no shame attached. But he can't tell me people don't have a different reaction to folks with diabetes than to folks with bipolar. Might as well say leprosy.

I don't use the term "bipolar" unless Walt brings it up first. Except to explain things to Gerrit, whom I trust to use the word correctly.

Richard unlaced his slender fingers. "Based on my knowledge—and I'm no expert—you don't seem bipolar to me."

I interpreted that as a positive. "Actually, it's Bipolar II. The mania thing is there, but less of an issue than depression." He wasn't taking notes and I felt comfortable continuing. "It scares Walt," I tried to explain. "He thinks I'm some kind of Patty Duke or something. He makes a bigger deal of it than it is. On the other hand . . ." I laughed softly, " . . . he certainly can't tell people he's leaving because I want to be Lutheran, for crying out loud."

With eyes closed, Richard shook his head in slow motion. After a long minute, he added, "Then there's the 'in sickness and in health' thing."

Our backgrounds have similarities. The old neighborhood, his grandfather walking past our house on his way home from the factory. One of Meike's violin recitals had taken place in his and Kristine's church that held the same Calvinist foundation I'd been brought up with. Where a vow was a vow was a vow.

"I should have told you earlier."

"Don't worry, Jane. You're fine."

I didn't feel so fine. In spite of his kindness, I felt exposed and picked up my folder. "I need to go." I fumbled through my purse for my parking ticket.

Richard stood when I did and held the conference room door open. He accompanied me to his secretary's desk without a word or any fuss and waited while she stamped my parking ticket. Grateful for his quiet calm, I extended my hand to signal goodbye. He shook it firmly.

"Call me in a week or so. I'll send the report to Hofstra."

I walked through the hallway and, at the elevator, pushed the down arrow.

~

Daylight Saving Time ended, and we turned the clock back an hour. Two days later, dusk snuck over the kitchen table while I was still measuring angles in my word problems. Sam and Meike were at Walt's. It felt like eight o'clock. I closed the geometry text and packed it in my book bag, and then shrugged when I passed the microwave. Only six-twenty-eight.

Odie followed me into the den. Instead of reviewing Dutch vocabulary for tomorrow's quiz, I scuffed the piano bench across the shag carpet and sat down. My right hand rolled a few C Major chords on the spinet, tinny and barely in tune.

I'd purchased the Lutheran hymnal a year ago. Holding its pages open with *The Psalter* on one side and *Let Youth Praise Him* on the other, I ran through "O Blessed Holy Trinity" five times, once for each verse.

Before long, I lost myself practicing a Chopin nocturne. Opus 72 is composed in a haunting E Minor, slipping from bittersweet to sweet and back in a few measures. Correct phrasing is absolutely necessary. By wrong phrasing, Chopin said, the pseudo-musician shows "music is not his mother-tongue but something foreign and incomprehensible." A dilettante, I did know exactly how it was supposed to sound from my Arthur Rubinstein CD.

An hour of careful fingering slipped by when Odie perked his ears and rose to all fours. I stopped in the middle of a phrase and slid the piano bench back. Reaching through the door, I hit the button on the outside casing. The garage door rumbled up its track, letting the autumn night into the hallway while, Sam, Meike and Walt climbed from the pickup.

"We had tuna casserole," Sam said as I held the door.

"With yucky peas." Meike pulled a face and stuck out her tongue. "Mrs. Lamar dropped it off."

I rolled my eyes and looked at Walt.

He laughed and said to Meike, "You sure liked the bread sticks, though."

"She ate six of them." Sam picked up Odie with one arm, scuffed his ears and apologized to him. "We could have taken you along, boy. Thought we were going to Windemuller's for a shrimp basket."

"We'll go on the weekend," Walt said.

"Better say goodnight to your dad," I said. "We're letting cold air in."

"Got a minute?" Walt asked. He gripped the door, smearing the glass, and followed me in.

His eyes scanned the kitchen, the den, the half-bath as if he expected it to look different than a few weeks ago when he was last inside.

"Stay on the rug, please," I said.

He wiped his feet like I cared about dirt on the floor, when really I just didn't want him any further in the house.

The kids said goodbye. Since it was a school night, we said they should go up and get ready for bed. Walt bent down and held Odie by the collar, scratching the fur on the side of the dog's belly. "Smells like you need a bath, Odie."

I sighed, impatient. "So, what's up?"

"Talk to your lawyer lately?"

"I'll see him on Thursday."

"There's an orientation by the Friend of the Court. Anyone getting divorced in Michigan is required to go. Mine's scheduled for next week. Yours, the week after."

"Fine."

Walt straightened up. "We'll have to sit through it. Hofstra says it one of those things geared for welfare families and so on. Suppose they don't know their rights and that."

"I suppose." I was learning better how to ignore Walt's condescension.

He zipped his nylon parka and turned to leave. Tipping his head sideways, he did an about-face. "I filed for custody."

My chin doubled as I jerked my head back. "You're not serious."

He just stood there.

I had to look down, down at the floor, down at his huge brogans trampling the innocuous rag-rug, before I plucked up. "Well, that was stupid."

Ten

As often happened, the hushed surroundings of the law firm's reception area settled the jitters that had arose on my way to Richard's office. Expressways, city traffic, parking ramps, elevators didn't intimidate me. I knew my way around town. Meeting with my attorney . . . having an attorney . . . that's what still felt uncomfortable to me, what I couldn't get through my head.

I shook his hand and followed him to the conference room. We sat at the mahogany table. He laid a fresh yellow legal pad next to a manila folder at his right hand and pushed the hold buttons on the phone. I placed my purse on the floor, folded my hands in my lap. He straightened his tie. We got right down to business.

"I've received a notice for the Friend of the Court orientation." He opened the folder, took out a single sheet of paper and showed me a letter. "It's mandatory in Michigan. You're assigned October 27. Walt's on the 20th."

I nodded. "Walt gave me a heads up the other night."

"They tell you what procedures are necessary, options for settlement without attorneys, realistic time expectation, what public resources are available. Things of that nature. Nothing we haven't already talked about."

"Okay."

Richard turned the letter over and set it to his left.

He opened the folder again but didn't remove the contents. Instead, he folded his large hands on the table in front of him and seemed to study the papers for a moment from that angle.

My intuition said to speak up. "He said he was asking for custody. I didn't take him seriously."

He picked up what turned out to be three pages stapled together.

Richard doesn't slide things across the table. He went ahead and placed the page right side up in the exact spot where I could read it.

"MOTION FOR TEMPORARY ORDER Plaintiff moved that the court: 1 – Award Plaintiff custody of the parties' minor children . . . 2 – Waives Defendant pay support . . . 3 – Refer matter of permanent custody to an independent agency . . ."

My body slumped. This wasn't my macaroni and cheese Walt was complaining about. This wasn't blowing off dinner by candlelight or falling asleep on the couch with indifference. Moving to his own apartment, even filing for divorce—none of it was this poor.

I moved my chair closer. Elbow on the table, I rested my forehead in my hand and scanned the order.

"This reads as if he wants this to take effect right away."

I focused on the city's skyline through the window. Richard waited, patient and still.

"What was he thinking?" I finally asked out loud.

Richard took the opportunity to move things along again. "You're quite certain there's not another woman in the picture? Someone he wants to marry?"

"I doubt it. Walt's ambitious, but not when it comes to that kind of thing. Does it make much difference? Custody wise, I mean?"

"It could." He smiled a derisive smile. "You know. Another, nice happy family."

"Geez." I imagined some well-endowed woman, pretty, but wide through the hips. Minnesota type, in love with her kitchen. I shook my head slowly. "I still don't think so."

Richard sat back and folded his hands across his chest. "Sometimes the father acts just for the record."

"How do you mean?"

"Well, kids grow up. Ask questions. How would it look if Walt never made some sort of attempt, if there wasn't some sort of petition?"

"I see what you're saying."

I breathed a little easier before glancing at the Motion once more. A wisenheimer smile was hard to suppress. "He spelled her name wrong."

"How's that?"

"Meike." I set an index finger on the page. "Meike Anne. He spelled it 'A-n-n.' Without the 'e.'"

For the first time that afternoon, Richard made a note on the legal pad.

~

Walt and I agreed Sam and Meike should continue to attend Fourth CRC. Walt would take them on his weekends, and I would take them when they were home with me. As far as I was concerned, catechism classes were mandatory and, since they were held after morning services, the kids kept up with those as well.

If Jesse caught me in the vestibule, we would visit until our children were dismissed. Otherwise, I felt conspicuous hanging around church. A mere three-quarters mile away, I'd scoot home, let Odie outside, down a cup of coffee, and turn around again.

One Sunday morning while the kids and I munched our cinnamon toast at the breakfast table, the Tjepkemas called. "It's been a while since we've seen you, Janie. Keith and I were hoping you could stop by after church this morning," Cindy said. "I'll have the coffee on."

We had been friends with the Tjepkemas for over twenty years. Our families camped together, we sent our kids to the same school, belonged to the same church. New Year's Eve meant celebrating at each other's place with the kids, and over spring break we rented adjoining condominiums on the ocean.

The autumn day flushed golden and burnt red in the late morning sunlight. I left my sweater in the car and strolled up Tjepkema's driveway, reminded of other years, other mild October days in peak color season when we lodged together on Crystal Mountain as a foursome.

Cindy answered the front door. "Can you believe this gorgeous weather?" She was a tall gal, taller than her husband, Keith, sturdy but not overweight. Her hair was cut in a straight pageboy to flatter her round face and deep eyes, the color of maple syrup.

Keith had changed from his suit and tie to a short-sleeved crew he tucked in baggy jeans with a stretchy canvas belt. During our twenties, Keith's stocky physique stayed powerful, but now a middle aged belly was evident, though not as prominent as Walt's.

His face wrinkled into a smile. "Good to see you, Janie." We shook hands and when he sealed our grip with his left hand, any awkwardness I'd anticipated disappeared.

We sipped hot coffee just ground, brewed and poured into China cups with saucers. I breathed in the vapor and began to feel rejuvenated after a long and boring sermon.

Like all good Dutchmen would do late Sunday morning, Keith asked, "What'd you think of Art this morning?"

"Reverend Byker's a nice guy and all." I rolled my eyes and sighed. "But his sermons are mostly goo."

With a hearty laugh, Cindy stomped her foot and gave me a look of appreciation. "I knew you'd say something like that. You hate touchy feely."

"God, yes. 'Go ye, therefore, and be well adjusted.'" I said, my arms raised.

Keith got up and opened the French door half way, letting the autumn air whimsy on through. It smelled like summer again, only drier. "Get to the cottage at all, Janie?"

"Nah. The kids and I set up a tent next to Jesse's clan on the beach one of those ninety degree weekends." I watched Cindy pour refills from the thermos server. "Walt's gone to the cottage alone a couple of times. He pulled the boats out last week and parked them at the shop with For Sale signs."

"He told me the cottage is going on the market," Keith said.

"We'll wait until after the holidays, but, yeah, that's the plan."

I knew Keith saw Walt around town, and I knew Walt's accountant, Larry Koening, belonged to the same golf league as Keith. I also knew the time and place to defame Walt wasn't around Tjepkema's dining table with Sunday coffee and bundt cake. But just the thought of Walt's finagling irritated me, and I'm sure Cindy and Keith could tell.

I turned to check the wall clock. "Five to twelve. The kids are almost out."

"I'll go get them." Keith snatched his keys from the counter. "Be right back."

Four glasses were already set out on the counter and Cindy slipped a few ice cubes in each one. Keith was back in five minutes with Sam, Meike, Ricky the red-headed spitting image of Keith, and Cheryl, who, except for having Cindy's eyes, looked like Keith, too. Cindy filled the glasses with soda.

"Thanks," Sam said. He looked at me and I winked.

"I heard Meike play her violin at Mother's Club last week, Keith," Cindy said. "It was lovely. What do you call that song, Meike?"

"Minuet in G," Meike said. She toyed with the end of her braid. When I stretched an arm around her waist, pulling her close, she relaxed and leaned against me.

"Sam, want to check out my baseball cards?" Ricky asked.

"Sure do." Sam polished off his soda. "I got Jim Abbott last week."

"We need to go in a few minutes, Sam," I said.

Cindy folded her arms and made an attempt to sound bossy. "You should stay for dinner." As if she hadn't already set me up, she added, "It's so nice outside we're going to grill burgers. There's plenty."

Sam and Meike raised their eyebrows and looked at me, expectant.

"Meike's wearing her prettiest dress," I said.

Cindy shook her head. "Oh, she can put on some of Cheryl's jeans."

"I already thawed pork chops." I tried to avoid Sam's eyes, but Meike stuck out her lower lip, and I felt stingy.

"They'll keep 'til tomorrow," Cindy said.

"Yeah, they'll keep 'til tomorrow," Sam said, like it was as simple as that.

And I suppose it was.

"Okay." I bonked the counter with my fist. "Then I guess we're staying."

"Yes!" the kids cheered.

We watched them chase off—the boys to Ricky's room, the girls still in their dresses to a swing in the yard. I turned to Cindy and Keith with a clumsy smile. For some reason, tears slipped down my face, and I looked away, not wanting them to see.

Eleven

Walt's motion for temporary custody led The Friend of the Court to schedule a conciliation conference that November. The purpose of the session was to discuss the possibility of joint custody. The notice stated that if the Plaintiff and the Defendant were unable to agree, the conciliator would submit his own recommendation for custody to the court.

Even prior to Richard's call to inform me of the meeting, the idea of joint custody between two people unable to manage a marriage seemed implausible to me.

"You and Walt need to talk about the prospect," Richard said over the phone.

"According to that dopey motion of his, joint custody isn't what Walt has in mind either," I said. "Besides. If we were given joint custody, what's to keep Walt from his usual 'I know better than you' attitude?" The thought of that eternal battle exhausted me.

I might have wiped off the front of the refrigerator or set out an after-school snack for Meike and Sam like moms do in movies when they're on the phone. Instead, I stood there business-like in the kitchen, waiting while Richard considered his reply.

"Jane, I do understand your concern, and you're probably right," he said. "But when it comes to the 'Best Interest of the Child,' as they say, joint custody is the trend. It's become the court's preference. Also, they would see an attempt in that direction favorably."

I played with the extra-long cord and untangled it enough to reach the kitchen table. "Well. All right. I'll bring it up to Walt." I pulled out a dining chair and sat down. "I'm having a hard time imagining such a thing. Honestly, seems I'd be at a disadvantage. What's your take on joint custody?"

A beat of rain on the kitchen window distracted me, drawing my attention to the backyard. The random maple saplings beyond the lawn were for the most part leafless. The gym set, hand-built of lumber, stood deserted and stark, the sand beneath it spotted deep brown by the downpour. In the interim before Richard answered, I gathered the hood of my sweatshirt further around my neck and wondered if the phone cord would reach far enough for me to turn up the thermostat in the living room.

"In a marriage where the husband has defined himself in a role of the head of the household, treating the ex-partner as an equal is likely beyond him." Richard paused as if making a note on his legal pad. "I can imagine fairness would be limited."

"Yeah." I nodded to myself. "Another thing. Isn't joint custody confusing for the kids?"

"Interesting you would say that. There have been significant studies made. Some experts say instead of the benefit of two parents, in the long run the children have neither. Not uncommon. There are documented cases. You could find them in journals at the library."

The next morning after Dutch class, I spent time in the college library researching the subject. Several articles reviewed cases where joint custody proved to be a disadvantage in terms of the "Best Interest of the Child." I made some photocopies. About an hour before Sam and Meike returned home from school that afternoon, I called Walt at the shop.

Walt sometimes tries to make small talk with me when he phones, which is way more often than I phone him. Straight to the point is my theory, no matter who initiated the call. Too late for niceties.

"Has your lawyer told you about the Friend of the Court conference the week after next?" I asked.

"For talking over joint custody, right?"

"Uh-huh. Do you want to talk about it?"

"Not really," he said.

Not a surprise. I believed Walt thought he had custody all wrapped up anyway. But maybe we should sit down the two of us and talk about it. So, I clarified. "I mean, you and me. Discussing joint custody."

"Not particularly."

"Well, me either."

~

In an attempt to brace for November, I added two extra appointments with Dr. Jennings along with our weekly sessions. Seasonal affective disorder technically wasn't my diagnosis. But as November's chilly rains fell through what little daylight there was, I worried depression would clinch me harder than ever. I fought the temptation to set my lithium aside and let the neurotransmitters in my brain open their gates wide.

The night following Thanksgiving, Sam and Meike wanted to roast hot dogs and marshmallows in the fireplace. Walt had taken off on Monday to spend the holiday in Minnesota with his brother and aunts and uncles who still lived in the small town where Walt was born. My mother and father had joined the kids and me for turkey and all that goes with it, and after days of preparation earlier in the week, the suggestion for an easy supper sounded good to me.

"The absolute first thing is to open the flue," I explained. "Sam, see if you can pull the dingus on the brick there."

The damper scraped against the chimney. Meike tossed a handful of kindling on the grate.

"The newspapers go first," I said and gathered the pieces up again. "Like we did camping this summer."

We crumpled the newspaper. With a half dozen wads in place, Sam and Meike laid the kindling back on top, making sure each piece touched another.

"I get to light it." Sam slid the box of kitchen matches open and took one out.

"Careful," I said as he leaned forward and grazed the match head on the side of the box. It lit on the first try. "Right on the edge of the newspaper."

The kindling caught and flared. Odie got up and moved as far away from the hearth as possible without leaving the room.

"It's okay, boy." Sam crawled to Odie and rubbed the dog's belly.

I laid a short stub of applewood over the whole works and when it started to snap, topped it crosswise with a bigger, split piece.

A card table we'd set up at one end of the den held paper plates, buns, relishes and potato chips. Meike and I both put our hot dogs on one wiener fork and took turns holding it above the fire.

"Yours is getting black," Meike told her brother.

"That's the way I like it," he said.

We ate two hot dogs each, then broke open the marshmallows. After Meike's first one fell in the fire, she let me hold her arm while together we roasted another, golden brown and puffy.

Grinning at the black gob at the end of his fork, Sam said, "I love my marshmallows well done."

Meike licked the end of her fingers. "Dad sure missed good turkey."

Sam glared at his sister and sighed hard. "He wouldn't have come anyway, dope."

"Meike got an 'A' on her science report," I said. "She's pretty smart, actually,"

Meike stuck her tongue out at her brother. "I can play the violin and you can't."

"And I can play the baritone."

"No, you can't," she snapped back.

"That's enough, you two."

The chunk of log on the grate broke in pieces and flared when I poked and turned it. At Sam's suggestion, I chose another, one that took me two hands to lift and place on the coals. We sat down on the carpet to watch the flame grow.

Odie licked marshmallow off Sam's hand. Sam lay back and rested his head in the dog's curly fur. "Why'd Dad have to go for a whole week, anyway?"

A mom can't just answer a question like that. Without sharpness, without whining, without anything but doleful honesty. Sam was only looking for some explanation as to why his holiday was messed up. He deserved a reasonable answer. I couldn't give him one.

"Your dad and I used to go to Minnesota for Thanksgiving more often. In fact, we went when you were babies, too. But you wouldn't remember. We went once when you were one, Sam, and Meike was a little bitty four-month old. Want to see the pictures?" Most of our photo albums were organized chronologically in an upper cupboard next the hearth. It took me less than a minute to pull out "1983."

"We usually stayed at Uncle Harry's." Waiting until Meike wiggled to a comfortable position in front of me, I reached around and opened the book across her lap. Sam scooted close. "Oh, yeah, but that year we stayed in Iowa at your Grandpa and Grandma's first. That's Aunt Linda." I pointed to a lady wearing a happy expression, a baby propped in her arms so that their cheeks touched. The baby's feathery dark hair stood straight up, wild in all directions, emphasizing bright attentive eyes set in her perfectly round face. Fist in mouth, content, the baby stared back at us. "That's you, Meike."

Recognizing the photo, she grinned proudly and nodded.

My mother had crocheted the dress Meike wore in the picture. An old-fashioned cap sleeve, a waist set off by a satin ribbon woven through the soft green fibers, folds of the umbrella skirt reaching over her snug white booties. "You look like a beautiful China doll. Doesn't she, Sam?"

He shrugged and I pointed to the shot of him at the dinner table with a cowboy bib tied around his neck. "Looks like cranberry sauce all over your face. Wouldn't Odie like to lick that?"

We flipped a few more pages. "The day after Thanksgiving we drove up to Minnesota."

We sat bunched together on the floor, looking through pictures of Minnesota cousins, the farmhouse, a go-cart Uncle Harry promised we could ride if we'd come back in the spring. I set the album aside. Meike curled up, sleepy, and nuzzled her face against my sweatshirt while Sam and I stared at the fire, now more glow than flame.

"It was ten-below zero on our way home that year," I told Sam. But I didn't tell him how we waited on the Interstate in Wisconsin for three hours while the state police cleared a semi that had jack-knifed in front of us on the icy highway. Or how afraid I was that we were all going to freeze to death, two babies in wet diapers, hungry in their car-safety seats in the back. And I didn't tell him how the next year at Uncle Harry's, we were snow-bound for two extra days before it was safe for us to trek out on the highway back toward home. Or how during the snow squalls in the approximate vicinity of the Wisconsin

Dells, I pledged up and down and out loud that I would never make that trip again unless it was the middle of summer.

I reached for Sam's hand and folded it under my arm. "We sure made a nice fire tonight."

The three of us dozed off and an hour later, dragged ourselves to bed without brushing our teeth.

Twelve

By the first of December, I fulfilled my geometry prerequisite with a "complete" from my tutor. Dutch class proved more challenging than I expected. My parents spoke a Groningen dialect interspersed with regional slang, which made learning the official language confusing at times.

A week before the final in Dutch 101, our class was invited to our professor's annual St. Nicholas Day party. "And bring the children," he made a point of saying, though all the other students were more or less kids themselves.

My mother remembers celebrating St. Nicholas Day, December 6, as a child in the Netherlands. In the Dutch tradition, St. Nicholas, *Sinterklaas*, arrives already in November, on a steamer ship from Spain along with his helper, *Zwarte Piet*. *Sinterklaas* has been busy visiting around the country on a white horse, determining if the children had been well-behaved. My mother likes to tell us how, on the eve of St. Nicholas, children fill their wooden shoes with carrots or hay and set them out for the horse. The next morning, the children find in their shoes a chocolate initial letter or chocolate coins, *pepernoten*, and little gifts. Or they find a lump of coal.

When I was growing up, Christmas meant the birth of Jesus, but the story of St. Nicholas had commingled enough that even Sam and Meike knew who *Zwarte Piet* was.

A merging of that sort would never happen in Walt's family. Now and then when a word of Gronings slipped from my mouth at the dinner table, Walt would say, "Don't talk Dutch!" Then he'd tell Meike and Sam, "Even though my grandfather came here from Germany, no one ever used any German on the farm. My mother was told, 'We are Americans and we speak English in this house.' So when I was growing up, we never spoke German in our house either."

No wonder Sam wasn't interested in "a silly Dutch party" and said he would rather spend the night at Walt's. Meike, however, looked forward to the party and asked if we could get dressed up for the occasion.

A wet snow fell but didn't accumulate as we drove the ten miles to the college on St. Nicholas Eve. Meike and I had made a compromise. She wore her favorite Sunday dress with tights instead of her violin recital dress, and instead of jeans, I wore an angora sweater with a black corduroy skirt that reached to the top of my boots.

We buttoned up our coats against the wind and took each other's hand while crossing the parking lot. Entering the nearest building to get out of the cold, we walked the east hall. "This is where we have our Dutch class," I said. Although Room 207 was locked, we peeked through the glass door.

A pleasant aroma, the blend of ginger and cinnamon and roasted nuts, welcomed us outside of the Dutch Department. We hung our coats with the others on a portable chrome rack.

Professor Leitsma himself greeted everyone at the door, his brogue warm and genuine. Only a few years away from retirement, he had stayed fit and handsome, with a full head of straight, silver hair. "Janie!" he said like he'd never seen me this side of the ocean. I offered my hand and he pulled me into an unexpected stiff hug, which, by the look on her face, surprised Meike, too.

"This must be the lovely daughter you're always talking about!"

Meike looked at me instead of him, her face turning pinkish. I slipped an arm around hers and touched a long loose wave of her hair. "Yes," I said, hoping she'd catch the admiration in my voice. "This is Meike."

Inside the main conference room, a reception area was sectioned off by a large table covered with a cloth of white Dutch lace. The table held a sparkling bowl of red punch and several untouched platters of wurst and cheese, breads and pig-in-the-blanket. A silver tea cart displayed fancy licorices, white chocolate, cookies and *banket.* Several rows of chairs with an aisle in the center took up three-quarters of the rest of the room.

Most guests were already seated, maybe thirty adults, none of whom I recognized, a dozen or so students and, from what I could tell, three children besides Meike. She and I found two empty places in the last row.

At the piano in a corner, a lady began "Santa Claus, Good Holy Man! Put Your Best Robe On." Her large bosoms reached as far as her elbows when she played. She stopped after the first few bars and began the stately tune again from the beginning. People started singing along.

> *"Sinterklaas, goed heilig man! Trek je bete tabbered an,*
> *rif er mee naar Amsterdam, van Amsterdam naar Spanje . . ."*

Meike is four years past believing in Santa Claus. But when a figure appeared in the doorway and paraded down the aisle, she knew—we all knew—it was St. Nick.

St. Nicholas wears a long red cape over his white bishop's dress. His long hair the color of snow, blends into a flowing beard and moustache, so that the three look as one. The tall miter on his head is red with gold brocade and a cross of ruby jewels in the center. It reaches to an inch above his pure white bushy eyebrows.

He holds a long golden staff with a fancy curled top called a crosier.

And he carries a black book.

I heard Meike catch her breath, her eyes fixed. Acted out in front of my daughter, the pageantry my mother had been talking about all these years made my throat thick and my eyes watery. Until a short little man darted into the room with a large burlap sack over his shoulder.

"*Zwarte Piet!*" Meike grabbed my arm and danced in place on her tiptoes.

In the traditional story, *Zwarte Piet* was a black slave. In an attempt toward racial sensitivity and to save a little face while still continuing the tradition, Black Pete is now referred to as a chimney sweep. His clothes and frizzy dark hair seemed covered with soot, and his face was black with charcoal dust. He stopped halfway in the aisle, and leaped up several times to look over the gathering. Then he skipped to where Professor Leitsma sat and jumped behind the professor's chair, pretending to hide.

We sang a song of St. Nicholas coming on a steamboat from Spain, with ". . . *appeljes from Oranje . . .*" and another song about *Zwarte Piet* riding his bike in the countryside and getting a flat tire.

Professor Leitsma had us sing "*Sinterklaas, kapoentje, Gooi wat in mijn schoentje,*" that asks Santa to leave "something in my shoe."

St. Nicholas opened his big black book and ran his finger down the pages. *Zwarte Piet* sprang up and out of hiding. He was the one who never spoke a word, but opened his sack to dig out presents, making a big show of it. Everyone must have been good. Except Professor Leitsma. His pretty box from *Zwarte Piet*, wrapped in red and silver foil, held nothing but a lump of coal.

"Grandma should be here," Meike said, laughing.

Her face beamed as we stood in line to taste the *saucijzebroodje.*

"Grandma told me there wouldn't be *oliebollen*," she said.

"Did she tell you why?"

"Because they're for New Year's."

"That's right. The Dutch don't make fat balls for Christmas."

St. Nicholas and his helper went on their way, and the party geared down. Hot chocolate was served in glass mugs and we sang, "*Stille Nacht, Heilige Nacht.*"

On our way back through town, Meike stayed quiet. Without the radio or cassettes playing, we could almost hear the enormous snowflakes land on the windshield before the wipers pushed them aside. I thought Meike had fallen asleep, but a half mile from home she asked in a hushed voice, "How did *Zwarte Piet* know what chocolate letter to give me?"

I smiled in the dark, keeping my eyes on the road, not wanting to spoil the little bit of magic in the December night. "Hmmm. That's a good question," I whispered.

We had left an extra light burning and the house looked cozy as we pulled in. After letting Odie outside, he followed us upstairs and jumped on Meike's bed while we dressed in our flannels. Meike's eyes were heavy as I gathered the blankets and quilt around her. I kissed her cheek and sat down on the edge of the bed, smoothing her hair.

Her droopy lids blinked. "I had fun, Mom. It was different, but fun."

"Different is good." I tucked her hair around her ear. "Different's okay."

She curled up on her side, snuggled further under the quilt and let out a long, faint sigh. "You and Daddy are different," she murmured, her eyes already closed.

~

My first choice would have the holidays over with or skipped altogether.

My next idea was to go for painless. Maybe new holiday festivities with Sam and Meike, without the tugs to the past.

A third option called for a traditional Christmas as normal as possible.

Tradition won.

A fresh-cut blue spruce, the Nutcracker on the shelf, cookies we cut and iced. Felt stockings hung on the mantel—Sam, Meike, Janie, Odie—four instead of five. My stocking was over thirty years old. My sister made it back in 1959, complete with "Janie" embroidered in cursive on the cuff. I copied her pattern twice, eight years ago, and had embroidered the cursive "Sam" on one and "Meike" on the other.

I added a new ritual this year. The Lutheran church I had been attending supported a cottage industry. From the display table in the back of church, I purchased a hand-crocheted starched mat that served as a base for an Advent wreath. Sam, Meike and I covered the circumference with evergreens, set it in the middle of the kitchen table and placed tapered candles inside—three purple, one pink, one white. We carried out a little ceremony each week, reading from The Book of Common Prayer, lighting candles in order of their significance until the anticipated center candle on Christmas Day. Hope. Love. Joy. Peace. Light.

None of which felt close at hand.

~

The snowfall overnight measured eleven inches. Jesse had us out to the country for sledding, hot chocolate, and braided coffeecake.

"Maybe I'm trying too hard," I confided to her. "Christmas is bound to suck. No point pretending."

"But it doesn't hurt to soften it a little when you can," Jesse said. "Though I imagine the whole time might be harder for you than it is for them."

"I don't know." I appreciated my friend's effort, though I doubted her observation.

Nothing manic about a moderate spending spree on my part that lay wrapped in festive paper and bows under our tree. Two warm sweaters, Legos, American Girl Doll desk, books, colored pencils, two board games, a new deck of Uno cards.

Typically, I fret when Walt indulges the kids. But this Christmas he could buy them a trip to Disney World for all I cared.

Walt agreed to wait until Christmas morning for his share of custodial time. I agreed to Sam and Meike spending New Year's Eve with him. He promised to return the kids by 5 p.m. Christmas Day so that, in spite of Walt's repulsion to "our Dutchy ways," they could come along with me to my extended family's celebration at Gerrit's. I insisted we make our trade-offs privately. I didn't want my kids feeling like baseball cards.

Meike, Sam and I spent a quiet Christmas Eve together at home opening gifts, popping popcorn, keeping some of our wolfish sadness at bay with hardwood crackling in the fireplace.

On Christmas morning, Walt picked up Sam and Meike for church. They invited him in to show off their gifts.

"Looks like Mom went all out," Walt said, all smiles and Christmas cheer. "And there's more at my place." He winked my way, and, in his endlessly optimistic eyes, for a second I saw a sparkle, a glimpse and reminder why I had ever loved him in the first damn place.

Walt and I had celebrated New Year's Eve with Keith and Cindy each year since Meike and Sam were born. The kids and I went to their place without Walt last year, since at the last minute he "excused" himself, deciding not to go.

I remember how last year Cindy encouraged me to come anyway with the kids. They were all looking forward to it. And so we did. Last year, somewhere during the evening while Meike and Sam had gone off upstairs with Ricky and Cheryl, I quietly relayed to our friends that Walt had threatened to move out.

"Walt won't go through with it," Keith said at the time.

This year, after I told Cindy the kids were going to be with Walt on New Year's, she kindly said for me to come and mark the year's end with them anyway. I said thanks a bunch but no thank you. I had also declined an invitation from Jesse.

During the afternoon of New Year's Eve, Gerrit called.

"Come on over," he said.

"I'd really rather not. I think I'd just as soon be alone. Mope."

"Is that a good idea?"

"It'll be fine."

"Want us to come over there?"

"Nah. I'll be okay."

"Call us if you change your mind."

"Thanks. I'll do that."

Around 10 p.m. I put on Eric Satie and poured myself a good two fingers of cognac. At 11 p.m., another two fingers.

Then I descended to the Barcalounger, oblique.

Thirteen

The kids returned to school the first Monday of January, Sam to his second half of fifth grade, Meike to the rest of third. My semester didn't start until February when, after this month's interim, I would continue my Dutch class and begin one toward my English major.

January is a month of drifting snow and single-digit temperatures when anyone can be reclusive and nobody seems to notice. I took the incentive to invite Jesse over on a Tuesday night while Meike and Sam had their weekday with Walt. The snappy temperatures conjured up images of last summer when Jesse talked me into buying a tent. Sam, Meike and I had joined her and the boys camping in the woods, where she taught us names of trees, wildflowers and grasses I didn't recognize as we hiked in the dunes along the sun-drenched shore of Lake Michigan.

In the middle of a sub-zero January weather pattern, Jesse came that night with a pint of vanilla ice cream and her recipe for hot fudge.

Butter, sugar, sweet milk and cocoa had to boil in the pan for ten minutes. I stirred them constantly with a serving spoon while Jesse chatted.

"If you saw my kitchen right now, you'd die," she said.

"Your membership at the art museum's current?"

"Yes. And the connection is?"

"Jesse, you grow a significant garden and tap trees for maple. Your Thoreau's handy, your camera's always loaded. I admire that. I don't care about your kitchen."

"Okay, okay. But my house is a pig-sty compared to yours. And you're going to college." She divvied the ice cream into two dessert dishes. "I'm supposed to tell you Art says hello."

I turned the burner off and continued stirring. "I haven't been to church since before Christmas."

"He only asked how you are. He knows the holidays can be hard."

"Well, tell him thanks." I slapped the air with my hand as if dismissing those last few weeks of December. "I made it."

When my mother makes hot fudge sauce for Christmas, she makes it thick and gooey. Jesse and I prefer it hot, thin and runny. While Jesse put the empty container in the sink, I ladled the sauce in generous amounts over the creamy white scoops. We picked up our creations, carried them to the couch in the basement, wrapped the down quilt around our legs and watched *Like Water for Chocolate* on the video player.

~

In the early afternoon, three Artic-stiff days later, I dropped a load of bath towels still warm from the dryer at the edge of the dining table as the phone rang.

"I received the Temporary Order," Richard said.

I pushed the towels to the center of the table and pulled out a chair. "And?"

"And I'll read it to you. 'This matter having come before the court pursuant to the Plaintiff's motion for temporary custody: Court having heard arguments of counsel and being otherwise fully appraised on the premises, now therefore, it is hereby ordered as follows: 1) The parties shall have joint physical and legal custody of the minor children. 2) The children will principally reside with the Defendant. Plaintiff's custody time shall be, at minimum, as follows . . .'" Here Richard stopped reading and summarized. "It's the same as the previous ruling."

"So, what's it mean?"

"The joint physical and legal custody—like I predicted—it's about expected. Sole custody's less likely these days. While the term 'joint' should satisfy Walt, the phrase, 'the children principally reside with the Defendant' says Holton hasn't seen a reason to change anything."

A relief, more like a fervent thaw, ran through every part of my body. I lifted the corner of a towel and dabbed my eyes.

"There's more," Richard said.

"Okay."

"Under number three. 'The parties to this case shall submit to counseling pursuant to Act 16 of the Public Acts of 1980. The attorneys shall immediately contact Family Services Association's office to arrange for an appointment. The parties shall comply . . . the willful failure of any party to follow such procedures may be treated as contempt of court."

"What the heck?"

"They do that on joint custody rulings. Hold on—Quote . . . 'the parties shall bear the cost of the counseling. . . . Plaintiff shall continue to pay spousal and child support directly to the Defendant . . .' It's four pages all together. You can look it over when you're in next week."

I thanked Richard for the information.

"We did well, Jane," he said before ending the call.

Shaking out a towel, I brought it to my nose, inhaled deeply and buried my wet face in the absorbent cotton.

When I finished folding and putting the towels in a neat stack on the closet shelf, I splashed my face with cold water, then went to the phone and dialed Gerrit's number. Laura picked up.

"Hi, it's me. Walt's picking up Sam and Meike for the weekend later."

"We can order out for Chinese if you want to come over."

"How about you come here?"

"Sure," Laura said. "We can do that."

"Cool. Bring champagne."

~

Sam and Meike shed their heavy coats, hats and mittens and pulled off their boots on the shag carpet in the den. "Let's bake cookies," Meike said sniffing, her cheeks blotched from the cold.

"But, Meike, your dad's coming at five o'clock to have you for the weekend," I said. "We'll have to wait until next week."

She stomped her foot. "I don't want to go to Dad's. I want to make cookies." She sank to the floor and sat stubborn like she was there to stay. Odie wiggled out of Sam's hold to nudge under her arm.

I checked the hands of the clock above the sink. Sam followed my gaze. "I suppose if we get right to it. You game, Sam?"

He shrugged before smiling. "Sure."

We measured and mixed and took turns flattening the stiff batter on the baking sheet. Promptly at five, Walt knocked and walked in. By that time, our first batch of oatmeal chocolate chip cookies had cooled. Meike placed them carefully in the round Tupperware and I sealed the lid.

"Mmmm. I recognize that smell," Walt said.

Sam picked up the container and handed it to his dad. "Mom said we could take these along."

"Got your hat? Where are your bags?" Walt asked from his place on the rug.

"Just hold on. I'm getting them," I said.

Sam clipped the leash on Odie when I brought the backpacks to the door. We locked together to say goodbye. "Love you, Sam," I said. "See you Sunday."

Dragging her coat across the floor, Meike slipped it on. I zipped it for her then drew her knit hat around her head and tugged it carefully over her ears. We hugged until I drew away. She let me run my fingers along her face before I smooched her cheek and pulled her hood halfway over her eyes. "Love you, Meike."

Walt and I watched through the storm glass door as Sam and Meike tromped through the driveway. "The violin needs to stay warm," I reminded Walt. The kids climbed in the pickup, still running, and I waved. I turned to face Walt, straightening my back, and with a slight smirk, crossed my arms and folded them in front of me. "So. The motion came through from Judge Holton."

He pulled on a pair of gloves and picked up the instrument. "Yes. So what?"

"Looks like the kids will be staying here where they belong."

He leaned his elbow against the door handle, ready to push. "Oh, this isn't finished, Janie."

"I'd say it's finished. It's the judge's order."

“And I’m going to fight it. I’ll fight and I’m going to win. The kids will live with me.”

“Walt.” I snorted and shook my head. “That’s ridiculous.”

“No, Janie. It’s not.” He pulled his rugged eyebrows into a fierce, jagged line. “My attorney says I have a good case. I think you do the kids more harm than good. You’re unstable and unfit.”

“Yeah, right.”

“I’ll prove it. You’re still seeing Dr. Jennings. Over a year now.” Walt sneered. “You’ve been in the hospital twice. Janie—you don’t stand a chance.”

I stuffed my fist into my pockets and straightened my arms, pulling my sweatshirt taut as I looked out at the truck. “The kids are waiting.”

“Take those journals of yours, for example. Line after line, rambling, page after page, up the margins . . . ”

“You read them?”

“They’re freaky.”

“You read my journals?”

“You leave the key right on the safety box.”

“The box is in case of fire. You were in the house and read my journals?” My hands opened palm up and like a claw, questioned the air. “When?”

“There you go, making a big deal of nothing. I needed something from the basement storeroom. You and the kids were gone.”

“Unbelievable.”

“It’s still my house, too, you know.”

“Get out.”

I stood numb watching through the glass door, now frosted at the edges, until the pickup turned the corner. I had the wherewithal to push the remote for the garage door, close the storm, pull the main door shut and find the handrail along the basement stairs.

My stocking feet over the plush carpet of the steps and basement floor were silent, almost slippery, and it felt like I was sneaking around in my own house.

In the office, I pushed open the wooden bi-fold to the closet and dropped to my knees. The miniature key turned easily, its little chain dangled as I lifted the cover of the Sentry 1170. Inside, a half dozen folders held smaller, unmarked manila ones. Behind that, three 5 X 7 spiral notebooks and one stenographer-type lay on their sides. They were all there.

I tugged the cardboard off first, then yanked large stubborn sections of ruled paper from the spirals. My fingers ached before I finished and at some point tears started to run down my face while hushed sobs choked my throat.

I just sat on the floor ripping, ripping, ripping.

Fourteen

Nothing bigger than one-inch pieces was left of the journals. I put the whole pile in a wastebasket and carried it to the fireplace in the den. Once the newspaper and kindling were lit, I fed scraps into the flame by the handful and watched them burn away.

At last, with a generous log in place, I went to the kitchen to pack up the cookie dough and make a grilled cheese sandwich. I made myself eat it, sitting cross-legged on the floor in front of the fire while it flicked shadows in the otherwise dark room.

Gerrit and Laura came around seven o'clock with the champagne, and I greeted them with puffy eyes and a blotchy face. I took the bottle from Gerrit and set it on the counter. "Whadayasay we have brandy instead."

"You look like hell," Gerrit said. He poured brandy into three snifters I took out of the cabinet. "Let's go sit by the fire."

I stepped on the switch for the floor lamp and turned the Barcalounger toward the fire. Laura helped me pull up the couch and set a small stacking table in front of it to hold our glasses. I put on Rachmaninoff and we listened for a while, quiet until the music, the fire and the brandy I breathed deeply before swallowing, loosened my constraint.

"This afternoon I heard from Dekker that the judge turned down Walt's motion. Couple hours later, Walt picks up the kids and tells me he's going for custody anyway. Primary. Permanent." I raised my glass and nodded a silent salute to all things reneged.

The Concerto in F-sharp Minor filled the blank space of the room for a while until Laura spoke up. "I don't understand. If he can't get temporary custody, why does he think he'll get permanent?"

Gerrit scowled and uncrossed his legs. "'Cause he's an asshole, that's why."

I shifted in the Barcalounger and stared at the flames, mulling. "He'll smear me all over the place." I spoke without expression as if dictating notes. "Call on my history. The hospital. Dr Jennings. The whole bipolar song and dance." Looking at my brother, I added, "He says I'm unfit."

He shook his head slowly. "Judas, man." He got up and brought the brandy from the kitchen. Without further comment, he poured another splash for me, then Laura, then himself, then put the cork back in and set the decanter on the mantle.

"It won't work," Laura said. "You've got way too much going for you."

Whether she was underestimating Walt or only trying to reassure me, she made it sound matter-of-fact enough.

"I don't know what to tell the kids." My voice cracked. "What to say to them . . . what should be told . . . or not . . . what Walt said . . ." With the back of my hand, I wiped my eyes. "I don't know what this kind of crap'll do to them . . ." I choked up altogether and watched the applewood burn.

Gerrit poked the fire, added to it, sat back down. As "Rhapsody on a Theme of Paganini" came to a head, tears flowed down my face natural as can be.

"Who's playing this?" Gerrit whispered.

"It's Sergei himself," I answered, rubbing one side of my face on the upper sleeve of my sweater, then the other side on the other sleeve. "Philadelphia. Eugene Ormandy. 1934."

We didn't speak until the rhapsody finished and the second concerto began.

"Do the kids even need to know about this?" Gerrit asked.

I found the remote and lowered the volume. "No. Not right now anyway. But you know Walt's a blabber. Church. School. Neighborhood. You know how this community can be. The kids could pick it up second-hand. That'd be cruel."

"Did you and Walt ever talk more about joint custody?" Laura asked.

"Legally, we already have joint physical and legal custody. But the order says the kids will principally reside with me. I'm leery of set-ups with equally shared time. It's a strain on the kids. Back and forth, back and forth. Different rules. Inconsistent. And often instead of two parents, children end up with none. Those are documented facts." I sighed. "But it's 1993. The trend leans to joint custody. Seems like an easier solution. Until the long run. I don't think Richard's inclined to it either."

"Richard could draw this out—make more money off you."

"No. I doubt it. And he seems to have a moral sense about all this. Especially when I talk about Walt's bully side. Walt's the one who'd take advantage of me. And Richard's up on that."

I swallowed the rest of my brandy and rubbed my tummy.

"You hungry, Janie?"

I shrugged. "Guess I am."

"What can I fix you?"

"I don't know. You guys want something?"

Laura intertwined her fingers and stretched her arms. "We had a big dinner."

"It's after nine. I could stand something to munch," Gerrit said.

"I'll get out crackers and cheese." I got up from the Barcalounger and remembered. "I made a batch of pea soup earlier this week. Sounds good to me right now."

"I'll take a *vlut*," Gerrit said raising his hand, thumb and forefinger a couple of inches apart.

"*Ik ook*," Laura said and went with me to the kitchen.

When the soup was hot, we poured it into three oversized mugs and took them to the den with a plate of *kaas* and crackers. Gerrit selected Brahms from my stack of CDs while I added wood to the fire.

Exaggerating a long slurp, Gerrit smacked his lips. "Delicious."

I concentrated on my soup. With a couple of spoonfuls and a cracker down, I paused and waited for an adverse reaction in my stomach. When nothing happened, I ate the rest—steaming bits of celery, carrot, potato, a little onion and a chunk of ham—without a problem.

Laura reached for a piece of cheese. "I'm trying to think about the possession being nine-tenths of the law thing."

"It's from English common law when landowners ruled. I believe it's nine points of the law." My brother looked at me and seemed to notice the weariness in my expression. "Not about people, though. And yet under your circumstance, it seems one advantage you have among many, Janie."

"I'll call Richard on Monday. He'll have plenty to say, I'm sure."

Our eyes went to the fire. Brahms switched to another violin concerto.

I truly wanted to change the subject. "How's the Theology Department, Gerrit?"

It was going on 11:30 when we brought the dishes to the sink. By then we concurred with Luther—"Gospel" impels man to faith. "Law" impels man to his vocation, namely serving his neighbor.

"You want us to stay over, Janie?"

I shook my head. "Frank's waiting for you."

"I'll go and warm up the car, then." Gerrit pulled his gloves from inside his coat sleeve before stepping outdoors. He returned with a breathy whistle. "Fricking sharp out there. The windshield will take a minute."

"Will you call Dr. Jennings tomorrow?" Laura asked.

"Probably not. It's Saturday. We'll see."

Gerrit checked once more. "You'll sleep? Be okay?"

"I'm exhausted," I said. "Might just curl up right by the fire until morning."

"Call you tomorrow," my brother said as they headed into the brutal night.

Fifteen

I know why people don't allow guns in their homes.

My intention at the time I brought Walt's hunting rifles to the police station was to protect us all—myself and the kids. Even Walt.

Walt is the non-confrontational type. He walks away to turn on television when he's angry. I stomp and yell, slam cupboard doors, or try to pound out Beethoven's "Pathetique" on my spinet. Walt would insist he didn't want to argue, but then go pout. I would want to have it out and over with.

Although Walt is slow to lose his temper, he's rabid when he does. He has never hit me or pushed us around, and I seriously expect he would never shoot anyone. But I hadn't expected our separation or his moving out either. These were strange times in our marriage. People erupt in all kinds of behavior in strange times.

I had acted in fear regarding the rifles. After a first thought to drop the rifles in a dumpster, I drove to the police station and asked at the desk if they'd take them off my hands.

"You did the right thing bringing them here," the policeman said when I simply told him I didn't want guns in the house anymore. Standing behind him in the office, his partner nodded.

If Walt really put us through an actual custody battle, then he certainly deserved to be shot. If he won—if the kids weren't with me—maybe I'd need to shoot myself.

It was the right thing, bringing those rifles away.

In the ongoing task to assess and divide our assets, Walt and I decided he would work with a realtor to put the cottage and lake property on the market. He'd sell the pontoon and motor boats through a newspaper ad. I wanted as little to do with the transactions as possible but included them in notes for Richard and my accountant. A couch, two chairs, the beds, a dresser, and a vacuum cleaner had already been transferred from the lake house to Walt's apartment. I called dibs on the kitchen set, dishes and a couple of framed posters.

A delayed January thaw broke the first week of February and gave Jesse and me an idea to drive out to the cottage one morning to make a pick-up. Meike and Sam had just boarded the school bus when the phone rang.

"Art wants to come along," Jesse said. "He'll give us a hand with the table."

We rarely took the opportunity for a girl's day out. Although I'd been hearing from her how Reverend Byker wanted to be seen as a "regular guy around town" instead of only the minister, I was disappointed Jesse let him intrude.

"We don't need him. We'll never get the table in the trunk anyway. Walt said he'd drop it here on the weekend."

"He bought donuts."

It would mean fewer trips up and down the steps. "Well, in that case, guess we'll put him to work. I'm about ready to leave. Be five minutes."

"Pick us up at church. I'm already here."

I waited while Odie did his thing in the backyard, and when he came in gave him a biscuit. Steering the old Lincoln Town Car through the wet snow on Sun Valley Court, I flipped the visor down to block the morning's glare. Even in February, True-Green lawns on the cul-de-sac poked through mossy, not brown.

When I pulled into the lot, Jesse and Reverend Byker came out of the church decked in jeans, their down jackets open. They carried their hats and gloves, a waxed bakery bag and a thermos.

"Going to be 40 this afternoon," Jesse said, scooting across the bench seat to make room for Reverend Byker.

He closed the car door, set the donuts on his lap and grinned his boyish grin. "Hello, Janie."

"Good morning." I nodded once. "Nice of you to volunteer."

"Just thought we could make a little fun out of a not-so-nice circumstance."

A huge puddle had formed in the drive so I turned the car around and left the way I came.

"This is quite a car. Pretty luxurious," Reverend Byker said. "What year is it?"

"'87. Walt bought it from a buddy who gets repos now and then—Lambert's, over on Division." I turned onto the highway. "Hope that's coffee in the thermos, Jesse. Although we'll have to wait until we're ready to leave again to enjoy it. The place is winterized. Nowhere to go to the bathroom or anything and you know how that is."

"That's fine," Reverend Byker said.

"Wait until you see all the steps," Jesse told him. "How many are there, Janie?"

"Sixty-seven. But there's a landing in the middle with a bench around the edge." I kept my eyes on the road. "We built it that way for my dad—he has emphysema. And am I glad we did. Comes in handy when hauling groceries and stuff. It'll be cold down there. Let's hope the sun stays out."

The exit is fifteen miles south of town, then five miles east and a good mile south to the cottage. It's only a half-hour drive from home, one of the reasons we bought it in the first place. The last three-quarters of a mile is a narrow dirt road, cleared along the sides of saplings and brush every nine hundred feet or so for parking. I pulled in our clearing where, with all the leaves down, we could see the roof of the cottage and the lake beyond.

"Very nice," Reverend Byker said when we stopped on the landing half-way down and took in the view.

"Yes. It is." More doleful than I expected to sound, I took off down the steps to avoid any wistful sentimentality.

I unlocked the door and, once inside, climbed the ladder to the loft, found a half a dozen empty boxes, the kind that hold reams of paper from the printing company, and brought them to the kitchen counter. By that time, Jesse and Reverend Byker had come in.

"Take a look around," I said. Jesse and her kids had visited each summer over the years. She began taking dishes out of the cupboard while I found newspaper in the pantry for wrapping and Reverend Byker took a short, self-guided tour.

In less than an hour, Jesse and I filled the boxes with glasses, mugs and service for ten Corelle dishes. Reverend Byker carried up three dining chairs one at a time so as not to have to set them on the melting snow before arranging them in the trunk. On one of his trips down, he brought the thermos and donuts with him.

"Still think we better wait with those," I said. "So, I brought a couple bungee cords to hold the trunk closed." We had left our coats on while working but now Jesse and I stuck our hands into mittens, ready to transport the boxes up the steps. I took the heaviest one, the one with a tray of silverware at the bottom.

We reached the top and I said, "Reverend Byker, you've already made four trips. You pack these and we'll get the others."

"Sure. But Janie, why don't you call me Art?"

"I don't know. Just doesn't sound right to me." I turned and headed back down before he could answer. I held the screen door for Jesse. We each lifted another box and mounted the steps again.

"One more trip to go," Jesse said after we caught our breath at the car.

"Except I still need to grab those two framed posters on the wall. And the coffee and donuts are down there."

"Well, then," Reverend Byker spoke up, "I'll come too and we'll be finished. I'm getting cold without the climb."

At the bottom, we traipsed across the length of the deck making tracks in the undisturbed snow. I took a giant step away from our footprints and deliberately lay down on my back like I was sun tanning, but instead made an angel in the snow. Jesse copied me and called out. "Come on, Art. Don't be a stick-in-the-mud."

"No, thank you," he said. "That stuff is wet. You'll both be drenched." We watched him disappear around the corner of the cottage.

I got up, stood at the railing, and looked out over the frozen lake probably for the last time. Jesse came and stood next to me.

"You okay?" she asked.

I nodded.

A slushy snowball just cleared over our heads and landed, splo-osh, near the edge of the lake.

"You're lucky you missed us," I said, calling in the direction toward a grove just beyond the storage barn. "It's a long walk back."

"Really lucky," Jesse said when Reverend Byker came out from behind a bare tree and joined us on the deck.

We went inside and I lifted the posters from the wall—a little girl in a sundress picking up stones along a waterfront, the other a young boy up to his shorts in the lake pulling a toy sailboat by a string. The frames and glass were light-weight enough, but I stopped in the middle of the room, setting one against each leg.

"Give me a minute," I said and sighed heavily, staring at the lake through the front windows of the cottage.

"Meet you up top," Reverend Byker said. "Take your time."

As the screen door closed, Jesse said, "I got the frying pan and wastebasket. Don't forget the goodies."

Once alone in the cottage, I didn't want to dawdle long after all. My eyes burned and started watering, but I took a deep breath and blinked most of it away. Outside, I held the frames under one arm. With the thermos between my legs and the bakery bag between my teeth, I dug in my pocket for the keys and locked the door's bolt one-handed.

Up above, Jesse and Reverend Byker had packed a quasi-snowman together using broken sticks for eyes, a nose and a smile. "Bye, Ralph," Jesse said to the snowman and took the bag and thermos from me. I wondered if the donuts were crushed after all that carrying around. Jesse sat on the passenger side while I carefully wedged the pictures between one of the chairs and a box in the back seat. I took my place behind the wheel and, when Jesse scooted over and Reverend Byker got in, started the car.

"Let's get out of here." Without waiting for an answer, I drove away. "We can have coffee at the rest area. I need the facilities anyway."

Our feet were wet through our boots, the bottoms of my jeans damp. I left the car running with the heater on while Jesse and I used the bathroom. Reverend Byker managed to find the box with the coffee mugs. It was just past noon, and though the donuts were stuck together with chocolate icing, they hit the spot along with the coffee.

As we arrived at the church, I pulled up to Jesse's car and let mine idle. "Well, thanks for helping, Reverend Byker. And tell Betsy thanks, too. You've been gone half the day."

"Oh, I won't tell Betts where we went," he said with a quick chuckle. "She wouldn't appreciate my going on an outing and her staying back with the babies." He opened the car door and his face became serious. "Probably shouldn't say anything to anybody. Might not look good. You know how people talk around here."

I waited for Jesse to say something. In a few seconds she nudged across the seat and got out without a word.

"Well, okay. Thanks again," I said as the car door closed, as I decided to mind my own business.

Sixteen

Walt's pickup is a diesel. I heard it as soon as it turned on Sun Valley Court a little after seven Sunday night.

Meike rushed in first, her snow boots squeaking across the vinyl in the hallway. "Mom! We're going to Disney!"

She dropped her backpack on the floor as we locked in a hug. "Wouldn't that be fun," I said like she was describing some recent dream. "How did your weekend go?"

"No, really. For spring vacation. Dad said."

"Hey, Sam. Hey, pooch." I hugged my son, unclipped Odie's leash and ignored Walt as he stepped inside.

"Tell Mom where we're going," Walt said, excited as Meike.

I shot him a suspicious look. "Something about Disney?"

"Orlando. My turn for spring break. I found a great package. Air, on-site accommodations. We stay four nights, get the fifth night free."

"Well, this is the first I've heard of it."

"But it's okay, isn't it Mom?" Sam asked when he heard me snip at Walt. "We're going to Epcot Center. And, Mom—I've never been on a plane before."

"Mom doesn't like to fly," Meike said. This wasn't news to any of us and it seemed like she was making excuses for Walt. Or maybe she was trying to take care of me. Or maybe I need to stop analyzing every single little thing.

Meike set her hand on her hip. She began to wiggle her behind around like an adolescent floozy and flipped her other wrist. "I'm going to love flying," she said emphatically. I beamed at her confidence and laughed at the same time as Walt.

"You're going to do just fine," I said. "They have little trays that pull out and the stewardess lets you order soda and peanuts or crackers from your seat."

"So, it's okay?" Sam asked as his sister clapped. "You won't be mad if we go?"

I set my hands on Sam shoulders and crooked my neck down a few inches until our eyes were level. "No, honey, I won't be mad at you." I stood straight and gently pulled him toward me. "Sorry if I was mean," I whispered in his ear.

He let me rub his back but in a second, pulled away. "You'll be mad at Dad, though." Sam stared at the floor instead of his dad shuffling on the rug, instead of me who understood that he understood any artificial schmaltz at this point was useless.

"People get mad at each other, Sam," I said. "It's not your fault."

Then I refrained from kicking Walt in the groin.

"All right, guys. Say goodnight," Walt said. "Don't forget, I'll be gone for almost two weeks." He took a folded paper from his shirt pocket and handed it to me. "Here's the itinerary for Vegas and Harry's number in case you have to get ahold of me."

I set the schedule on the kitchen counter unopened, leaving the three of them to say their goodbyes.

"I'll call you next week after the conference—when I get to Uncle Harry's," I heard Walt say. "Be good for Mom," he added. I looked up at the ceiling, rolling my head and eyes with my mouth open.

"Tomorrow's a school day," I reminded Meike and Sam from the kitchen. "Get on your PJs and slippers first and we'll have banana muffins and milk."

They trekked on up. "Odie, come," Sam called from the top of the stairs.

"Come on, boy," Meike repeated to the slap of her hand on her thigh.

Halfway out the door, Walt stopped when I caught up to him in the hallway. "Thanks for setting me up." I stood on the rug, in the way of his coming back inside, with my arms crossed against the cold.

"What are you talking about?" he asked.

"Don't ever do that again, you son-of-a-bitch."

"It's my turn for spring break so I decide what we do and where we'll go."

So, he did know exactly what I was talking about. "You can't make plans like that without checking with me."

"That's what you think. Why can't you just let us have a good time?"

"And. You certainly can't take them out of state without telling me."

"I'm telling you now."

He had to hustle to beat the automatic garage door.

Every year the Cement Cutters Association attended a nationwide conference held by various manufacturers of diamond blades, saws and cement-boring equipment. I had gone with Walt several times—Indianapolis, Las Vegas, Detroit—where lots of all-expenses-paid wining and dining and high living went on.

Most anyone from Michigan would enjoy lounging at a Las Vegas poolside in seventy-degree weather during February. I didn't begrudge Walt the vacation; in fact was happy to see him go. Flying frightened me. I hated it. And the extravagant flaunting that took place at the association events made me uncomfortable. I envisioned two weeks without Walt's interference. Without shame, I went so far as to envision a plane crash. Just for a second.

A week later, Walt was still out of town as planned. The kids had needed to skip their weeknight sleepover at their dad's on Tuesday. Typically, Sam also spent another few hours at Walt's the night Meike and I went to her violin lesson and on to youth orchestra. Sam had come with us this week without complaint, finishing his homework while his sister practiced, and ordering a burger and fries when we stopped for supper.

A few days later, I woke at 2 a.m. to an unnerving, high-pitched screech coming from Sam's room. I vaulted barefoot across the carpet. Odie's sharp barks interrupted the outcry. A white glow of winter night through the window revealed Sam sitting up in bed, covers aside, terror smeared across his face, his eyes attending some invisible alarm.

"Sam. Sam," I whispered. I drew closer, dropped to one knee next to his bed, and reached to pick up a corner of the quilt. His eyes followed my hand as I pulled the blanket over his arms, snug around him. Some of the distress left his expression, a look of recognition took its place.

"May I sit on your bed?"

He shifted and moved toward the other side of the mattress butted against the corner. I took a place at the edge, and Odie sprang on top of me. He sniffed around the quilt and eased his way over to Sam's lap before settling down, curling into a half-circle.

"You must have had a nightmare, hon, a bad dream."

Sam's hand found Odie and began to smooth his fur, though his face still looked tight and frightened. Taking his other hand, I rubbed the top of his fingers with my thumb and felt him relax a little. "You want to tell me?"

"I don't remember," he said with a hushed voice.

We sat quietly for a minute or two before the tears building in Sam's eyes dripped slowly down his cheeks.

"Miss your dad?" I whispered.

He answered with an ever so slight nod. I wrapped an arm around him, his head drooped to my shoulder. Then I held my son in both arms as he sobbed like no one was there.

With his sadness let loose and his tears gone over to sniffles, Sam lay down on his bed once more. He rolled to his back and sighed, staring at the ceiling with dry eyes blinking hard and delayed. I ran my fingers lightly through the front of his hair, stroking it off his face.

A melody from years ago floated in my head . . . *the birds upon the treetop* . . . "You know," I said, keeping my voice low. "When you were little and woke up in the night, I used to sing to you until you fell back sound asleep." I caressed his cheek and tucked the covers around him.

"Go ahead," he said.

Seventeen

The State of Michigan Public Act No.16 requires parties in a divorce with children meet with Friend of the Court to evaluate problems involving custody. Noncompliance is contempt of court. If the parties couldn't agree, the Friend of the Court's conciliator would submit his own recommendations.

Since Walt was not awarded temporary custody in November, I had dismissed the section in Walt's motion where he asked the court to refer the matter of permanent custody to an independent evaluating agency instead of to Family Services. After Richard reminded me, I acknowledged my concern for any needless bureaucracy or maybe even possible incompetence from a free, public agency. Like Walt, I guess I carried some sort of middle-class suburban bias—I thought a private service might be more professional, if only because of the high fees involved. I agreed that rejecting Family Services and finding a private agency made sense.

"I will if you will," I put it to Walt.

Yet the next week when Walt and his attorney proposed a specific agency that pitched itself as a Christian association, I balked.

And Richard wanted to know why.

I took a long, deep breath and hoarded it. I focused on snowflakes outside the tenth-story window. Across the table from me, Richard sat patiently, his pen resting on a fresh yellow legal pad. I sighed loudly and watched a few of the white patterns catch on the glass. "It's a long fricking story."

My attorney rolled his chair closer to the table and ran a hand over his tie. "Jane, you've been up front with me. I know you have a history with the hospital. And the adoption agency. We're both familiar with these organizations. We've both put money in the collection plate toward their support." He checked his tie again. "Cynic that I am, I can imagine some shortcomings with these places."

I laughed outright. "That's an understatement." Richard's grin encouraged me to say more. "A person can't question motives in these places, you know. They play God. Or they assume what they do is God's will simply because they might mean well. Or since they prayed about it. Drives me crazy." With that, my mouth clamped shut and I stared at the floor.

Richard cleared his throat and spoke kindly. "I can help you better, Jane, when you're free to speak your mind."

I nodded without looking up, feeling his patient scrutiny anyway.

People can't just reveal these kinds of things to other people. More accurately—people ought never have to reveal these kinds of things to other people.

I went with it. "My mother was in Pine Rest . . ." I said like my mouth was muffled. My brain defaulted to covert mode. "Two of my sisters . . . well . . . it gets complicated."

Not like it fazed him.

"If Walt pursues this," Richard said, "and my impression is he will, I'll eventually need a better picture, more details, about all this." He pulled his earlobe. "Meanwhile, you may want to put any animosity—and by this I don't mean to imply your animosity isn't legitimate, I don't doubt that it is—but meanwhile, you may want to put it aside for the sake of cooperation."

I tipped my head slightly and squinted. "Meaning?"

He took his time. "We don't want to rock the boat." Folding his large hands, he rested them on the legal pad and drew his eyebrows together. "If only for the sake of appearances, my advice is that you agree to hire this agency to make a referral."

I pay $120 an hour for his advice. That didn't have to mean buying everything he said. Fidgeting in the pocket of my blazer, I felt the corduroy knap and a loose peppermint I resisted sticking in my mouth. Surely Richard would appreciate my caution. "How do we know they're any good?"

"I'm not aware of anything negative on their record, although prior to now, there's been no call for my clients to use them. Dr. Jennings would know. He could verify their reputation for you."

"Couldn't he just do it for us? Or the folks from that office? They're credible in the community."

"We could never convince Walt's attorney they'd be neutral," Richard answered like he'd already considered the possibility. He picked up the ballpoint and turned it. "I have some homework for you. I want a summary. Your marriage. Include when you were hospitalized, the adoption, when you started the businesses. Write it out." With a sympathetic smile, he added, "The more information I have, the easier my job will be, and the better I can help you."

I was learning not to underestimate Richard's instruction and I sat back in my chair to think. "Any idea what the supposed professional review from this agency would involve?"

"Likely some private sessions with you. And Walt. Separately. A couple of psychological tests."

"Fuck," I whispered exhaling.

"They'd spread it out over a number of weeks. They'll want to meet with Sam and Meike."

What I wouldn't do to spare them that.

~

On Thursday afternoon, with one more day of classes remaining before spring break, Sam and Meike's school held their annual roller skating party. We waited in line next to Sam's best friend, Matt, his sister and mother near the entrance of the rink.

"Aren't you going to skate?" Stacy asked her mom.

"There's no way," Ruth said. "I'll bet Mrs. Weber will skate with you though."

"Sure will," I answered. "Soon as Meike and I warm up."

"All packed for your trip?" Ruth asked Meike.

"Yup. We're going to Disney with my dad."

We paid our money, received our tokens and rented skates. After I tied my own, I helped Sam and Meike lace up.

"You going to want some help out there, Sam?"

"Don't even think about it," he said and proceeded confidently across the carpet and onto the wooden floor to join his buddies.

Holding hands, Meike circled the rink with me three or four times, squealing whenever she thought we were moving along too fast. We stopped to pick up Stacy and made a threesome, rolling along on the outskirts like several other groups of students and parents. A few songs later, I pulled Meike and Stacy's hands together and broke away for a few laps on my own.

I was comfortable on skates, relaxed. Without my usual self-consciousness in this meddlesome suburban group, I rolled along, gliding and swaying to the old Beach Boy tune "I Get Around" blaring on the loudspeakers.

Meike and I rested from time to time, buying soda, chatting with Ruth and Meike's friends. Sam wound up skating with Sissy from his class during the Grand March, in spite of Matt's teasing. About a half an hour before the end of the party, Meike and I made our way back to the rink for the umpteenth time. Although stopping remained difficult, she was getting better on the curves and we skated faster than when first starting out.

But stopping proved altogether impossible when two boys in front of us collided and fell. I saw it coming, tried to swerve. Within a few seconds, we screamed and crashed. Meike fell first. When I fell on top of her, I broke her leg.

Eighteen

The examining table was raised at one end to support Meike's head and back. Her leg was propped by several pillows. I stood with my hand over hers, playing with a few strands of her hair that had loosened from her French braids. By now some color had returned to her pallid complexion.

"Well, Puddin'," the doctor addressed her as he clipped up the x-ray, "let's put this here so I can show you the picture of your bone."

Sam set his book down on a chair. The doctor clicked on the light and ran his finger vertically along the image. My stomach tightened. I could see the crack immediately.

"The smaller bone alongside is called the fibula. As you can see, the fracture is here in the tibia." His finger stopped on the crack. "It's a complete fracture, the bone is snapped in two. Fortunately, not displaced. But we'll need a cast to keep it that way."

During the time the technician set a plaster cast, Walt caught up with us. As he entered the room, Meike brightened. "Daddy!" She quickly told the doctor, "He's taking us to Disney World on Saturday."

"A pink cast!" Walt said. "How do you like that?"

"It's fuchsia," Meike answered.

Walt and the doctor shook hands. Displaying the x-ray again, the doctor pointed out the break to Walt, then dug in the pocket of his jacket and produced a black magic marker. "Usually I get to sign the cast first, Puddin', but maybe you'd like your dad to do the honors?"

The doctor handed me a page with some general instructions. "Starting out, it will be hard for her to sleep with the cast. Aspirin every four hours will help and act as an anti-inflammatory."

Walt printed "Dad" in bold letters and passed the marker to Sam. Drawing a dog's paw, Sam wrote "Odie" next to it before signing his own name.

"A child's bone typically takes six to eight weeks to heal," the doctor said. "Next week you'll need to make follow-up appointments with an orthopedic doctor who will keep you posted on the progress." He signed Meike's cast and pulled out a business card. "I recommend Dr. Bates. Rumor has it he pays a dollar for every signature on a fuchsia cast." Meike grinned, and he set a hand on her shoulder. "The leg must be immobilized and elevated. This is imperative. Not only to avoid more swelling, but to keep it aligned and prevent any deformity." He squatted so Meike's eyes and his were level, taking her hand as he spoke. "That means, Puddin'—no Disney World."

She accepted the news relatively well. A throbbing leg can block a lot of other misery. Through some quiet tears and an extended lip, Meike nodded as the doctor explained to her if she took the trip, she might permanently damage her leg. "Follow my orders and back to gymnastics by summer."

"Actually, she's a shortstop," I said as I smoothed her hair from her face.

Walt rubbed his hand over the leg without a cast. "We'll go again next year, Meikee. Maybe Jason can use your ticket."

The same technician who took x-rays returned with a pair of crutches. He eased Meike off the table, loosened and retightened the screws to adjust the crutches and walked with her around the room as she tried them out.

"Sam. Think Jason would like to go?" Walt asked. Sam didn't answer but looked at his dad and shrugged as if he felt awkward discussing it in front of his sister.

"Take it slow and easy first, Puddin'," the doctor said and left the room.

~

Although Sam might prefer that his best friend Matt took Meike's place, Ruth's attitude toward Walt wasn't a secret on Sun Valley Court. So Walt knew better than to invite Matt on the trip. The next morning, when Walt left for the airport with Sam and Jason, Meike seemed indifferent to the whole excursion. Her injured leg bothered her more than anything. Leaning against me, she hobbled to the couch where I helped her spread out among the extra pillows and gave her more aspirin. Odie nestled beside her and with one arm on top of him, she slept until early afternoon.

Walt called Meike at dinnertime and almost every night they were in Florida.

Meike and I read books together, drew pictures with colored pencils, ate ice cream in the afternoons. My parents came on Tuesday and while I went to class, Meike cut out paper dolls her Grandma brought and played Rummy with her Grandpa. In the evening, we watched "The Lion King."

Meike's discomfort had lessened to the extent that by Wednesday, when sun shone on the window and fresh spring air puffed through the screen, we went out on the sidewalk to practice with the crutches.

That night was the first time Meike actually grumbled about not being at Disney World. I pictured Walt watching the boys at the pool of a ritzy hotel, reclining with a gin and tonic, absorbing rays, absorbing the neighborhood's admiration, absorbing our son's loyalty.

Meike stretched out on the bed and patted the mattress to signal Odie. I adjusted the pillow under her foot and joined them on the bed while Meike said her prayers. The soft flannel of her nightgown covered her little arms, and little print roses on the ruffle embraced her wrists. She folded her hands on top of the quilt.

When she finished her prayer, she asked, "God knows that I can't kneel while I have my cast on doesn't he?"

"He sure does."

"Just like he knows some kids are too sick to pray at all?"

"That's right."

She stroked the top of Odie's head as a worried look came across her face. "And that sometimes people are too hungry or too scared to pray?"

"He especially knows those people."

Her brows relaxed and a smile showed in the corners of her mouth.

I leaned forward and smooched her cheek. "Maybe instead of Grandpa and Grandma coming tomorrow, you would like to go with me to school. You're doing pretty well on those crutches of yours."

"We'd see Mr. Leitsma from the Christmas party?"

"Yup. But I have English class, too." I tried to read her face, wondering if the outing would be too exhausting for her. "You could bring your notebook and pencils in your backpack."

"Can I take my trolls?"

"You can."

"And have lunch in the student center?"

"Sure."

"We'll forget all about Dad and Sam and Disney."

My sigh came out a wobbly rasp, my voice subdued. "Meike, honey, I'm sorry you couldn't go." I put both arms around her and pressed her head on my chest. "I'm sorry we fell at the roller skating party, and I'm sorry I broke your leg."

"Don't worry, Mommy. It was an accident."

Mature. Innocent. I didn't know. But a lump scraped my throat as I swallowed.

If only I practiced that kind of clemency.

~

On our nineteenth wedding anniversary just over a year ago, when Walt had already moved into his apartment, I presented him with a sentimental card as a small token toward a possible reconciliation. "You're a loon," he laughed. "Stop trying to kid yourself."

I had confined him to the rug in the hallway by that time. But then and there, I vowed never to set myself up for a rebuke like that from him again.

As I happily pampered Meike that first week in April, I postponed the assignment from my attorney. But once spring break was over and Sam and Meike were back in school, there were no more excuses. Daunting as it was, I outlined twenty years of marriage in nine hand-written pages and sent them by mail for Richard to look over before our next consultation.

As if it were March and not April, a strong wind blew that day. I parked in an open lot across the street from the downtown office building and braced myself against a stiff gust before reaching the main entrance. I thought of Meike, bold and brave on her crutches in the blustery air as I escorted her into school that morning.

On the tenth floor, the receptionist took my coat and offered me coffee, which I declined. Richard ushered me into the conference room. He passed a document across the large mahogany table.

"The Stipulation was received and filed and this is the corresponding Order." Twisting his pen open, he ran it along the edge of the first page and commenced his review. "The first paragraphs state that you have agreed a counseling and custody evaluation be done by Psychiatric Consultation Services. You will each pay half the cost." He looked up. "The Order notes the court reserves the right to modify that part, based on the ability to pay."

I scanned the paragraph and shrugged. "I won't give Walt the advantage of being the only monetary contributor. I'll pay my half. But no one can tell me this counseling service is necessary."

"All right." He noted it on his yellow pad. "Next paragraph. 'The parties shall cooperate with PCS, who upon termination of counseling shall submit a written report, evaluation, and recommendation to the court and shall furnish copies to the attorneys for each of the parties.' Then it explains after the recommendation is received, an order 'conforming to the written recommendation—agreed to by both parties—may be submitted to the court.'"

"Meaning Walt and I have to agree on what we disagree about it?"

"No. More like consenting to the recommendation, with you and me and Walt and Hofstra working out the details."

"Well, fine . . . except I'm still leery of the whole evaluation thing."

Richard nodded, leaned back in his chair and folded his large hands on his lap. "Sure." He blinked slowly, an indication he was weighing his words. "I understand. And I appreciate your concern all the more since I've read the summary you sent me."

I pursed my lips before setting my mouth in a straight line, looked at the floor and massaged the back of my neck with my hand, wishing Richard would have said something like, "Don't worry about it."

He sat forward. "Notice the next section. It might help you some." He turned the page. "It states either party has the right to object to the written recommendation and present additional proofs as may be appropriate and that either party may schedule the matter for a hearing."

"Everything's all covered, isn't it," I snipped.

His touch of sarcasm came through. "All in the 'Best Interest of the Child' as they say." He collected the pages and aligned the order neatly by tapping it on the table before putting both copies in the folder. He set his elbows on the table, intertwined his fingers and rested his chin against them. "So, you'll need to call PCS for the appointment."

"I suppose."

In the window behind Richard, small pieces of debris whipped the air. Street cleaners hadn't swept the winter's mess yet and I saw dry leaves, last year's litter and a plastic grocery bag disappear between the buildings. The sun kept coming and going behind puffy clouds.

"Oh, yes," Richard said and reached for another sheet inside the folder. "I have a note dated March, '93." His eyes searched the paper. "Being the nice guy that he is, Walt . . . let's see . . . 'Plaintiff moves the court waive Defendant's obligation to pay support during the pendency of this cause.'"

"I don't get it."

"He won't ask you to pay child support."

"How very gallant," I said softly.

My usual stamina while meeting with my attorney now slipped to fatigue. It had been over an hour. I probably needed lunch.

"Let's call it quits for today," I said, and Richard agreed.

When I stepped out into the street, a full realization hit me like the gust of wind.

How I mothered my children wasn't all I'd have to defend.

I'd have to defend my sanity.

Nineteen

Maybe since they carried so much power to make decisions for others, the interior of the Psychiatric Consultation Services reminded me of one of those new kind of suburban churches. Exposed brick, stark, bonded with grayish mortar easily shattered with the tap of a chisel. Carpeting over cemented floors connected the one-story sprawl. The lobby was vast like a vestibule, partitioned off in one corner with a brick wall reaching halfway to a low-hung ceiling. Opposite, an office had been designed without sliding glass in the window opening, some fake-ish effort to appear accessible.

PCS promoted their enterprise as a Christian establishment, but they were not a non-profit organization. I paid a $1500 retainer fee prior to the initial visit when I filled out preliminary forms and scheduled the first appointments. Altogether, I was to undergo three individual sessions, three diagnostic interviews, three psychological tests, two conferences with the entire team, two meetings for interpretive explanation, and one for legal consulting. The same regimen would apply to Walt.

"We need to have you sign this release for your medical records," the assistant in the office said before I left. She handed me a form on a clipboard.

I politely passed it back. "I'll need to check with my lawyer first."

Her original cheeriness vanished. "The team will want them before your first appointment."

I scanned a calendar on the counter. "That gives me two weeks and three days." My comment came out rather impertinent, and I quickly tried to dilute it, weighing what was at stake here. "If I come back and sign by Thursday, will that be enough time?"

"I suppose," she said.

I wished there was one of those little glass panels for her to slide between us.

I went straight home and called Richard.

"They want me to release my medical records."

"I'm not surprised," he said.

"Thanks a lot. Now you tell me."

"I wasn't certain and didn't want to put the cart before the horse. I expected you could handle it. Are they asking for records from the hospital or from Jennings?" he asked.

"Just the hospital. They might not know Jennings is involved yet."

I heard a soft, repeated click of his tongue like he was thinking.

"There's so much history there . . ." I cut myself off. He knew all that.

His answer sounded regretful. "You don't have a choice, you know."

A silence while the reality sunk in.

"So tell me," Richard said. "All in all, how did it go?"

"Okay, I suppose. Agitating as heck."

"No doubt," he said. "I know this is hard, Jane, but don't let them get to you. Cater to them. Give them what they want. If you have to roll the windows up in your car and scream all the way home, so be it."

"I understand."

Understanding and doing are not the same.

Two and a half weeks later, after a twenty-minute wait that I considered their test to measure my patience, a PCS receptionist ushered me into a small room for my first meeting with the psychologist.

He was seated near a round table, no bigger than a card table, paging through a typed report. He barely stood up half-way and nodded toward the chair across from him. I smoothed my skirt behind me, sat down, and hung the strap of my shoulder bag on the back of the chair.

The man wore a shabby suit of material shiny with ironing marks. His white shirt was pressed, but I noticed the dingy neckline since he didn't wear a tie. By his receding grayish hairline, I guessed him to be in his late forties, early fifties. Short and round, his girth seemed cumbersome and explained why standing upright might have been too much effort to grant me. No wedding band, but a gold ring with an onyx setting choked his finger. His breath was labored, and I pictured that his pinky stuck out kind of like Jackie Gleason whenever he held a beverage.

"Jane Weber," he said. His eyes gave me a quick once-over.

"That's right," I answered.

"I'm Jay Riley."

I nodded once. "Hello."

He looked back at the report in front of him. "I was just going over the records we received from Pine Rest."

"Yes. I signed the release last week." I forced myself to smile.

He thumbed through a number of pages. When he stopped to read, his head moved back and forth with the lines. Flipping to the beginning, he licked his finger and started through the pages again. "Hmmm." He continued to search. "Seems to be a section or something missing." Finally, he quit riffling through the papers and raised his head. "You know anything about this?"

"About what, exactly?"

"The gap in this report. You know anything about it?"

"No. A gap? What kind of gap?"

He laid the report on the table and folded his stubby arms across his middle. I looked away, crossed my legs and studied the pattern on my skirt that, just as a mother's would, draped modestly over my calf, almost to my sandals. I reached for my bag and held it on my lap like a child holds a pillow for security.

"What's in there? What are you hiding in your purse, Jane?"

"Excuse me?"

"You're hugging your purse. If I had you empty your purse out on the table, what would we find? More records from Pine Rest?"

I grimaced and pulled back in my chair. My inside clenched, my eyes narrowed. What in God's name kind of test was this, I wondered. Anger flushed through me and settled on my face. I thought a moment, trying not to let some wicked spiel run from my mouth I'd regret later.

I wished my purse held poker chips, cigarettes, tampons. I'd dump them all out in front of him.

Maybe this was tryouts. I told myself to simmer down, be a good sport. Finally, with a weak smile, I managed a firm chin and said, "Of course not. How could that be?"

If staring could bore a hole into someone's brain, he'd have read my mind. But I knew better from experience. There were limits to the power of probing.

I didn't flinch. He looked away first.

The rest of our meeting consisted of relaying family history. Riley divided it in two parts—before I knew Walt and after. The facts were in the record on the table and Riley verified them systematically.

"You grew up in Grand Rapids. Attended parochial schools. Graduated from high school 1970. No college. Joined the work force."

"I'm in college now."

"Oh?"

"Part-time. While the kids are in school."

"Two brothers, four sisters."

I'd been wondering how the transcript read on that one.

"Your parents were born in The Netherlands. Your mother is a housewife, your father a butcher."

"My father was born in the United States. When he was one, my grandmother went back to The Netherlands for a time and took him along. The First World War broke out and they had to stay longer than planned."

"Interesting," Riley said with a blank look that told me—not pertinent. "Your parents are still with us?

"Right. Retired."

"I see your mother was in Pine Rest."

I knew it was coming, but could he be any more blunt? Before answering, I wondered if the record said how many times. "Yes. Years ago. Depression." I wanted to know if it mentioned my sisters.

"You've been diagnosed with bipolar disorder?"

"Bipolar II."

"I see. Your doctor?"

"Thomas Jennings."

"Medication?"

"I take the lowest therapeutic dose of lithium daily. Actually, with Jennings' permission, a little less."

"A little less?"

"I'm a student. I don't want my brain fogged any more than I have to. I don't weigh much. Wouldn't take long for more lithium to kick in if needed."

"Jennings would confirm this?"

"Sure."

"Other medication?"

"150 mg of Wellbutrin once a day for depression." And for agitation, damn good thing given this Riley guy.

He confirmed the dates Meike and Sam were born, where they went to school, that Walt and I were married twenty years ago.

"And now you're getting divorced."

"His idea, not mine." I congratulated myself on taking that opportunity.

The statement didn't seem to faze him.

"The children are living primarily with you?"

"Yes."

"They're happy about that arrangement?"

"Yes." It occurred to me that might have been a trick question. Before he could ask another, I began again. "Well, they're not what I'd call 'happy' about the overall situation. I mean, Sam and Meike would rather we all lived home together. One big family." I hesitated a few seconds. "Given that's not likely . . . their living with me is best."

Riley shifted in his chair, and I guessed I said too much. Checking his watch, he cleared his throat. "We can start with that next time. Your next appointment is scheduled?"

"With you on Tuesday."

"Be sure to sign a release for Jennings' office. And check with Jill if you can squeeze in an MMPI before Tuesday."

I waited for him to get up, but apparently he wasn't going anywhere. I stood and hung my bag on my shoulder. I opened the door, and with my back to him said "Thank you" for some reason.

"Have a nice afternoon," I heard him say as I escaped to the lobby.

I didn't rev the engine or squeal out of the parking lot. I didn't play the whole scenario over again in my head, only the part about the purse and whether I should tell Richard. I didn't scream all the way home with the windows rolled up. Just gripped the steering wheel until my arms hurt from squeezing.

~

During the half-hour drive home, my frustration lessened. I exited the freeway, lowered the window and let the warm afternoon air rush in my face and mess my hair around. I turned onto Sun Valley Court, drove past the houses along each side of the street and into our driveway. In the yard next door, Judy reached from a step ladder, attacking her front windows with a spray bottle. She turned my way and flapped her paper towel like a flag. I waved back before pulling in the garage.

With winter behind us and summer coming on, it would be harder and harder to avoid the neighbors.

I went out on the back deck in the sun and waited for Odie to piddle. Instead of the interview that afternoon, my thoughts stuck on a whole cluster of folks and the lopsided picture they must hold. Walt would have told them the agency was involved. He'd see to it his entire network knew, working up sympathy as he relayed the heartbreak of being married to me for twenty years.

From there, my thought broadened. Maybe I shouldn't even try for custody. Maybe Walt was right. Maybe I should stop fighting him and let the whole business go. Move far away . . . .

Odie jumped from the grass, to the steps, to the deck, and brushed against my legs. "Good dog," I said, stroking the top of his head. I crouched and held his muzzle loosely with one hand while scratching behind his ears with the other. "Good dog. Stupid Jane. Can't think that way, can we boy?" I opened the door and followed Odie inside, quite aware of the new dent in my confidence.

That night during supper, conversation turned to the end of the school year.

"Where's your report card, Mom?" Meike asked. "You didn't let us see it."

"I put it away in the desk."

"You must have got a bad grade," she said.

Sam picked up his glass of milk and told her "*Gotten* a bad grade" before he took a swallow.

"A 'B+' in Dutch and an 'A-' in World Lit, I'll have you know." I smiled at both of them and waggled my head, cocky and proud.

Sam blew on a fork-full of hot tuna casserole. "Did you talk to Tjepkemas? We going camping?"

"The first week after school's out," I said. "Same place in Ludington we went last year."

Meike swallowed a bite and looked at Sam. "Remember Mom made us sleep in the car?"

"That was quite a storm we had that night," I said in my own defense.

"Yeah. Odie jumped in the front seat and started barking when it hailed," Sam said. "Mr. Tjepkema said there was a tornado warning." He popped the rest of his dinner roll in his mouth and played with the rhubarb sauce on his plate. "Do I have to eat this stuff, Mom?" He took a small taste and made a face. "It's too sour."

"I hate it." Meike stretched her mouth in a frown until her neck tightened.

I found the cinnamon sugar we use for toast some mornings and sprinkled it on their rhubarb. They each managed a couple more bites.

"Aunt Lynn wants to know if we want to camp with them and the Berends a few days."

"At the Conference Grounds?" Sam asked. "Is the new pool ready?"

"Yes and yes," I said.

Meike's cast had been removed two weeks ago and she swung her legs back and forth beneath the table. "Dad wants to take us fishing in Lake Michigan."

I picked a few crumbs from the butter dish with my knife. "There'll be lots of time to spend with Dad." I hesitated and considered bringing up the two appointments Sam and Meike would have with PCS toward the end of June. Our original plan, that Walt and I would wait until school finished to tell them, made sense to me at the time, but now I wondered if we were holding out on them. Quite possibly the neighbors were already jabbering about it, maybe even in front of their own kids. Sam and Meike would hear of it second-hand. For all I knew, Walt would have informed Sam and Meike without telling me.

With the exchange at the counseling service that afternoon still fresh, I realized anything said tonight would reflect my current shabby attitude. Instead, I reminded Meike about her violin practice. "If you buckle down after supper we could take a bike ride to the Dairy Freeze before it gets dark."

"Can Matt come along?" Sam asked.

"If it's okay with his mom."

Sam read a page out loud from the Bible Story book, about the time when the walls of Jericho fell after Joshua's army blew their trumpets. I read a short prayer from *The Book of Common Prayer.* While Meike started her lesson, Sam and I packed the dishwasher. We waited to push in the bottom rack so Odie could lick everything first. His tongue jiggled the silverware around and the clinking blended with the Offenbach ballet Meike worked on in the den.

We had a good two hours before the sun would disappear. The air was still warm. I stuffed our sweatshirts in my bike basket anyway, just in case. We rode single file on the sidewalks, Sam and Matt led with Meike and me in the rear. After our vanilla and chocolate swirl cones, we biked back and braked in front of Matt's place. Ruth stepped from off the lawn and approached us.

"You're doing a pretty good job with that leg of yours," Ruth told Meike.

Odie barked from the screen door when he heard our voices three houses down.

"Time to say goodbye and put your bikes away," I said to Meike and Sam. Going to bed before dark wasn't easy for the kids, but it was nearly nine o'clock. "Brush your teeth and I'll be right there."

Ruth turned to Matt. "Did you remember to tell Mrs. Weber thank you?"

Matt gave his mother a firm nod and I said, "He sure did."

As he headed indoors, Ruth set her plastic pail of uprooted dandelions on the cement and tossed the miniature spade in. "How's it going for you, Janie?"

Straddling my bike, I let go of the handlebars and stuck a hand in my pocket. Ruth usually didn't pry, and I hadn't told her about PCS.

But she could know from hearsay, and I wondered if she was prompting me. I glanced up and down the street scanning the flourishing maples, the lilacs almost finished for the season, some late blooming tulips, pretty lawns peaceful and quiet in the twilight. Sam and Meike had turned on the lights upstairs.

"You know what, Ruth?" I said. "Feels like the neighbors are always paying attention. Every move I make. Taking notes. Reporting back to Walt."

She nodded with a sympathetic expression. I let the bike lean against my thigh and scraped my foot along the pavement with my tennis shoe.

"I just play dumb if people get nosy," Ruth said.

"Thank you for that." Setting my bike upright, I balanced on the seat by alternating the tips of my toes on the sidewalk. "But I didn't mean you."

"If this business ever goes to court, I'll vouch for you."

I shrugged before saying, "Appreciate it." Then I pedaled home.

Twenty

Trying to envision a custody trial challenged my imagination like nothing ever had before. When I asked Richard at the end of May if he thought things might come to that, he set his ballpoint on the yellow pad, clasped his hands on the table and, with a serious expression, answered yes.

"The more I learn about Walt, the more I believe that unless the two of you agree to joint custody, he will contest you every step of the way." Richard offered a quick grin. "Of course, from what you've said in our previous conversations, even with joint custody, he'll contest you every step of the way."

I left my attorney's office that day determined to consider the feasibility of a trial.

The first Saturday in June, three days after school let out for the summer, Sam, Meike and I packed the car and drove to Ludington State Park to camp for a week with the Tjepkemas. Our adjacent lots lay on the north end of the campground, situated between Hampton Lake and Lake Michigan. Cindy and Keith, with Cheryl and Ricky, had already set and leveled their Dutchman Denali when we pulled in.

The kids and I set up a four-man tent for Meike and me, and Sam's two-man tent where he and Odie would sleep. Keith offered a hand, but I wanted to prove self-reliance and declined. An hour later, Meike helped me wrap a heavy orange electric cord around the leg of the picnic table and spread the cotton tablecloth. Sam poured fresh ice into the cooler. I placed a rag rug on the sand at the entrance of each tent. We were finished.

I worried about it already before we left home. But during the entire week, I never felt like a fifth wheel. Keith and Cindy respected what privacy I needed while I appreciated their company. Already chums, the boys' alliance went unbroken. The girls became inseparable. We took only a couple meals together, my preference, but shared a campfire each night.

With the fire dwindling on our last night, the kids admitted their exhaustion and settled into their sleeping bags with hardly any coaching.

Keith rose from his lawn chair. "Well," he said, "there's two logs left and I sure as heck don't want to transport them back home. You ladies game?"

Cindy spiked our decaffeinated coffee with brandy. "Chilly night," she laughed.

On the second round, we skipped the coffee.

I have tried to be sensitive with Keith and Cindy when it comes to Walt, remembering Keith and Walt had been classmates in high school, their friendship made long before either Cindy or I showed up. But when we reviewed the day, the week, love and life in general the campfire way, the spirits loosened my tongue.

"In the hopefully remote chance Walt and I go to trial, would you testify?"

In the glow of the fire, we could see each other's faces.

Keith answered quietly, his lips barely moving. "I don't think we can do that, Janie."

Cindy's reply came out hushed. "We've tried not to take sides."

I waved my arm back and forth through the air. "Sorry I put you on the spot." Lifting the hood of my sweatshirt, I drew it closer, like a fur collar, around my neck. "I understand."

And though disappointed, I really did understand. The past week had confirmed their caring. I would make that enough for me.

~

When we returned from Ludington, in an unusual moment of cooperation, Walt and I together informed Sam and Meike of the upcoming appointment with PCS.

"The first time, on Thursday, Mom will go with you. The next time, next Thursday, I'll take you."

Sam stood in the hallway, the backpack over one shoulder weighed with clothes for the weekend and a few of his favorite, carefully chosen belongings. "But I don't want to see a counselor," he said. "Not Mr. Palmer, not anybody."

Mr. Palmer was the Phys Ed and Bible teacher/pseudo-counselor at the Junior High. At least once a week, Palmer stopped Sam in the hallway to ask how things were going and reminding Sam that he was available if he needed someone to talk to. I had encouraged Sam to feel free to speak with Palmer if he wanted, keeping to myself that if he did on a regular basis, I'd seek a professional for Sam instead. Not anyone from PCS, certainly, and certainly not a teacher from the community who fancied himself qualified given self-help books he'd absorbed.

Walt crossed his arms over his chest, one foot on the rug, the other trespassing to the linoleum. "It's not for counseling." He laughed as if counseling was taboo.

I gave him a dirty look. "It's more like a check," I said. "Sometimes when kids' parents are getting a divorce, kids need someone from outside the family to check on things. Food. Money. Sometimes kids act out at school and —"

"Sometimes the dad beats on them or the mom's boyfriend wants the little girl to kiss him," Meike said.

"Geez. Where'd you hear all that?" I asked her.

"Becky Zandstra."

Walt and I looked at each other and shook our heads.

"Sam's game is at seven," I reminded Walt. "I take it you'll have supper first."

"You're going to be there, Mom?" Sam asked. I have never missed a game, but he still wanted the verification.

"Wouldn't miss it for nothin'. Don't forget to grab your glove."

"I'm taking Odie along," Meike said.

I hugged her goodbye. "Come sit with me in the bleachers."

The following Wednesday with my PCS appointment looming in the morning, I resolved to face Jay Riley pleasant and self-assured, no matter how insulting his questions were, no matter where or how he nosed around. And I prayed Dr. Jennings' encouragement from the previous day would fortify me through this next phase of scrutiny.

Riley could hardly get close enough to the table to take notes, and I wondered first off why he didn't just go ahead and press on his abdomen to write.

"It's okay to call you Jane?" Riley began.

That's what he'd already called me last time. I smiled sweetly and told him, "That's fine with me."

He wanted to know more about my religious upbringing. I chatted easily on the subject, referring to our Reformed tradition, our Dutch neighborhood and my love of the catechism. I threw in a few theological terms Riley didn't seem to have a clue about.

"Now that you're an adult, what is your impression of your parents' religiosity?" Riley asked. "Overall."

"Good." I answered without hesitation. I thought for a moment before adding, "They are probably some of the most sincere Christians I know."

For better or worse, Riley's questions were more precise than during our first interview. "Name something your parents did when you were a child that you make a point not to do with your own children."

"You mean, besides washing my mouth out with soap?" That won a smile from him. I looked up at the ceiling, taking a moment to think. "Keep too many secrets." As soon as I answered, I felt manipulated and wished I had said something simpler.

"Care to explain?"

"Well, they didn't exactly hide things. Just assumed I knew family history when I didn't."

"Like your mother's illness?"

"No. I knew about that." I picked something random. "More like, umm, my dad's first wife died." I was getting in way too deep here and wished he'd move on.

He seemed driven by the subject of my mother's health. And mine.

"Tell me about your bipolar."

"First of all, it's Bipolar II." I had told Riley that before, and it pissed me off that he didn't make the distinction. "I don't try to fly off rooftops. I don't go on shopping sprees or come home with three homeless dogs from the shelter. I don't act promiscuous. Don't lock myself in the bathroom and slit my wrists."

His voice became stern. "All right. Tell me what it is you do. Describe the mania to me."

"I don't sleep well. I lose my appetite . . . talk fast . . . play the piano a lot."

He breathed heavily, writing all this down. Maybe if his chair had wheels, he'd move around more, change his posture now and then. "And the depression?" he asked.

Because my mother had a background with depression, I already understood as a child that one of the worst consequences consists of other people's boilerplate ideas about it and the stigma attached. As an adult, I knew about withdrawal, diminished self-worth or purpose. I've experienced the dull dreariness and melancholy. That didn't make me a poor mother. A good mother could actually know feelings like disappointment, frustration, anger, sadness, and not always try to fix them. She would dare to observe the dark side of reality, not deny it. Heck, I was at an advantage.

There was no way to impress Riley with any of this.

"General gloominess," I answered. "Not very social . . . lack of energy."

"Stay in bed all day?"

"Nope. Never. I always get up, shower . . . don't let myself go."

As if reading from a check list, he asked, "What happens at home when you are angry?" At least he had moved on some.

"I yell . . . slam doors."

"Ever hit Sam or Meike?"

"No."

Both Walt and I spanked the kids on the behind when they were toddlers, when they were dangerously naughty. Like against our warnings of getting too close to the woodburning stove or continuing to tease the dog.

What I did not admit to Riley was the impatience I have had with Meike's backtalk. About a month before Walt moved out, I overreacted and slapped her face.

"Does Walt?"

"No."

"Walt ever hit you?"

"No."

"What was your sex life like? You and Walt?"

"None of your business."

"Pardon me?"

"I said, none of your business."

He appeared taken aback, like no one in his career had ever challenged him before, and sat up straighter. Looking to the side, he raised his eyebrows and shrugged like a gesture to some unseen colleague.

"Okay. One more area to cover for today," he announced next. Whether that had been his original plan or lazy Jay already had enough didn't matter to me. The appointment was nearly over.

He went on to ask about the adoption proceedings Walt and I underwent during the late 70s and early 80s.

"It was a hard time," I said. "They kept postponing things. More than four years."

"That's when you went to Pine Rest?"

"Yeah."

"Then you got pregnant so the adoption was cancelled."

"Actually, they cancelled the adoption before we knew I was pregnant." Twelve years ago and it was still hard. But I managed to say it. "It's in the records. They cancelled *because* I went to Pine Rest."

"I see." He seemed to take that in for a minute. "The pregnancy was Sam?"

"Yes. One of two best things that ever happened to me."

"And the other?"

"Meike."

Twenty-One

Like the day before, we walked the seven-minute trail from the campsite to the beach and spread our blankets in the sand already warm in the late morning sun. Jesse set our lunch coolers side by side and covered them with a beach towel. Lake Michigan glimmered in front of us. Behind us, miles of dunes with poplar trees and cut-grass poking through the sand ran north and south along the shore. As much fun as we had yesterday lunging and body surfing in the waves, we weren't disappointed that today the lake's edge lapped with a slower, restful pulse.

While Sam and Meike and Jesse's two boys, Joel and Billy, horsed around in the water most of the afternoon, Jesse and I stretched out on the blanket facing the kids and lazed in the sun.

"Meike holds her own pretty well with the boys," Jesse said, setting her book aside.

"She does all right. Joel and Billy don't treat her like a sister."

Jesse unscrewed the cap and reapplied sunscreen to her face. "But Sam's good to her, too."

"He usually is. Especially when he sees your boys appreciate her."

"How are they doing since those interviews?"

I rolled over and leaned back on my elbows. "Hard to say. Last time, Walt brought them, and they stayed at his place that night and the next day. When I took them the first time and asked them how it went, they didn't say much. But later, after supper, while we were watching *The Simpsons*, Meike swiped the remote out of Sam's hand. He yelled bloody murder and socked her.

"That seems unusual for him." Jesse offered a feeble smile. "But might happen anyway."

I sat up straight and drew in the sand with my finger. "Jesse. You know the guy asked them their stupid hypothetical question."

"Which is?"

"Which is, 'If you had to choose whether to live with Mom or Dad, which would you pick?'"

"Good God. Are you sure?"

I nodded. "PCS told me ahead of time they might. I never mentioned it to Sam and Meike. I wanted them to be free to say whatever they wanted without worrying that I'd ask them about it. Or what the consequences might be." I picked up a handful of sand and let it run through my fingers. "Hell, what kid can do that?"

The first of several high cirrus clouds passed in front of the sun. I watched Meike, knee-deep in the water, fold her arms and hold them like she was chilled.

"So, of course they're frustrated," I said. "Not sure they realize why."

We looked at each other and Jesse nodded, deliberate, like she understood. I sighed and looked back at the kids. "You notice anything?" I asked her.

"Not a thing."

I considered that for a moment. "It's great you and I have done this together for a few years now. It seems so natural that I doubt Sam and Meike even think about how the guys aren't here."

Meike came out of the water and I wrapped her panda towel around her.

After a time, when the boys had dried off and started throwing the Frisbee back and forth, Meike and I decided on a hike along the shore.

"Keep an eye on Sam?" I asked Jesse as we pulled on our shorts.

She flipped her hand, signaling us on. "No worry."

We set out south, hand in hand, purposely bumping each other into any wave that meandered toward our bare feet.

"In July, Dad's taking us fishing in Lake Michigan," Meike said. "You ever fish in here, Mom?"

"Sure have. When I was your age, Grandpa took us on the pier in Holland to catch perch. We used minnows for bait."

"Minnows? Did you catch them with a net first?"

"No. We stopped and bought them on the way. Grandpa put them in a bucket."

Meike ran ahead a few yards then picked up two shiny flat stones out of the sand. "Billy will show me how to skip these over the water," she said when I caught up and she put them in her pocket.

"Better yet was when Grandpa took us fishing in a rowboat." I bent down for another smooth stone and handed it to her. "The night before, Grandma would run the sprinkler on the grass, and after midnight, Grandpa would get us up and we'd catch night crawlers with a flashlight."

Her eyes got big. "You did?"

"Yup. You have to snatch them between your fingers before they scoot back into the ground. We'd put them in a coffee can with dirt. After we had three or four dozen at least, we'd go back to bed. Then Grandpa would get us up at four o'clock in the morning. He always wanted to get to the lake before the sun came up. 'Best fishing time,' he'd say."

"Grandma, too?"

"Nooo. Just Grandpa and Uncle Jerry and me. Later when he got older, Uncle Gerrit, too. Grandpa would knock on a cottage door, I don't remember the name of the lake or where it was, maybe Coopersville, and the man would come out and give him a set of oars. Grandpa would pay him three dollars. The rowboat would be up on the shore and when we loaded it with our poles and the coffee cans—plus the sandwiches Grandma packed us—Grandpa would tell us to get in. I always had to sit in the middle. Grandpa would put one leg in the boat and push us off with the other. There were lily pads all over along the shore. He always got wet. By then, the sun would be coming up."

Meike had stopped walking, listening to me. "That must have been really cool!"

"It was." I smiled at the water in front of us. "It was beautiful." I looked at Meike and made an awful face, stern and frowning. "Of course, we couldn't talk. We had to be quiet the whole time." I laughed. "And I'd always be the one to have to go to the bathroom first and

Grandpa would whisper to me to hold on a little while. Finally, he'd have to row to shore so I could pee in the weeds."

Her grin was as big as a roasted hot dog. "Serious?"

"Serious. Then we'd go back out on the lake for a while."

We'd been gone walking almost half an hour. "We have to go all the way back, too, you know," I reminded her.

We turned around and by the time we spotted the others, a cool breeze picked up from off the water.

The temperature dropped that evening, but the rain held off until after our campfire and marshmallows. With Sam and Odie settled in their tent, Meike and I reorganized ours inside, then dressed in our sweats.

"Burrrr," she said as we zipped up our sleeping bags.

We snuggled up closer together and lay quietly, listening to the rain drip on the roof of the tent.

"Dad wants us to live with him," Meike said softly in the dark.

Easing my finger alongside her hair, I tucked it behind her ear. "I know he does." I waited a short minute, in case she wanted to say more. "That's because he loves you," I whispered. "Just like I do."

Twenty-Two

Odie heard someone at the front door before I did. We were out in the sun on the back deck. He barked twice, and I pulled my t-shirt and shorts over my swimsuit and went to answer.

Through the screen, I saw Reverend Byker dressed in jeans, a gold t-shirt and tennis shoes.

"Hi, Janie," he said with his usual boyish grin.

"Well, hello." Instead of holding the door for him, I slipped through and stood barefoot on the stoop. "This is a surprise."

"I was over at Betty Jensen's dropping off the costumes we used for Bible School. Thought I'd stop and see how you're doing." He looked up at me from two steps down.

"Well, that was nice of you. I'm fine." I smiled, in case there was any doubt. "I'm doing fine."

"May I come in? You have a few minutes?"

"Umm, okay. Sure."

He followed me through the door and stopped just inside when Odie sniffed at his shoes. "Should I take these off?" Bending down, he scratched behind the dog's ears.

"That's all right." I hesitated between a fragile uneasiness and my good manners. "Would you like a glass of iced tea?"

"Sounds great."

I keep a full pitcher on hand when it's hot outside. Boil the water on the stove before steeping, and chill it overnight in the refrigerator.

"Have a seat," I said, nodding toward the kitchen table. He pulled out a dining chair while I filled two glasses with ice and poured tea at the counter.

I sat down across the table from him. "Hope you don't mind, there's a little sugar already added."

"Not at all. Thank you."

"Bible School went well?"

"Always an interesting week, but pretty busy." He sipped from his tea. Our glasses were sweating, and I reached for a couple paper napkins. "Sure glad we have Jesse on staff," he said. "She's not the most organized person, but she certainly is creative." He beamed with a suggestion. "Ever think of volunteering?"

"Nah. Did that for years in the city. Before I met Walt." I felt a hint of nostalgia. "Wouldn't be the same here in the burbs."

Odie lapped noisily at his bowl like he wanted to participate in our conversation. I went to the freezer for some ice cubes and dropped them in his water. "There you go, boy."

"Taking classes this summer?"

"No. Staying home with the kids."

Through the window facing the backyard, Reverend Byker glanced at the gym set. "Are they around?"

"They're out of town with Walt. Minnesota. Where Walt grew up."

"Long trip."

"They're staying over the 4th. It's Walt's favorite holiday. Big out there. Not just fireworks, but a parade, animals, apple pie. It's a really small town. Patriotic. He thought the kids should have the experience."

"Hard for you, though."

A faint buzzing on the screen caught Odie's attention and I watched a yellow jacket hover outside the mesh and zoom off again. "I try not to make a big deal of it," I said, my throat swelling.

Reverend Byker shifted in his chair and sat on his hands. Keeping his goodwill expression, he raised his brows. When I didn't say any more, he frowned.

"My impression from Jesse is that things are getting tougher for you right now," he said.

I shrugged one shoulder.

"I'm a pastor, Janie. You can talk to me."

I really didn't want to get into this with him. Spill my guts like milk all over the kitchen table. "I appreciate it, Reverend Byker—"

"Please. 'Art.'"

I waved off his comment. "I have good support. A professional therapist—doctor in psychology. A lawyer—trustworthy, well-respected. Jesse. My parents. My brothers." There was Cindy and Keith. My neighbor, Ruth. That was about it. Ten people . . . I could add my sisters.

"Divorce is certainly upsetting and painful," he said, trying a new approach. "Marriage takes effort and work." I thought him imprudent. He went on. "Harmony is a difficult thing. And I believe Walt gave up too soon."

"He just wanted out, one way or another." I didn't remember articulating that before. Accurate or not, it got me thinking aloud. "I might have agreed with you about the harmony a year or two ago."

"You mean you don't think Walt gave up too soon?"

"Sure he did. We could have made it work. I would have gone along with the harmony stuff, staying in tune and all that." I checked under the table for Odie before crossing my legs. "But now, I don't think of marriage that way."

"Oh? How would you define it?"

I smiled just a little, dropped my head down and shook it slowly with my eyes closed. "You wouldn't like my definition."

"Try me," he laughed.

My smile fell away and I spoke earnestly. "Marriage isn't harmony. It's counterpoint." I sighed, maybe too heavily. A sigh of impatience. "Harmony implies a main melody with added subservient notes. Counterpoint is two independent melodies played simultaneously. Like a fugue. Like Bach."

"I see. Hmmm." He jiggled the ice around in his glass, disturbing Odie, who got up and settled at the other end of the kitchen. "Interesting."

I should stand. A hint for him to head out. Instead, I slouched down a few inches in my chair, pretending indifference. He finished his tea with a few swallows and no further comment.

I pushed away from the table, still in my chair.

"Want to say a little prayer together?" he asked.

Maybe he felt obliged to ask. I squirmed and said, "I don't think so." He laughed, pushed his chair away from the table and headed to the entryway. I walked along out to the driveway. "Thanks for stopping," I told him.

He turned to face me. "Maybe a little hug?" he asked.

I didn't move one way or the other, kept my arms at my side. He stepped forward, reaching an arm behind me. I pulled away and with my fist to my mouth, fled to the house.

Five weeks of summer vacation had already slipped by with six more to look forward to. Sun and warm temperatures enhanced my outlook. When the day came for the last interview with PCS, I arrived confident. I knew I was a good mother. No way could they not get that.

Jay Riley began our appointment by inquiring after Sam and Meike.

"They're with Walt for three days. Going to Wrigley Field."

"Sounds like a good time," Riley said, "though not a Cubs fan myself."

These excursions had advantages for Walt, such as leverage, power and favor from Sam and Meike. But I didn't point this out to Riley. "White Sox?" I asked. "Or just hanging with the Tigers, like me?"

"Not big on baseball."

I accepted that without comment. He opened his black notebook, breathing like he just ran a few bases himself.

"When I review my notes, Tina, I see you mentioned earlier something about your attempts to reconcile with Walt since the two of you separated." He was looking at the page, not at me. "I want to give you a chance to say more on that."

"Actually, my attempts began before he moved out. He knew I didn't want him to go. We did start with a counselor. Only went twice. Then Walt quit.

"I remember another time. Walt didn't want to go to our traditional gathering on New Year's Eve with our friends, Keith and Cindy. I tried to persuade him. We could make it fun. This was two months before he left. Looking back, I suspect Walt had already made up his mind about leaving and didn't want to face them. Of all the couples we hung out with, they knew us best, most honestly. Walt knew they'd likely question his reasoning eventually."

The air-conditioned room was freezing and I pulled my cardigan around my shoulders as I talked. "Ended out, the kids and I went anyway. When I explained on the phone that Walt wasn't coming after all, Keith and Cindy insisted New Year's wouldn't be the same if we didn't. And the kids were counting on it."

Riley paged through his notebook in search of something. While I waited for him, I decided Riley didn't care to know the rest, where I told Keith and Cindy that Walt might move out and that they didn't believe he'd go through with it.

Riley look up. "Other times?"

"Let's see. Our anniversary came around a week or so after Walt left. I bought him a romantic card. He just laughed at it." I tipped my head back and looked at the ceiling, not admitting to Riley how once after Walt moved out, I called him in the middle of the night, asking him to reconsider. And there was the time I stopped by his shop for no reason, other than that's what I used to do to say hello, tell him what was for dinner.

Probably a good thing Riley didn't notice I teared up.

I told him of a less embarrassing time. "After Walt's initial announcement that he filed for a divorce, I reminded him that a divorce wasn't what I wanted. I said if he ever changed his mind or had second thoughts, I'd want to know."

"So, you don't want this divorce. In your opinion, the two of you should get back together?"

A trick question. A yes—honest. A no—also honest, but uncooperative.

Since asking Reverend Byker the sense of staying married to someone who didn't want to be married to me, I'd decided no more begging. Besides, Walt's idea of resolution consists of having one more chance for me to do things his way. I couldn't trust the agency to understand or believe that. Nor could I let PCS know that putting Sam and Meike and me through this hideous rigamarole with their damn agency was unforgivable.

So, maybe a yes wasn't a more honest answer.

"I believe we could have made it work."

"Could have?"

"I'm not so sure anymore."

There was a chance Riley might have picked up on the sadness in my voice or heard me swallow or just acted in kindness. At any rate, he moved on with his agenda. "You won't consider joint custody as an option?"

I bounced my answer right back at him. "That's incorrect. I *have* considered joint custody."

Feeling a need to explain, I slowed down. "Walt would take advantage of me. He wants the upper hand. He would not see me as an equal."

Riley scratched in his black notebook, presumably duplicating my words.

"Another thing," I said. "You must know there's plenty of research out there documenting how often with joint custody, each parent assumes the other has taken care of things, or even will just hope so. The children end out with no parenting at all." I sat up straighter, but he had already stopped writing, as if my point carried no validity.

"And why is it better for you to have custody than for Walt?"

We were where I wanted to be. The bottom line. Where, right then, I had no doubts. "There are several reasons," I began.

"Okay."

"Not necessarily in order of importance."

"Okay."

"It's what the kids are used to. It's consistent. I'm the stay-at-home mom. Walt is self-employed, works fulltime plus."

"All right."

I clicked my tongue, thinking. "At their school, I was vice-president of Mother's Club for a year, then president for another year. Before Meike and Sam were born, I was housemother in a group home. I am legal guardian for both my brothers' children."

For all these weeks, I had wanted to get this information in somewhere. Now given the opportunity, none of it sounded particularly impressive to me.

"There's the kids' music lessons. For Walt, music is entertainment. Other than that, he doesn't appreciate it. It's not that important. He claims to be tone deaf. He doesn't catch the nuances. He can't understand the necessity of music as expression, for instance, as a healthy outlet. Or the work involved . . . ." I caught myself and took a deep breath. If I wasn't careful, this could sound like mania, not passion. "What I'm saying is he won't do justice to their music or their lessons. Music is way down on the priority list for Walt.

"Another example. When the kids were babies—they were eighteen months apart—Walt wouldn't stay home alone with both of them at the same time. He said he couldn't handle it. Like, if I wanted to go to church at night, Walt would be willing to stay home with Meike, but I'd have to bring Sam to the church nursery. Or vice versa."

"That was over eight years ago," Riley said, dismissing me. "The kids are older now."

Despite his blatant defense of Walt, I managed a smile and nodded. Yet during the next few minutes, articulating what remains so obvious to me became increasingly difficult, as if I had checked my belt and noticed what few bullets I carried. Even so, with little shame, I continued turning pieces of our lives into ammunition.

"I'm careful not to slam Walt in front of the kids. Walt doesn't take the same precaution."

Expecting Riley to want examples, I crossed my legs, moved my foot up and down in a nervous jitter, and waited for him to ask. Instead, he sat breathing loudly, looking at me and thumbing the corner of his notebook.

"Unconditional love," I said finally, forgetting about specifics.

"Pardon me?"

"I love my kids, period." We were eye to eye. "They don't need to earn it, don't owe me anything in return. They know I love them, no strings attached."

"Interesting. Anything else before we move on?"

I shook my head. What the hell more did he want.

"There are still a couple questions I'm required to ask you."

Shifting in my chair, I planted my feet and waited, my self-assurance sneaking a way back to me. "Okay. Shoot," I said.

"What's the most important time for a parent to be with their child?"

I answered without hesitation. "Well, there's early morning. There's after school. Dinner. Bedtime. Consistently. They're all important."

He appeared to write my list down. The same information would be asked of Walt, and, as vindictive as it was, I took a second to relish how Walt would falter at the question.

"This is the last one," Riley said as if more relieved than I was. "In your mind, what is one negative thing and what is one positive thing about each of your children?"

"Oooo." I brought my hand up to my face and scratched my chin. "A negative thing about Sam and a negative thing about Meike. Hmmm. I guess a negative thing for Sam is teasing his sister."

"He often teases his sister?"

"Sometimes." I grinned. "Meike would say a lot of times."

Tugging my lower lip, I considered something negative to pin on poor Meike. "She screams bloody murder when I brush through her hair. She just hates it." I cleared my throat. "It is a negative, but not really her fault. She can't take good care of her hair herself. I usually braid it before she leaves, but it gets so tangled after a weekend at Walt's." That slipped out. I didn't say it on purpose.

"And the good? A positive thing for each?"

"Sam's so smart. He loves books. Started reading before preschool. Gets good grades, plays piano and baritone, lots of friends. Intelligent yet very intuitive. Sensitive . . ."

"Stop. That's more like four or five."

With a short nervous giggle, I added, "Yeah. Well, moms do that." I needed to be careful and hold back. "Seriously, it is a good thing. Being intelligent and sensitive at the same time."

Riley might not have bought that, but the interrogation was nearly over and the evidence clear. The rest of the interview—a piece of cake. I would stop for ice cream on the way home whether or not the sun was out. I had made my point. Riley was getting it.

"And Meike?" he asked.

"She's smart, too. Reads a lot. She's beautiful. Plays the violin . . ."

"One."

"Okay," I said. "If I have to pick one . . . she's intense."

His reaction couldn't have been worse. "That's a good thing?"

Twenty-Three

Eighty-five pages stacked neatly on the corner of Richard's mahogany desk told the story. Not the part of the story where I was forced to abandon Sam and sit in the hallway while the child psychologist questioned him. Not the part when after her turn, Meike clung to me as we both fought tears. Not the part of the story where I didn't pump my children to learn what they said during their interviews. I had bit my tongue until raw rather than speak evil of their father in front of them, but that part of the story wasn't included either.

None of the eighty-five pages noted the advantage an extrovert might have. Nothing mentioned psychological tests with multiple-choice answers are unfair to people whose brains just don't operate that cut and dried and simply. None of the pages described the boorish Jay Riley passing judgment while taking notes with his pinkie in the air.

In his tall leather chair, Richard's expression remained serious, his back to the office window, his arms stretched on top of his desk.

Every part of me winced. Unless we settled on joint custody, the recommendation went to Walt.

I looked away, outside through the glass ten stories high, through the August air heavy with humidity, and into nothing.

Soon, the nothing spread over me. Not a dazed, dull-witted numbness, but an actual keen sensation of painful vacancy.

I sat very still until making myself draw a deep breath. Lips compressed hard together, I tapped them with a clenched fist. Eyes crimped shut, I exhaled and opened them again.

Richard waited patiently. After a time, I managed some cerebral calm. Evidently my posture relaxed a little, and he spoke up. "It's only a recommendation."

He said it with courtesy enough, but I twisted my mouth toward one side of my face and shook my head slowly a few times, pretty much dismissing whatever consolation he might have intended.

Richard wasn't easily offended. "This report is a perfect example of excessiveness," he said. He lifted the stack of pages and slapped it down on the table in front of him. "The interviews with you, the interviews with Walt, even the ones with Sam and Meike. The testing . . . evaluations. Seems to me, the whole shebang." He leaned back, the top of the chair pointing to the window. "In my opinion, it's overkill."

My attorney might have aimed only to cushion the bad news for me. While trying to absorb the result of the evaluation, let alone the implications, I was still aware of his mitigating skills. I grabbed his impression and clung tightly.

"You really think so?"

Richard nodded. He pushed away from his desk a few inches and leaned back further. He folded his large hands over his chest, and I glimpsed his gold wristwatch. It reminded me of my father's.

"For example," he said. "They point out Walt's personality type makes him a possible candidate for alcoholism. What kind of bullshit is that? A possible candidate? 'We give a nod to Walt.' Not too final, seems to me."

"I want to read it," I told him. "Is there a copy for me?"

He sat up and reached for the report. "If you want to." He thumbed an upper corner of the pages, frowning, speaking with caution. "They quote the children, you know."

"Of course." I looked down at the floor, trying to collect myself, running the back of my thumb under my eyes over and over, wiping it on my skirt. "Sorry."

"Not at all." Richard waited while I found a handkerchief in my purse. "Any child's going to prefer the Disney Dad, you know."

The air-conditioning seemed harsh, set high to compensate for the muggy outdoors. Shifting in my chair, I folded my arms, rubbing them through my sweater. With a faint voice, I asked, "So, what do we do?"

Richard blinked slowly. "We wait." He held his earlobe. "Quite frankly, our previous conversations indicate Walt will use this as points to boost his agenda." His mouth stretched into a mischievous grin. "Or this might suffice. He's had his ego stroked. He could just wise up and let it go at that."

Another something for me to grab and cling to.

Three steps into the parking ramp, the humid air reached me, surrounded me, comforted me. Walt had picked up Meike and Sam earlier in the afternoon for an overnight at his place. Tomorrow evening, the kids and I would set out for one last camping trip of the summer. I drove mindful of the traffic, the sultry sunshine, the sand and swimming and roasted marshmallows on the coming weekend. I dared not think any further.

I listened for Odie as I came in the door, forgetting he'd gone with Sam and Meike. Changing quickly into a t-shirt and shorts, I left my slip, camisole and sweater out on the bed. Pouring a glass of iced tea, I set it on a paper napkin on the kitchen table, pulled out a chair and opened the manila envelope.

While I read every word of the eighty-five pages, my insides ran through a gamut of emotions I'd be incapable of identifying even to Dr. Jennings. It took me an hour and twelve minutes. My share of the evaluation cost $5,745.00.

When I finished reading, I ripped the whole thing to pieces.

~

Packing the Town Car took up most of the evening. A couple duffel bags with our clothes, along with some towels and pillows, fit in the back. In the morning, I would wiggle the cooler in the open spot behind the driver's seat. The tents, sleeping bags, grill, clothesline and a few tools went in the trunk, firewood stuffed in between.

The task didn't take a lot of concentration and the PCS evaluation kept invading my thoughts. "In the Best Interest of the Children . . . . In the Best Interest of the Children . . . ." While I worked, I continually replayed what Richard had said. The report was only a recommendation. The recommendation will stroke Walt's ego. With his ego pumped, Walt might give up the custody issue altogether.

When I finished packing, I put some Dave Brubeck on the stereo and mixed an almond coffee cake to bring along camping. While it baked, I combined peanuts, raisins, pretzels and M&M's in a jumbo freezer bag. I wrote peaches and melon in big letters on the grocery list, in the best interest of the children as if fruit was an exception.

My brother Jerry called just before ten and wanted to know if they should swing by on their way to the campground in the morning.

"The forecast is good and hot so we're aiming for just before eleven," he said.

"You go on ahead. Walt's not bringing the kids back until noon. It'll be close to three before we get there."

"You want the big sandy lot on hill C if I can get it?"

"That would be perfect. They wouldn't promise it when I made the reservation, but nobody else seems to like it up there."

We said good-night and I started cleaning up my mess in the kitchen, thankful Jerry hadn't asked about PCS. He knew about the agency's involvement but not the details or the time-table. Even I hadn't known exactly when the report would be completed and sent to my attorney, only that the court had set a deadline for the end of the month.

When I drizzled glaze over the coffee cake, I supposed I should let Gerrit know about today. Except I didn't feel like talking about it. He and Laura were picking up my folks on Tuesday and visiting the campground. I decided to postpone telling him. Maybe on Tuesday we'd get a few minutes alone to talk. By then, maybe I could discuss it with a little objectivity. Maybe by then Walt would have changed his mind.

A few minutes before midnight, I went to bed and, in the best interest of the children, repeated a checklist through my head. Soap, shampoo, sun screen . . . I fell asleep calculating the easiest place to stop for ice, and didn't wake up until daylight.

It was early enough that I went for a jog before coffee and a shower. My mother called to tell me not to buy hamburger for Tuesday since Dad wanted to bring enough for everyone. Really, she just wanted to check how I was doing. Her calling was okay with me. Face to face, my mother could read me pretty well, but over the phone, I could tell her I was fine.

The diesel pickup pulled into the driveway. I went to hold the door open for Meike, Sam and Odie. Walt followed them, but once the leash cleared the threshold, I let the aluminum storm door shut between us. We could talk through the screen if he had anything to say.

"All packed to go, huh?" he asked.

"Yup," I answered.

"We went out for a late breakfast so they should be all set."

Sam retied the lace on one of his tennis shoes. "I need to grab my baseball glove."

"It's on your bed. You guys grab your books. We can leave after you have a drink of water and use the bathroom."

"Can we go swimming?" Meike asked, jumping up and down.

"That's the first thing we'll do," I said. "Even before we unpack the car."

"Yippee! Come on, Odie." Off they went, Odie barking as he chased her.

"Have the kids call me on Wednesday night," Walt said. "And say hi to Jerry and Lynn for me."

"Right."

"Case and Denise are going too? Man, I haven't seen them for a while."

"Uh-huh."

Walt put his hands in the pockets of his shorts and took a step back. "The evaluation's finished, you know."

"I know. I read the whole thing."

Through the screen, I could see his expression turn.

"You must be really bad, Janie. They never choose against the mother."

In the best interest of the children, I slammed the door in his face.

Twenty-Four

Jerry was able to hold three adjacent spots on the sandy hill of section C. The wooded property along Lake Michigan was owned by the Christian Reformed Church and run mostly by their volunteers. Over the last two decades, cement slabs had been added to lots in sections A and B of the campground, accommodating the increased use of trailers, 5th wheelers and motor homes by second-and-third generation immigrant Calvinists. An old airport hangar on the grounds had been converted into an auditorium where gospel concerts were held twice a week. Church services were held there as well, one every Sunday morning and one every Sunday evening.

A camp store sold basic supplies, along with Hudsonville ice cream and homemade Dutch pies. Closed on Sundays. Attached to the office, a fellowship hall served breakfast on weekdays until 10 a.m. if you wanted to buy it. After 10, the room was cleared for Bible study. Topics for study were listed for each week of the summer and posted with a thumbtack on a bulletin board outside the store: Christianity and the New Millennium. Christianity and the World Market. Christianity and Your New (W)Holy You.

A Calvinist either takes advantage of an opportunity meant for edification or risks a reputation of slothfulness. Fortunately, tent camping on the overflow hill separated us from the mainstream. We were farthest away from the hub. No one had to walk by our campsites to attend anything. We came along with Case and Denise and their three children, my brother and his wife and their boys every year for the beach. And the shuffleboard.

Complex playground equipment, bright yellows and reds connected with bridges and tunnels, made adults wish they were eight years old again. One rainy afternoon, we watched "Milo and Otis" at the recreation center. Bible school, organized sports and hayrides were available if Sam and Meike wanted to participate, but I didn't push it. They usually went if their cousins wanted to. We did attend one of the Sunday church services, in the best interest of the children.

First thing on Sunday, I had to drive into town to get ice for the cooler. Later that hot afternoon, we all piled into Case's van and drove to the county park to avoid the "No Swimming on Sunday" posted at the access to the campground beach. If we wanted wine or a brandy, we drank it at the campfire from coffee mugs.

My low spirits that week had little to do with where we were camping. Walt's comment followed me around like smoke from a damp campfire no matter where I moved my lawn chair. The more the words troubled me, the less I wanted to tell anyone, afraid what measly hope was left would disappear if I admitted them.

My attitude of keeping things to myself continued when Gerrit and Laura brought my parents on Tuesday. I wanted to forget about Walt. I wanted everyone to enjoy their day.

Promptly at coffee time, my mother called from the bottom of the hill. "Yoo-hoo!" she waved.

Gerrit walked alongside her, toting a small cooler and a white waxed box from a bakery. My father strolled a ways behind with Laura on his arm. His emphysema seemed less troublesome this spring and summer, although he kept his portable oxygen in the car on outings just in case. With temperatures cooled a good ten degrees since the weekend and the humidity diminished, he could conquer the hill if he took his own sweet time.

Including Case and his family in our gathering was a natural fit. He and his parents and siblings immigrated from The Netherlands, first to Canada then to our neighborhood and church, when we were twelve. Case Berends and I had been classmates. We dated the first year in high school but became each other's best friend instead. Our parents often visited to talk Dutch, discuss theology and the old country. Jerry and Case's brothers served in Vietnam at the same time.

I think we all assumed the Berends would join us for burgers, but my father made it official when Gerrit lit the charcoal.

"You're to eat with us, *hoor?*" my father said to Denise.

"Are you sure there's enough?" she asked with polite shyness.

"Dad brought enough burger for the whole campground," I teased, guessing he likely sacrificed a little coffee money, a couple tanks of gas for his Olds. My father played piano, read books, studied theology. But he had worked hard all his life, a butcher and meat counter man, to make his living and remained, rightly so, proud of it.

"Judas, man," Gerrit said after my father opened our meal with a prayer. "Ya have to sign the three forms of confession to camp here?"

"If you want the discount," I answered.

Jerry helped himself to potato salad. "Janie paid full price, of course."

In the sand under the oak trees that beautiful August afternoon, conversation around the picnic table turned to school days just ahead. Each of the kids took a turn telling what grade they would be starting.

"You're all growing up too fast," my mother said.

"And what class will you take this fall, Janie?" Denise asked.

"Christianity and RV Maintenance," Gerrit answered for me.

My parents still struggled with the idea of their daughter attending college, but my father laughed heartily until we thought he might need his oxygen.

We cleaned up and boiled water for dishes, then agreed a shuffleboard tournament was in order.

"Of course, Grandpa and Grandma are going to win," my father warned.

As we walked down to the camp store where the courts were, I heard my father tell Sam, "You'll be Granddad's partner, *hoor*?" He'd never used the word "Granddad" before and I'm not sure Sam or anyone else caught his heartfelt offer to sub for Walt.

We hogged the two shuffleboard courts for over an hour. A small audience from the campground gathered on the wooden benches in front of the store. For the play-offs, my mother in her pedal-pushers teamed with Gerrit, and my father in his red *pije* teamed with Sam.

The prize, mile-high Dutch coconut cream pie, went to Sam and my father.

Some of the loveliest sunsets of all times and places are here in western Michigan along the lakeshore. But my mother liked to be home before dark, even though Gerrit did the driving that day. Our group parted at the bottom of the hill. Meike and Sam and their cousins squeezed their grandparents in hugs and said goodbye. I walked with my father while Gerrit, Laura and my mother went on ahead, waiting for us at the car.

"I remember the year we rented these cottages," my father said as we leisurely passed the row of one-room cabins at the edge of the woods. "Sam and Meike were still babies."

"It rained a lot that week," I said.

"Walt and I spent a good deal of time with the chess board between us."

I hadn't thought of Walt so kindly in a long time. I kept my eyes on the gravel under our feet.

"You played the organ in the auditorium, and Mom the piano. Remember?"

"Seems like a long time ago, Dad."

"It was a good summer," he said.

I knew my father. He wasn't rubbing it in, just acknowledging his sadness. I stopped and nodded slowly. My father stood still. Gerrit must have noticed and backtracked across the parking lot.

"All set?" Gerrit asked, meeting us.

My father and I hugged. He tried one of his old-fashioned bear hugs, and the strength of his arms under his thin frame surprised me.

"So long now, little girl," he said.

Before the steep climb back to the tents, I waited alone in the restroom until my sobbing finished. Then I headed up to join Sam and Meike at the campfire.

~

I kept the evaluation and Walt's remark to myself the rest of the week. As we packed up on Saturday, the sky turned from platinum to deeper grey to inky over the lake. We loaded the car haphazardly in the rain. Because the thunderstorms caught up to us, the usual forty-five minute drive home took well over an hour.

Once home again, we had some catching up to do. School began in ten days, four of which included the Labor Day weekend Sam and Meike would take with Walt. While Sam griped because we needed to shop for jeans and tennis shoes after the orthodontist on Monday, Meike grumped about making up her violin practice.

If I had shouted at the night sky, or kicked up sand on the vacant beach, or at least complained about Walt at the campfire, maybe I wouldn't have squawked at Sam when I told him to be quiet and help me unload the car. Maybe I wouldn't have yelled at Meike that her "E" was flat, that she should slow down, use her fricking ear.

Three days later, Dr. Jennings used most of our session to finally coax the details from me. After I told him, we sat for a moment, silent except for the scrape of tissues against the cardboard whenever I'd reached to the end table for one. Our chairs faced each other, eight feet apart. He leaned forward eventually, feet flat on the floor, hands on his knees. "Jane, are you believing what Walt said?"

I dabbed my eyes and shrugged.

"How would Walt possibly know what kind of recommendations they make? Or how? Or when? He has some kind of psychic power?"

"Of course not," I admitted softly.

The only window in the room was to my right, almost behind me, a narrow double-hung window with a panel of sheer lace curtain on each side. Jennings' office was on the second floor of an elegant nineteenth-century home in the Cherry Hill area of the city, renovated with the center's goal of a tranquil, comfortable setting. I shifted sideways in my chair and looked out. The window offered a view to the back of the property and into a garden my friend Dorothy had initiated. Dorothy is not a pantheist. She would cringe at such a label. But she values the beautiful harmony, the cleansing rest and the mystery a garden possesses.

The calming effect works, even from up here.

Dr. Jennings spoke in a quiet voice. "Jane, you have great kids." I turned from the window and met his pleading look. "If you were a bad mother, how would Sam and Meike ever be who they are?"

I never answered. Just accepted the box of tissues Dr. Jennings handed over.

Twenty-Five

Richard called to let me know a draft of what he referred to as my "interrogatories and request for production of documents" had been forwarded to my accountant.

"Finally," I said.

"We now have a copy we can work with," Richard said.

"I'd like to talk more about the PCS report, too," I said. On Dr. Jennings' recommendation, I repeated Walt's remark so that, as Jennings put it, my attorney would know what we were up against.

"That brings up the other reason I called, if you have a minute," Richard said.

"Sure."

"I'm quoting Act 155. 'Upon specific referral from the court . . .' aah, 'counseling service may be instructed to serve as an impartial, unbiased resource in evaluating problems involving custody of minor children . . .' and so on and so on . . . Here we go. 'Either party shall retain the right to object to the recommendation and present such additional proofs as may be appropriate . . . either party may schedule the matter for a hearing' . . ."

"I don't get it," I said into the phone.

"Was PCS an impartial, unbiased resource? Especially if Walt is going to push this, I would argue they're not an expert witness."

"You're serious, aren't you."

"Serious about considering it. And you've mentioned Riley had it in for you in the first place."

"Yeah. First thing, he accused me of stashing some of my old records. So stupid. As if I were the transporter anyway." I twisted the phone cord around my fingers at the thought. "He asked me what would happen if I emptied my purse on the table, remember?"

"Ha! I saw that in my notes," Richard said. "But I'm also going on other information. I've heard—I can't reveal my sources," here he paused with a short laugh, "but they're reliable. The scuttlebutt is that Riley's gone through a rough divorce settlement himself recently."

"Geez," I said, shaking my head toward the ceiling.

"Anyway, something to think about."

"Definitely. And what about Riley's reaction when I told him Meike was intense?"

"I remember."

"There's no way he didn't stereotype me. He even asked me to pass his business card on to friends. Highly distasteful."

"Soliciting clients."

"Here's another thing that's been bothering me. Why the hell were there only men questioning me? Not even Sam and Meike were ever interviewed by a woman."

"Hmmm. Good point."

~

When Walt picked up Meike and Sam that evening for his extended Labor Day weekend, he stood on the rug without much to say besides "Say goodbye to your mom." He might have sensed my readiness to haul off and punch him in the face. He might have at least apologized.

No apology came. Two hours later, the phone rang.

"Mom," Sam said between whimpers. "I want to come home."

"What's wrong, Sam? What's the matter?"

"I stubbed my toe." He started crying. "Bad. It's bleeding!"

"Oh, hon, what happened? Where's your dad?"

"I hit it hard . . ." he caught his breath " . . . on the corner of the shower door. It really hurts and it's bleeding," he sobbed.

I heard Walt in the background. "It's not that bad, Sam. Let me talk to Mom."

"I want to come home," Sam repeated.

Walt took the phone. "It isn't that bad," he said to me, chuckling as if amused. "A little overreaction. He'll be okay."

"Walt, are you sure?"

"We put a cold washcloth on it," he told me. "Sam, let me see . . . looks like the bleeding stopped. It won't need stiches or anything."

"You sure? He wants to come home."

"It's not a big deal."

"Then why not, if it's not a big deal? He just wants his mother." Tears welled in my eyes, but I kept my voice steady. "What's wrong with that?"

"We can't have the kids running back to you over every little thing."

And why not, I thought.

What Walt said made some sense, and for a second, I supposed he was right.

But it didn't *feel* right. Sam is crying.

Why do I second-guess myself when confronted by Walt?

The tears began running down my face. My son wants to come home. Simple as that. For a hug, for a Band-Aid, for chicken soup, for whatever. What difference does it make why?

I sighed long and heavily into the phone. "Walt. Just let him come home."

"Fine," he said and hung up.

The day after Meike and Sam started their school year I began two courses for my semester. World Literature II and Intermediate Dutch, both on Mondays, Wednesdays, and Fridays.

An appointment was scheduled with my attorney on Thursday that same week to begin work on the financial aspects and to discuss the possibility of disputing the PCS report. But on Wednesday afternoon, Richard phoned to give me a heads-up.

"Looks like the agenda for tomorrow has changed." He paused before getting specific. "A few hours ago, I received a Praecipe for Trial."

I pulled out a dining room chair, dropped into it. Praecipe for Trial. Walt's invitation. Walt's damn stubbornness. His insistence on a nightmare. Elbows on the table, I tipped my head, clutched my hair, squeezed and released it again.

"And. In the meantime," Richard said, "there's a new motion to amend the temporary custody order."

"Can he do that?" I asked with a tight voice. "Amend a temporary custody order, I mean?"

"He can try. A request can be submitted anytime. But changes aren't usually made in the middle of things. And it looks like we're still pretty much in the middle of things here."

"Yeah," I sighed. "I guess we are."

"I wanted you to know before we meet."

"I understand. I appreciate that."

"Well, now that I've ruined your evening. . . . We'll talk tomorrow."

Tomorrow was a long time coming. A semblance of nonchalance with Meike and Sam all evening, eating supper, homework, wasn't easy. Yet, thank God, I believe they both fell asleep that night without suspicion of the new battle line forming. They would need to walk through the shambles soon enough.

Settling into the Barcalounger with a cup of herbal tea, I tried to get some homework done. I had to read the first four paragraphs of Thomas Mann's "Mario and the Magician" three times before I knew what I was reading. Dozing somewhere after the German narrator and his family arrived in the Italian village and when they were seated inside the arena, I jumped awake with a lingering image. A circus tent, with Sam and Meike in the front row between Walt and me. A man in the center ring—a stern man, a black-robed judge who snapped a whip. I closed the anthology and went up to bed, only to lie awake a good part of the night.

Ahead of schedule the following day, I decided to park near the center of downtown and walk the several blocks to the law office.

Some mothers in my neighborhood avoid downtown. They're intimidated by the city and the "ghetto" Walt supposedly saved me from. That morning as I walked, tall buildings, city buses, sidewalks and pedestrians reminded me of riding steep escalators with my mother in Wurzburg's when I was Meike's age, standing in line for S&H Green Stamps. Strolling with my father past the holiday windows in Herpolsheimer's.

The crosswalk flashed an orange hand. I stopped and waited, absorbing the energy of the city corner and a confidence I rarely felt in the suburbs. At Pearl Street, I pulled open the glass door of the Trust Building and took the elevator to the tenth floor. Then I entered the law office and its reassuring propriety.

Richard and I shook hands in the reception area. We remained silent as he escorted me to the conference room. Once we were seated at the mahogany table, he set the official document in front of me.

". . . demand is hereby made that the above entitled cause be set for trial."

Reading upside down, he followed the words with his ballpoint pen. When he finished the page, he glanced up before reading another. "We'll assume now that Walt means business."

I nodded and let him continue.

"This is a copy of Michigan Court Rules 3.210. It basically says a request for change in temporary custody may be made at any time, but not without a hearing. Unless the parties come to an agreement beforehand. The probate judge must hold a hearing within 56 days. The court must enter a decision within 28 days after the hearing."

Hardly any space remained between Richard's dark, bushy eyebrows. He set the page aside, and I looked away toward the autumn sun coming through the window. Richard waited patiently. When I faced him again, he placed Walt's new motion in front of me.

"The motion reminds the court Psychiatric Consultation Services has completed their evaluation . . . . The judge has a copy . . . . The recommendation is physical custody of the parties' minor children be granted to the Plaintiff . . . . Both children have expressed a strong and sincere preference to reside with the Plaintiff . . . ." Richard looked up. "Did you know this?"

I shook my head.

". . . have begun pressuring Plaintiff to conclude this matter . . . ." He paused, and we both shook our heads. "The first testimony-taking trial isn't set until May 5 and 6, 1994, and I quote, 'Plaintiff fears that the present living situation is harmful to the children.'"

"Jesus." I bit the tip of my thumb as if needing an excuse to wince.

Richard leaned forward in his chair. "Of course, we need to draft a reply to this." He ran his hand over his tie and frowned. "And we have to pay attention to this financial statement soon."

My shoulders rose and fell. A heavy sigh escaped me. "I don't care about the damn money," I told him in a calm voice. "I just want my kids."

Richard nodded several times, indicating he understood. Then he raised his eyebrows. "Jane. Has it occurred to you that might be the exact response Walt is aiming for?"

I stared at my attorney.

"We don't need to work on the financial today," he said picking up his ballpoint. "There is another thing, however."

I slumped back in my chair. I was still on *harmful.*

Once more, he read upside down following with his pen. "Let me see . . . 'Plaintiff prays that this Court amend the Temporary Order to provide . . .' Here it is, the third one. 'That Plaintiff be granted sole possession of the parties' marital home, effective 30 days after entry of Order.'"

"What the . . . ?" I pushed against the back of my chair, slam-crossed my arms and resisted an urge to get up and stomp around the room. "Why doesn't he go live in the damn vacant $300,000 house he talked me into building?" I spit out the question. Emphatic, I counted on my fingers. "He's the one who dropped marriage counseling. He's the one who wanted to separate. He's the one who left and filed for divorce." My eyes narrowed. "He wants to kick me out of the house . . . he wants the kids . . . . *Harmful*? What the hell?"

Richard laid his pen down and folded his hands as he listened.

"I was plenty great while he was out feeding his ego for nineteen years. But now, you see, I cramp his style." Tapping the mahogany table with my knuckles, I explained. "I won't play golf, won't spend any more time entertaining his employees or his clients. I don't want a two-carat diamond, a gas-guzzling car. I don't want a new house."

Just repeating the word hurt my throat. "Harmful?" I gulped, shoving the pain down where it gnawed my insides. As my anger resurfaced, the indignity somehow brought focus. "Which is why he brings it up a year and a half after he leaves home?"

Apparently, I hadn't been able to grasp it until now.

The implications fell into place.

"You know what, Richard?" I straightened while taking a deep breath. "This really isn't about bipolar. Or mental health. Or any of that. This is about Walt's intolerance. His damn intolerance that I've put up with for a long, long time."

I stopped to breathe and exhale.

"Walt doesn't want me to write stories. He doesn't want his wife taking college classes. He wants his supper served at six. Oh, and 'Don't talk Dutch to me' he tells me. Heaven forbid the kids pick it up. 'This is America,' he says."

Given the look on Richard's face, I kept talking. "He can't handle my wanting to join the Lutheran Church. He's the kid of an evangelical preacher. He even objected to sending money for kids in Guatemala because the organization is Roman Catholic." My smile came and went quickly. "We do anyway. I send a check every month, along with a pen-pal note that Sam and Meike write. We have a picture of—Hernandez is his name. At Christmas and Easter, he sends us a color crayon drawing and a few lines in Spanish.

"Walt has a cow about it," I said. "But I told him never mind because, for one thing, it was good for the kids, and for another, I didn't have to account to him for every damned dollar. We could afford it."

I hid my face behind my hands and forced my breath out hard.

"So you weren't always the perfect submissive wife," Richard said.

We both laughed, and I found his reference to our community's background comforting.

"Usually I was," I said. My torrent of words slowed. "I accepted that crap too long."

My hands open, I massaged my face, letting my head fall back against the chair. I stared at the ceiling some more. "Walt can't very well say our divorce is about his intolerance or that he doesn't consider a woman his equal. But he needs to justify the divorce. To his friends. To the community, his network. To his family. To himself. So now his wife is impossible to live with. A bad mother. Unfit. She's *bipolar* for crying out loud." I buzzed my lips in a phhft. "Even a Christian isn't obligated to a Crazy."

I looked through the tenth-story window, leaning my forehead on the tips of my fingers. "Wonder how long Walt's been planning this whole thing."

"Good question," Richard answered softly. Not so softly I didn't hear his sadness.

~

The second week of October ended by the time I focused on Walt's financial disclosure enough that Richard could draw up a reasonable response. In Gerrit and Laura's living room that Friday night after dinner, I gave them an update.

"It was getting to the point I didn't know what was what, who was who. When I stopped at the bank this summer—that little bank in Byron Center—they wouldn't let me take my name off anything. But the chauvinists suckers. Won't let me say no to any new obligation either. Still frickin' under coverture law.

"So I'm listed as an officer for the companies and yet they claim they can't release any information to me. Folks at the bank are more of Walt's buddies." I blew out my cheeks. "I can hardly keep up with it all."

"So what do you do?" Laura asked.

"Richard's asking for a restraining order."

"No shit?" Gerrit asked, a satisfactory smile slipping over his face.

"Yeah. And it asks the court to order Walt to pay me half of any returns received on any investments during the pendency of the divorce. Just since January, Walt's gotten over $200,000 on investments."

Frank wandered in from the kitchen, his paws clicking lightly on the hardwood floor. He sniffed and snorted along the rug in the center of the room before settling close to Laura's chair.

"What will a restraining order do exactly?" Laura asked.

"Keeps Walt from selling, transferring, releasing—that kind of thing—our marital assets. Otherwise Walt can renegotiate just about anything. He can even dispose of stuff whether it's ours individually or jointly."

Sections of the newspaper lay scattered next to me on the couch. I busied my hands and set pages in letter-order, lining up the corners. "There's a list of assets Richard's attaching. We've got two land contracts—one to the underground sprinkling company, another to Vander Baan's." I pushed the newspapers toward the other end of the couch. "Walt sold the house on Glendale and closed in April. Proceeds over eighty-two grand. He's got promissory notes from the cement-pumping company. And he collects rent from both of these guys. Then there's like fifteen thousand each year from selling the Concrete Cutting shares."

"You mentioned something about buying Michael out a while back," Gerrit said.

"The shares are to other guys. Employees. I can't understand all the finagling. Walt sells the boats from the cottage, buys a cabin cruiser and parks it in a slip in Holland."

"You've got to be kidding," Laura said.

I shook my head. "I'd never know except Meike and Sam mentioned a shower at a yacht club. When I asked Walt about it, he tells me that they need something fun to do on the weekends he has the kids." My voice thickened and the words came out slower. "It's so strange . . . their going places I don't know about . . . I'm not even sure they wear life jackets on that boat. Running with that elite crowd . . . ."

I clamped up with the thought of Sam and Meike who knows where. Shivering, I folded my arms and clutched them. The leather couch creaked as I shifted to cross my legs, wrapping one tightly around the other, resting my foot against the opposite ankle.

"Janie, would you like a shot of brandy or something?" Gerrit asked, getting up from the Sleepy Hollow. "It's only eight o'clock. Hon, how about you?" He headed to the kitchen, *te schooiken* in his slippers. A little tinkling of glasses, and he reappeared with a snifter of liquid amber for each of us.

The CD player purred and Dave Brubeck switched to Itzhak Perlman.

We listened to a Rebbe's frolic, the room otherwise quiet except Frank's occasional snore.

"Mom and Dad sure enjoyed Meike playing her violin on Grandparents day," Laura said after a while.

"They tell you about that?"

"Bragging her up to no end," my brother said.

"Meike wanted to do a fiddle tune, but her teacher thought a Dutch Psalm would be more appropriate. We settled on 'Amazing Grace.'" I drew up my shoulders. "People always like 'Amazing Grace.'"

"You play the piano for her then?" Gerrit asked.

"Yeah. No big deal, although some of her recital stuff is getting more complex, and I can't necessarily sit down and just sight-read the accompaniment anymore. She's coming right along. Double-stops and all that."

"Meike still like St. Cecilia?" Laura sometimes wished she'd kept up with playing her flute.

I nodded. "It's pretty cool for those kids. You can't believe the fullness of the sound. Lots of work, though. They're doing Offenbach this spring. You know, with 'The Can-Can.'"

Gerrit played the trombone through high school and still brought it out of the attic from time to time. "I got a nice picture of Meike with her violin last year," he said.

"At St. Cecilia? Her white blouse, long concert-black skirt?"

"No," Laura said. "That dress you made for her. Pastel floral, cotton sheen. Tiers in the back."

"Oh, and her hair's all French braided. That was her recital."

"I was showing Mom and Dad." Gerrit sometimes played an intercessory role for me.

Frank opened his eyes, stretched, shook his jowls, settled back in. Laura reached and clicked the floor lamp lower.

Itzhak pined a sweet Yiddish melody. I sipped my brandy, slowly, the warming sensation reaching as far as that place where painful things I swallow hid.

From the bookshelf a clock chimed softly under its glass dome.

"Don't tell Mom and Dad Walt wants the house," I whispered.

"We won't," Laura answered kindly.

"Don't ever tell them about the PCS thing," I said still hushed. "Or that Walt says I'm crazy."

"We would never do that," Gerrit whispered back.

With my fingers, I wiped tears from my face that sprang from nowhere. "Mom would only blame herself."

Twenty-Six

Owing to my World Lit class, I spent several October evenings with the don Quixote and his knight-errant chivalry. Other nights, wanderings of the young and innocent Candide temporarily distracted me in late hours after Meike and Sam's bedtime. I struggled less with the grammar usage of *de Nederlands.* Hundreds of words I'd memorized for class, written on cards with which the kids loved to drill me, as well as vocabulary I had known from my youth, began to flow readily. Sometimes I found myself thinking in Dutch.

Legal jargon, lines and menacing words of Walt's motion were tumbling around in my brain at the same time, sometimes randomly, sometimes not, but nearly always foremost.

Entered for a good cause. Entered for the best interest of the children. Plead the Court. Grant Plaintiff complete. The recommendation as a result of extensive, thorough and time-consuming efforts to determine the best interest of the parties' minor children. Children express a strong and sincere preference to reside with Plaintiff. Children have begun pressuring Plaintiff to conclude this matter.

The clause "Plaintiff fears the present living situation is harmful to the children" remained the most painful. The statement "Both children wish to discuss their preferences with the trial judge" nearly as troubling. I doubted Sam or Meike had even considered the possibility of the court interviewing them personally "in chambers," but I had no doubt whatsoever where the idea came from.

My having some sort of conversation on the matter with my children seemed appropriate. Avoidance would be worse. I could tell them a "be careful what you wish for" parable. I could explain that a father's good intention doesn't make an action wise. I could persuade Sam and Meike how they were too young to know what's best. I could correct them like when they make a mistake conjugating verbs. I could shed tears all over the kitchen to induce their sympathy or their guilt. I could bribe them, or shake them until common sense coursed through their heads.

What the hell was I thinking—they are just children.

~

My mother often uses Dutch idioms. *Kraab en de hals* is when someone "pokes in your hallway." That is, when someone picks your brain. Just like I taught the kids "Don't talk to strangers," when I was growing up and we left the house, my mother often warned "Don't let them *kraab en de hals.*" She worried that grown-ups would pump me or my siblings for information on what was happening under our roof on London Street.

Often disguised as caring, *kraab en de hals* is not a virtue. People need to mind their own business, my mother would say. Curiosity, nosiness, a penchant for gossip, malicious probing, *kraab en de hals* manipulates people to say more than they intend.

Children are especially vulnerable to *krabben.*

~

The kids usually ride the school bus, except on Fridays when Sam carries his baritone home. Middle school dismisses first.

As Sam approached the Town Car, I popped the trunk. He fit his instrument inside easily, then jumped into the back seat. A few blocks away at the elementary building, Meike climbed in the front with me.

With a forecast of cold, rainy weather most of the weekend, we had formulated a plan to make pizza from scratch. I pulled a grocery list from my pocket and handed it to Meike. She ran down the list with her finger.

"What is y-e-a-s-t?" she asked.

"Yeast," Sam answered. "It's for the crust. Mom, can we buy pepperoni?"

"We can," I said. "And I'd like Canadian bacon, too."

"Bacon on pizza? Icky," Meike said.

I held back a giggle. "It's ham," I told her. "You've had it before." We turned into the lot at Family Fare and parked.

Choosing soda pop to complement our meal took longer than locating the pizza ingredients. But we were in and out of the store in less than twenty minutes.

"We have to start with the yeast," I said when we set our grocery bags on the kitchen counter.

Sam found the bowl in the cupboard then proceeded to tease his sister, raising his arms, coming at her with a monster voice. "It comes alive."

"Huh?" she asked.

"Dry yeast is dormant," I said. "It is alive but inactive because there's no wetness. When it gets warm and moist, it wakes up." I checked the recipe in front of me. "Okay. We need two and a quarter teaspoons in the bowl, Sam. Meike, you measure a half teaspoon of brown sugar and add it."

We poured on the warm water. Meike stirred it slightly with a fork, and then we let it set. After ten minutes we added salt, olive oil, and most of the flour. The remainder of the flour Meike dumped on the counter. "So it doesn't stick," she said, remembering pie crusts we'd made.

"We don't roll it out yet," I explained. "Instead, we knead it." Each of us took a turn until the dough was no longer sticky. I oiled a clean bowl and Sam dropped the lump in. "Now we cover it with a towel and let it grow."

More than once during the process with the crust, I found myself tempted to ask Sam and Meike about their supposed request. Let it rest, let it rest, I reminded myself. I didn't want to *kraab.*

"Meanwhile, we can start on the toppings," I said. "Let's remember to grate the mozzarella, have it all ready before we spread the sauce."

Meike filled the sink with a few inches of water and gave the vegetables a bath. She fished them out again and set them on a towel. Sam and I started chopping. Tomatoes, green peppers, mushrooms.

"We're going to live with Dad," Meike volunteered, wiping her hands on the towel.

I set the paring knife down. Running fingers through my hair, I looked at the raindrops ticking the window before turning to Meike.

"Maybe," I said.

"We'll live here and you can live in the apartment," my daughter said. "You'd live in the apartment, wouldn't you Mom?" She looked at me, her petite little face framed by two braids in multiple hues of blonde. Her delicate little face expectant. Her heartbreaking innocence waiting for my answer.

Mute, Sam picked up the cutting board and swept the green pepper into the Corning dish with his hand. I took a few steps to the opposite counter and leaned against it, facing both of them.

"No. I won't live in that apartment," I said, my voice certain but not obstinate. "I belong here, you belong here, I want to live where you live." And I wanted to kiss them and to hug them and to hold them a long time and I worried it was controlling and so I didn't. "I'm your mom. I love you and I want us to live together. Here. In this house."

I moved and stood between them.

"But what about Dad?" Sam asked, not like he was pleading or taking sides. Just wondering.

Breathing deeply, I brought my hands to my mouth and spoke behind them. "I don't know."

I put an arm around Meike's waist and then the other on Sam's shoulder. Two seconds later, the timer dinged.

"The yeast," Sam announced.

He lifted the towel off the bowl we had placed near the furnace register.

A gleam lit in Meike's eyes. "It did grow!"

I winked at Sam. He poked the dough with his finger, grinning as Meike touched it carefully and drew back.

"What makes that happen?" Meike asked as I began to punch the dough down and squeeze it.

"When it's warm, the yeast gets tiny gas bubbles so it foams and makes little openings," I said.

Meike felt the dough again, less cautious this time. "It's soft," she said.

We rolled it out.

It seemed that for the kids, the subject of who would live where was done for the day. And that was okay. Maybe all I could do was cover them, keep them warm, make opportunity for little openings.

"About the money thing, Janie," Walt said from the rug in the hallway, although I hadn't brought it up. "It would be better for both of us if we just settle."

Richard had advised that I no longer discuss financial aspects at all with Walt. But that Tuesday evening, Walt stood so woeful and forlorn that, for a flash, I pitied him. A very quick flash.

For me to recognize the children's best interest according to Walt was impossible, and to consider he might have my best interests in mind, ridiculous.

"Not a good idea." I reached past him, opened the storm door, and followed him outside. After a second goodbye to Meike and Sam, I stood in the driveway watching until the pickup and my children turned the corner.

When Richard called the following day to confirm that Walt continued to pay me each month, I told him about Walt's suggestion that we just settle.

"Walt's received over two hundred and eighty thousand dollars since he filed for divorce," my attorney reminded me. "And that's from non-business investments. We have every right to worry he's reinvesting these monies without proper documentation, without your consent. Or dissipating the assets someway."

The second day of November, Richard filed for the restraining order.

That was the easy part.

In his office less than a week later, my attorney handed me a copy of the Memo in Opposition to the Motion to Amend the Temporary Custody Order. It was six pages.

We decided I would spend time going through the document at home before Richard and I reviewed it together. I locked the memo in my strong box to make certain Sam and Meike wouldn't accidentally come across it.

Friday afternoon was the mildest day in November that year. The sun, already low in the sky, still felt warm as we tied Odie out front and shot a few baskets in the driveway. When we heard the diesel engine coming up the cul-de-sac, we hugged goodbye and I went inside to grab Sam and Meike's overnight bags.

I returned to find Walt waiting in the hallway. He stood in one place wiping his feet on the rug although his shoes weren't dirty.

"The restraining order."

I folded my arms in front of me to brace myself. "What about it?"

"I can't do business that way."

"Hmmm."

"I only have a nominal amount in the bank accounts and not much cash either."

"Yeah. That's what Richard said your attorney told him."

Walt sighed heavily, but said no more.

I followed him into the driveway. Sam rolled down the window of the pickup and when I stuck my head in, Odie slobbered my face with licks. Sam grasped the collar and held the dog back.

"Suppose now I can't have any more smooches," I teased him. I pulled away and Meike threw me a kiss as her father backed up.

After a quick raisin bread sandwich, an apple and hot tea, I buzzed through my Dutch vocabulary for a quiz the next day. "No sweat," I thought and packed my cards away. I went to the basement office and unlocked the strong box to find the memo Richard had prepared.

I turned on the floor lamp in the den, settled in the Barcalounger and, with a pencil in one hand as if tackling my homework, I began to read.

The introduction stated that Walt requests the court interview the children concerning their preference regarding physical custody, amend the temporary order by changing primary physical custody from me to Walt, and further, that I be removed from the marital home and he be granted sole possession of the property.

A factual background took up the next two pages. It reviewed our age, when we were married, and when, after years of attempting to have or adopt children, Sam and Meike were born. Since their birth, our family has been a "traditional" home, the document said, and "though loving and caring for his children, Walt has primarily focused on his business interests. He currently has a 50 percent or larger interest in five businesses. During the marriage and since the filing for divorce, Walt's focus and energies have been directed toward the businesses."

With my pencil, I drew a star next to the paragraph that stated in March of 1992, the Plaintiff moved out of the marital home. "For the last nineteen months, the Defendant and the two children have resided in the marital home, where she continues to raise and care for the children, as she has throughout the parties' marriage."

Richard finished the factual background in two more paragraphs.

"When the Plaintiff filed for divorce in October 1992, the Defendant opposed it. The Plaintiff is unwilling to participate in counseling in order to preserve the marriage. At one point he indicated that he hopes to 'have a new life with a new wife.'"

"Although the children are not happy their parents are getting divorced and wish they could reconcile, they are happy and well-adjusted and continue to do excellent in school."

So far, so good, I thought.

In the center of the third page, Richard began a new heading. Law and Argument. It read that the "Plaintiff requests the court change custody without the benefit of an evidentiary hearing to determine the best interest of the children. The Plaintiff proposed that the court, prior to making this change, simply discuss with the parties' minor children, ages 10 and 11, their preference."

Richard quoted and documented a previous case where the Michigan court ruled a court cannot change custodial arrangements without an evidentiary hearing. If evidence presented shows that there is an established custodial environment, custody is not to be changed unless there is presented clear and convincing evidence that it is in the best interest of the children. In another, separate case, Richard documented that the court ruled the child's preference is only one factor to be evaluated.

I turned to the fourth page. "The Plaintiff, in his motion, expresses a fear that the present living situation is harmful to the children," Richard had written.

I stopped. The room had gotten chilly. I set the memo aside and bumped the thermostat to seventy. At the stereo, I selected a Brahms violin concerto and set the music on low volume. I walked into the kitchen, took the brandy from the cupboard above the refrigerator and poured two fingers worth.

Holding the throw blanket from the couch, I returned to the Barcalounger, set my brandy on the end table and with pencil in hand, began with the fourth page.

"The Plaintiff expresses a fear that the present living situation is harmful to the children. There is no basis for these claimed fears. The children continue to look to their mother for their primary care, love and affection. An indication of this situation is found in the PCS Evaluation Report. During a weekend at his father's house, Sam stubbed his toe in the shower. Sam's response was to call his mother to come and take care of him. On another occasion since the filing of this divorce proceeding, when one of the children became sick during father's custodial time, the child was brought home to mother."

I took a good hard swallow of the brandy—no sipping tonight. Richard actually quoted from that damned report. I thought we considered having the report pulled. My hand shook simply turning the page.

Noting Walt's contention that Sam and Meike express a "strong and sincere preference" to live with their father, Richard refuted the motion by saying not only was Walt's statement an exaggeration, but it ignored underlying factors which may be having an impact on "the perceived preference." I tittered at his word choice.

In the next several paragraphs and on to the last page, Richard again referred to the clinical evaluation.

He noted a review of Dr. Sonnevelt, the man who had interviewed both Sam and Meike. Sonnevelt reported Sam saying he didn't think he would have a preference of who to live with as long as he got to see each parent each week.

Leave it to Sam to try to please. Take care of us.

Asked what he might consider the advantages of living with his dad, Sonnevelt reported Sam saying his dad was more lenient about their activities in the home, therefore they could play more Nintendo and watch more TV, and that his dad took them out to eat more often "because he could afford it."

Richard wrote that with respect to Meike, when placed in the hypothetical position of a judge asking her with whom she would prefer to live the majority of the time, Sonnevelt reported that Meike responded, "I don't know. If I had to choose, I don't know how I'd do it." She was then able to spend a considerable period of time with me talking about both the good and bad of living at each of her parents' current homes. Sonnevelt said her basic thrust equaled seeing her father as basically less rigid and more flexible in terms of his expectations as well as the kinds of activities he will let them engage in, while on the negative side, he tends to have "more of a temper" than does mom. At the end of their initial interview, Sonnevelt reported, when brought to a session by mother, Meike volunteered, "I'd rather live with my dad because I don't see him as much . . . . It's a little more fun with dad at his place."

I rubbed my eyes, turned back a page, and reread the section. I set my pencil down. A few paragraphs buried among eighty-five pages of psychobabble, Sonnevelt's portion blurred or possibly even seemed irrelevant at the time I read the PCS report two months ago. Now I wondered if my anger with the report's conclusion caused me to miss some of its details in the first place.

Richard ended the document with one final paragraph—a concise, two-lined sentence. "Defendant respectfully requests that Plaintiff's motion for change of custody be denied, there being no legal or factual basis for granting the motion."

Brahms' violin concerto had finished. What was left of the brandy went down easily in one gulp.

The argument was strong. It rang true. It spoke for me. Richard didn't underestimate Walt or his cocky assumptions of deserving. I sensed Richard understood the weight of it all and that he believed in me and in my legitimate, established place.

This assuredness lasted about three minutes.

As well written as the contention was, only a few weeks ago my attorney had considered challenging the PCS report. His reversal, using it in our defense, might prove regrettable, rash, risky, reckless roulette, even a ruse—the "r" words popped in my head until I told myself, "Stop it." All I needed to do was wait until Monday to call Richard and ask. Friday night, Saturday, Saturday night, Sunday, Sunday night, Monday morning. I would call Monday morning.

From my chair, I reached and dimmed the light. With the room warmed, my face flushed. It might have been the brandy. I knew better than to pour another.

Sure, a beautiful autumn day. But already in the first week, November was working its way with me.

A shove on the Barcalounger and the footrest released. I walked to the piano, clicked on the reading lamp and again dug Chopin's Nocturnes from the pile of music I'd been practicing. I opened to the last composition, Op. 72, and ran the four octaves up the keyboard in an E Minor scale. After the first half dozen measures, I closed my eyes and let my fingers find the phrases on their own with fewer stumbles than expected. I turned off the lamp and began again at the first measure, concentrating on the crescendos and diminuendos, slowing to the varied intensity of the haunting, bittersweet music.

"If I had to choose, I don't know how I'd do it," my daughter had said, and I played the phrase over and over in the dark.

Twenty-Seven

Daylight Saturday morning was a spare, cheerless presence at the window. After coffee and toast, I jogged a mile and a half north, in and out of side streets. Turning back south through a different hodge-podge of suburbia and asphalt, I arrived home only minutes before the rain began, a rain that lasted the rest of the weekend.

Gerrit and Laura were expecting me for dinner. Later that gloomy afternoon, with the November rain constant, I thought about cancelling. After a long, hot shower, I toweled dry and felt somewhat revived. Just before five, I drove to my brother's, dusk already on the way.

Through the course of the evening the conversation turned to various topics, from Bill and Hillary Clinton, to Bosnia, to our mother's 74th birthday celebration the following week, to Walt's pending motion. When we cleared the table and settled in the living room, I informed Gerrit and Laura I would head home early.

"Last night's catching up to me," I said. "Restless. Didn't sleep well if at all."

"You wanna just stay over?" Gerrit asked. "Frank will be happy to share the guest room."

"No, no." I reached down near my feet and patted the top of the dog's head. "No offense, Frank."

"You don't seem restless," Gerrit said. "Chatty, though. Definitely chatty."

"As the daughter of Pearl," I said, my smile exaggerated, "I am practiced in not allowing outward appearances reveal inner matters.

This does, nevertheless, take a toll on one's guts. How about a brandy then, before I go?"

An hour later when Gerrit walked me to the door, Laura took another stab at the invitation. "You sure you'll be okay?"

"Wouldn't send a dog out tonight," Gerrit said.

"The rain's let up some since I came and the temperature's supposed to stay steady." I buttoned my coat. "Not that 40 degrees is comfy."

"But will you sleep?" Laura pressed.

"I have a deal with Jennings. I call him after the third sleepless night."

"Well," Gerrit said, "you can call me tonight if you want. I never sleep for crap anyway."

~

On Monday morning, Meike and Sam left for the bus stop at their usual time. 8:10. Soon after, before I had a chance to call him, Richard called me.

"Looking for your impressions of our Opposition. The sooner we submit our argument, the better," he said.

"I'm surprised you cited the PCS report."

"Hofstra tells me they are submitting it anyway. He's attaching it with the motion."

"I see."

"Those quotes from the kids are in there, Jane. Page 57, if you don't remember. If you haven't already looked it up."

"I ripped up my copy."

After a short pause, I heard Richard laugh. "I can appreciate that," he said. "Which is why you pay an attorney."

"Yeah, okay," I said with a stupid giggle. "Anyway, the rest is awesome, especially the Walt's 'perceived perception' line. Whether Walt purposefully lies or his warped sense of entitlement gets in the way, I don't know. You're a lot kinder that I am. I totally doubt his motivations."

Again, a pause, and I pictured Richard scratching on the legal pad with his ballpoint.

At 9 o'clock, we walked together to the Hall of Justice Building, only a few blocks from Richard's office. Any warmth in the morning sun was cut by the blustery November wind. Over my skirt and sweater, my long black trench coat gave some protection. Richard's charcoal gray suit with a tie, deeper gray marked with burgundy, was tastefully professional. He had foregone an overcoat. With one hand, he carried his briefcase and as we walked, he placed the other in the pocket of his suit jacket. His ears turned red in the cold.

We had been in the courtroom before, over a year ago when temporary custody was first granted me. Yet even with Richard as my spokesperson, when we entered, the scene immediately intimidated me. I realized that after twenty years of marriage, whatever the hell Walt and I were doing, we didn't belong here.

Walt had the nerve to gesture a quick bow of his head as if greeting me, but I looked away, feigning indifference. The Honorable Judge Holton entered. With the two of us looking on, our attorneys did the talking.

An order officially stamped by the county clerk on November 12, was given that day from the said court, "having heard the argument of counsel and being otherwise fully apprised in the premises, denies Plaintiff's Motion to amend Temporary Order at this time. The custody evaluation report, prepared by Psychiatric Consultation Services, is hereby admitted as evidence. The parties shall arrange for the children to interview with the Trial Judge in his chambers on November 19, 1993. After reviewing the report and meeting with the children, the Court shall meet with counsel for the parties to inform them of his recommendations as to a possible modification of the Temporary Order."

The entire session took less than fifteen minutes.

"It went well," Richard summarized once he and I stepped outside.

We said little more on the return walk, and I noticed calmness in Richard's long-legged stride. Although in my head, a line from childhood stories kept echoing as we stepped.

"Come into my parlor said the spider to the fly."

Twenty-Eight

"Art keeps asking about you," Jesse said when I had answered all her questions on how the hearing went. "He'd like to talk with you a while."

"Frankly, Jess, I'm tired of talking about it. You see him almost every day. You tell him if you want."

Other than Richard, Gerrit and Dr. Jennings, I didn't admit to anyone that Walt has used the word "harmful." Not even to Jesse. I supposed Walt threw the claim around freely, to get people used to it, to somehow substantiate it, and Jesse probably knew anyway. But I wasn't going to repeat the word to her or to anyone more.

During the week, Walt and I argued who would transport the children on the nineteenth to Judge Holton's. Although the interview was scheduled on a Friday when Sam and Meike were not at his place, Richard told me I needed to let Walt participate.

Considering Walt often put words in their mouth anyway, any last-minute coaching on his part wouldn't make a whole lot of difference. "Then he can bring them and I'll pick them up," I said to Richard.

Although Meike and Sam hadn't brought up the meeting, I'm their mother and I knew what was on their mind. "You're free to say anything you want to Judge Holton, you know," I reminded them the day before. "I won't ask you afterward what you said." I reached my arm around Meike's waist and pulled her into a hug she did not return, her body loose and limp. Over her shoulder, I locked eyes with Sam. "And no matter what you say, remember, I'll still love you. Always."

While we waited for Walt after breakfast in the morning, I explained how even though their dad was bringing them, I'd be there in the lobby while they were in the judge's chamber.

I had written and scratched out several excuses for Sam and Meike missing school. I simply told my professors ahead of time that Walt and I needed to be in court. But writing an appropriate note to the fourth-grade and sixth-grade Christian School teachers stumped me.

"Sam was unable to attend school on Friday because, as you probably already know, the court . . . Sam was absent on Friday in order to talk to the County Judge concerning his ruinous living situation that calls for . . . Please excuse Meike from class since her father needed her to vouch for his ridiculous . . . Please excuse Meike because her father is a . . . ."

Finally, I settled on school counting their absence as a personal day.

Thinking it best to wait, I entered a few minutes after their appointment was to start. I took a seat in one of the chairs lined up against the wall opposite the courtroom, as far away as possible from Walt, who sat alone along the opposite wall.

Forty-five minutes passed when a woman, a county clerk, according to her badge, came into the hallway escorting Sam and Meike. I didn't object that Walt waited until the interview was over, but once they returned, I shot him a nasty look that said, "Cut it short, mister." He promptly hugged our son and our daughter, said goodbye and left.

We stood there in the Hall of Justice, Meike with her fingers laced between mine, Sam's tucked just inside the pockets of his jeans. He looked toward the door, his eyes lingering—longing—on the exit and I ached for him, realizing now he had wanted to leave with his dad. I swallowed hard, ashamed of my selfishness for a moment, until my anger returned and I wanted to scream at Walt how stupid he was. How there was no way he had Sam and Meike's "Best Interest" in mind.

Pulling in a deep breath, I let it out slowly. "You guys okay?"

"Sure," Sam answered, his head still turned. Meike nodded, timid.

The hands on a black and white standardized clock in the corridor pointed to 11:25.

"Not much point going to school today," I said.

A grin appeared on Meike's face and Sam looked at me.

"Really?" he asked, and I couldn't tell if he was relieved or disappointed.

"Unless you decide you want to," I added.

At that Sam shrugged and some of the strain in his shoulders disappeared. We exchanged just enough of a smile that his face relaxed. This time, I turned away, eyes stinging with tears before I could face them again, a little brighter.

"Okay," I said. "Let's go home."

"How you guys doing over there?" Ruth asked when she called that afternoon. "Matt says Sam wasn't in school today." She paused. "Nothing contagious, I hope."

I laughed at her directness, one of many things I appreciated about Ruth. "We're okay. Nobody's sick."

"You know me. The over-protective mother."

Chances were Ruth already knew the latest. One could hardly live on our little cul-de-sac and avoid the grapevine. "The kids had their interview with the judge today."

"I suspected as much." She hesitated, giving me an opening. I didn't offer more and knew she'd respect that.

"Matt wants to know if Sam can come over. Play Super Mario Brothers."

I passed the phone to Sam. He said yes.

When Sam left for Matt's, I convinced Meike to practice violin so we'd be free after dinner to do whatever. We fine-tuned her strings to the piano. G D A E. She scraped the rosin back and forth across her bow as I went to answer the phone again.

"Getting ready to pack it in for the day," Richard said. The hint at keeping our conversation short didn't hide the concern in his voice. "How was it today?"

From the other room, I could hear Meike, her scale slightly off pitch. "About as sucky as I expected," I said, assuming she couldn't hear me.

"I suppose so," he said. "Well, I wanted to let you know Hofstra contacted me this afternoon. They took out the clause about you moving into the apartment and Walt moving into the house."

"Huh. I'll be."

"I think Hofstra started feeling guilty about that portion."

I thought about that for a moment. Besides Hofstra feeling bad, maybe he advised Walt how awful Walt would look, that only a total asshole would think of such a thing, let alone go through with it.

"When will we find out about the rest?" I asked.

"I have a feeling Judge Holton won't contact us until after the holidays. Where are the children this year for the holidays?"

"They're with Walt Thanksgiving Day and the entire weekend. They're with me most of Christmas vacation and on Christmas Eve. Christmas Eve is a given. We're going to share Christmas Day. At least we agree on that one."

"Good. Good. The more cooperation, the better."

I nodded as if Richard were in front of me. Meike stopped in the middle of a phrase and repeated a few measures before quieting her violin altogether. "Sounds like Meike could use some interference," I said. "You'll let me know if anything new comes up?"

"Of course. Have a happy Thanksgiving."

~

"I already practiced," Meike bragged to her brother when we finished supper.

"And you don't have to clean up, either," I told her. "What'll you do with all your free time?"

"Watch you and Sam do the work." She found a place on the kitchen floor and wrapped an arm around Odie until, once we opened the dishwasher, she had to let him go as he pulled away to lick the plates and silverware.

We watched television together after Sam and I finished cleaning up. An hour and a half worth. Sam picked *The Simpsons,* Meike picked *Family Matters,* and I chose an *Andy Griffith* rerun. "Oh yuck, that's so deformed." Sam rolled his eyes but sat through the entire episode with us.

"Did you watch *Andy Griffith* when you were a kid?" Meike asked when Sam hit the off button. Odie passed us on the basement stairs and waited on top.

"I did. And *Dick Van Dyke*."

The cold November air invaded the den as Sam pulled the sliding door open enough for Odie to get through. Meike and I plopped next to each other on the couch. Sam stretched out on the carpeting in front of the stereo.

"But my favorite was *Bonanza*."

Sam exploded. "That's so deformed!" He rolled over laughing, pounding his fist on the floor.

Odie scratched at the door. Letting him in, I clicked the door lock and sat down while Meike snuggled closer. "*Bonanza* always came on at 7:30 Saturday night. The whole family watched it," I said. "Aunt Reannie had a crush on Adam. Parnell Roberts."

"He's bald," Sam told us.

"Uh-huh. Very scholarly. Foot up on the hearth near the fireplace. Always reading. And Aunt Gretta had a crush on Hoss."

Howling, Sam pounded the floor again. "The fat guy?" Odie backed up, barking at him.

"Yup. Dan Blocker. He died in real life, but they were all really, really young then." I blinked dreamy-like into the air, smiling. "And I was in love with Little Joe. That's Michael Landon," I explained with a wink to Meike. "The dad on *Little House on the Prairie*." She raised her eyebrows, nodding as if my feelings back then were perfectly understandable.

"That is really, really deformed!" Sam sat bent over laughing, his head nearly touching the carpet.

"Well, wait 'til you hear this, Sam. Later, NBC switched *Bonanza* to Sunday nights at 9 o'clock—*after* my bedtime. I put up a fit. But Grandpa and Grandma would not let me stay up." I waved my hand in the air. "So, the whole family's in the den to watch except me and little Uncle Gerrit, who didn't care 'cause his favorite was *The Rifleman*. Well, when the *Bonanza* theme song started, I crept down the steps, snuck under the kitchen table and . . ." I stopped to laugh " . . . watched a whole five minutes before anybody noticed!"

Now we were all cracking up, crying we were laughing so hard, Meike jumping up and down. "Whoopee!" she yelled while Odie barked at the ceiling.

"Weren't Grandpa and Grandma mad?" Sam finally asked.

I shook my head and squeaked, "They let me stay up on Sunday nights after that."

I wiped my face with the sleeve of my flannel shirt, the soft absorbent plaid accepting my outburst, my silliness, my relief. Odie brushed against my leg.

"Sooo . . . speaking of bed . . . ," I said as we calmed down.

When Sam and Meike finished their turns in the bathroom, I joined them upstairs. Sam had propped his pillow against the wall, his head resting on it, one arm stretched across Odie. He set his book face-down on the bedspread and moved over for me to sit.

"All set, bud?"

He nodded once.

"Say your prayers?"

He nodded again. I placed my hand on the side of his face, brushing his cheek. Odie lifted his head and licked Sam's cheek noisily.

"Night, hon. I love you." I kissed the top of Sam's blond head where his hair, like mine, had already lost the lightness of summer.

"Me, too," he said.

Odie stayed put and I went in to check on Meike. She placed a bookmark approximately half-way through her story, *Next Spring an Oriole.*

"All set, sweetie?"

"Uh-huh."

"Say your prayers?"

"Yup. Mom, how come Odie sleeps on Sam's bed and not mine?"

"Oh, you know—it's a guy thing. Guys think they gotta stick together sometimes." I lifted her hair back and circled her ear softly with a fingertip. "Goodnight, Meike." I kissed her cheek.

"Mom?"

"Hmmm?"

"Dad says the day after Thanksgiving we're going to look at houses."

Twenty-Nine

I know why people skip the holidays. Thanksgiving and all that feasting and family. Christmas with Hallmark and glitz and glimmer and cheer. New Year's. Put all the old behind you. A new day dawning.

On the eve of Thanksgiving, I stood in the driveway wrapped in my corduroy coat, collar up against a stiff north wind. If every eye in the neighborhood saw me, I didn't care. Even if Walt checked his rearview mirror and made an addition to his list of my peculiar behaviors, I stood there riveted until the pickup rounded the corner, just in case the kids turned to wave.

The following day, in order to mollify my parents, I showed up at my sister's for dinner. Gerrit and Laura had gone to Detroit overnight to see a Lions' game. Otherwise, along with their spouses, all my siblings were there. And their children. And their children's children.

Everyone else had gone to a service that morning, although Thanksgiving isn't officially part of the church calendar. My father said a prayer before he carved the turkey, the same prayer he had said at the table for decades. Thankfully, we were a private family. No holding hands or going around the table, each of us slobbering about what we were most grateful for.

When our meal finished, my father read Psalm 100 aloud from the King James Bible, as he had every year for as long as I could remember.

Make a joyful noise unto the Lord, all ye lands.
Serve the Lord with gladness;
come before his presence with singing.

Know ye that the Lord he is God:
it is he that has made us and not we ourselves;
We are his people, and the sheep of his pasture.
Enter into his gates with thanksgiving and into his courts with praise.
Be thankful unto him and bless his name.
For the Lord is good; his mercy is everlasting;
and his truth endureth to all generations. Selah.

Not like the eerie chant Dutch immigrants often take on when they read a passage, my father's smoky-deep voice was crisp, the Psalm clearly articulated. I heard conviction in his words. A desire for that voice to once again fall on Sam and Meike rose inside me. What little mashed potatoes and turkey I'd eaten was threatened by a sour yearning.

No part of me blamed my family for enjoying the festivities, only I found it harder and harder as the day went on to have all this family in my face.

Our own annual football game takes place after dishes and before the pumpkin pie. As Jerry divvied up the teams, my father and I snuck away and shot four games of pool together in the basement. My mother even bundled up and went outdoors to cheerlead, ignoring our absence.

Nearly an hour later, we heard her back inside preparing coffee.

"And now I'm going home," I said to my father, my lips sealed into a faint smile. He returned the smile as if not surprised and gave me his famous bear hug. Then I went upstairs and kissed my mother on the cheek.

"You be careful, young lady. It'll be dark before you know it. I don't like you out there driving alone," she said, implying both forgiveness that I was leaving and her reminder that she loves me.

Forty-five minutes later, I pulled into the garage, turned off the Town Car and hit the button on my visor for the automatic door. A picture came to mind as the door rumbled down—the handsome face of Denny Opperwal, youthful, tanned, freckled. The man I worked for in the Michigan National Bank building when Walt and I were first married. Six months after Denny's wife filed for divorce, we learned the mortgage department was to merge with general finance and we would lose our jobs. Dear Denny lowered his garage door without shutting off the motor.

I went inside, locking the door and the picture of Denny behind me. Setting a share of leftover turkey on the top shelf of the refrigerator, I filled a mug with milk, mixed in some chocolate, and then accidentally scorched it in the microwave. I skimmed off the skin with a spoon and set the mug next to the Barcalounger without bothering with the lights.

The radio broadcast featured Gustav Mahler's Symphony no. 1 and I listened, wrangling with the beauty of the music and my awful sadness. When the piece finished, I went to the piano and, from the hymnal, began Bach's "*Nun Gott Wir Allein Danket*," sustaining each four-note chord as if I were playing the church organ in Germany instead of the hand-me-down spinet piano in my den, old and out of tune. Following one of the arrangements I have, I played a stanza in the lower octave, without harmony, followed by another stanza an octave higher.

I switched to Handel's piece, HWV34. Stretching my left hand in an open interval, I emphasized a three-quarter time with the bass clef, and with my right, began the stately hymn "Thanks Be to Thee."

God knows I was trying.

~

Meike and Sam phoned on Friday afternoon. They took turns telling me about the day before—turkey, cranberries, apple pie—and I reveled in their play-by-play. Sam had dripped gravy in Odie's dog food. His older cousins kicked soccer ball with him. Meike got to beat the egg whites for her grandma and won three games of Chutes and Ladders.

Thanksgiving had gone well with Walt and his family, and I hung up the phone sick with envy. I found the Barcalounger and sat watching dusk fall over the neighborhood, the backyard, the abandoned gym set.

They'd be better off without me. I should pack my bag, find a place like California, far enough away that Sam and Meike would be spared any more of this.

Kids heal. They would forgive and forget. If only I would conjure up enough courage. Give them up quietly. In their best interest and all that.

I tipped my head backward, forward, side-to-side, stretching my tightened neck as far as I could as if to literally rotate my brain and change perspective.

Over an hour passed. My thinking coiled very slowly around and around.

It takes courage to stay. Leaving is a coward's choice.

Staying is cowardly. To leave is courageous.

Give up.

No, insist.

No, run away.

No, stand with it.

I recognized the momentum. Leaning back in the Barcalounger, I pushed the footrest up and gulped three deep breaths in a row, exhaling each one at length like Dr. Jennings had demonstrated and I had dismissed at the time as gimmickry.

Sometimes a person just needs to get by for a day, an hour, a minute.

Tears ran down my face, didn't let up, and I welcomed the release, some sort of silent giving-in to an uncertainty.

Yet, a person could dehydrate.

The Friday evening was early with night looming impossibly long. I began a list of people who might help.

Jesse and family were in Minnesota for Thanksgiving. Gerrit and Laura were in Detroit. Dr. Jennings' emergency number would connect me to only a stranger on call for the holiday.

I went to the bathroom and splashed cold water on my face, letting it drip and run between my sleeve and my arms. Grabbing a hand towel, I brought it to my nose and inhaled the clean scent of laundry soap, which helped for about five seconds. As I dabbed the rest of my face, I remembered Reverend Byker.

The number of the parsonage was in the small church directory we kept in the drawer under the phone. He picked up on the fourth ring.

I kept my voice steady. "Reverend Byker. It's Jane. I know this is abrupt, but . . . I'm having kind of a hard time. If we could talk—"

"Hold on."

I heard him set the phone down and children's voices in the background. It seemed forever before I heard a door close and he picked up again.

"Jane, listen," he said quietly. "Give me twenty minutes. Come to the church and pull in the parking lot. A light on is the signal to come in. No light in my office means I couldn't get away." The receiver clicked.

I put the phone down, the tremor in my hands worse than when I first dialed. He had reminded me a hundred times a pastor could always get away or at least talk on the phone. That was his job, the sacrifice his family expected and lived with.

My intuition usually serves me well. Listen to it now, I thought.

I drew a glass of water at the kitchen sink. Despair wasn't the issue anymore. I had to calm myself.

I opened the closet, found my purse and dug for my wallet. From the coin pocket, I took out the scrap of paper with the hotel's number written in bright blue sharpie.

The phone rang a half dozen times. Please answer. Please answer. Please answer.

"Gerrit?"

"Yeah. What's up?"

"Did I wake you?"

"It's only 8 o'clock."

"Look . . . I know you're taking a get-away but no one's around . . ."

"It's not a problem."

"I didn't want to bother you."

"What is it, Janie?"

"I had to talk to somebody . . . No one's around . . . I called Reverend Byker."

I told my brother what the minister had said, word for word.

"You're not going, are you?" Gerrit asked, a sudden edge in his voice. "You stay away from him." There was a pause. When my brother spoke again, the sharpness had already dissolved. "That man is pathological."

I leaned against the wall and slid my back along it to the floor. "That's what I thought." Gerrit might have heard the relief in my voice. He couldn't see me crying but I couldn't cover a sob. "I just needed to check."

~

For the remainder of Thanksgiving weekend, the black adhesive wrapping my thoughts loosened somewhat. Each time I passed the book bag stashed in the corner of the den, obligations came to mind. In two weeks, the fall semester would end. My term paper for World Literature was finished and submitted, but Monday was the deadline for a requirement in Dutch class. I still had to read a novella, *En Bitter Kruid*, and write a book review.

Our Dutch Calvinist work ethic reaches beyond employment and how we make a living. My mother keeps an immaculate house. Basement to attic, under the sink and rugs, inside furnace registers and, with a good *modschep en stuba*, even the driveway, sidewalk and curb. My father keeps his Olds 88 top notch—premium gasoline, regular oil changes, a specific soft white rag under the front seat to touch up a side panel, fender or hood. Every scrap of two-by-four, baby-food jars of screws, nuts and nails aligned neatly next to rust-less toolboxes on specific shelves in the garage.

I believed that when Gerrit and Laura first encouraged me to earn a BA, they knew all along how seriously I would take my studies, how my courses would become second only to Sam and Meike.

On Saturday morning while I fortified myself with a bottomless cup of coffee, my concentration improved in half-hour increments. When distracted by thoughts of Sam and Meike or Walt or running away to California, I alternated between Joplin ragtime, Mozart's Piano Concerto no. 19, and my homework, completing the novella along with a draft for the required four pages by 9 p.m.

Polishing the review could wait until Sunday. In spite of the coffee, I crawled into bed exhausted and yielded to a much-needed restorative sleep.

~

The following week over a steaming cup of cocoa Saturday afternoon, I tried to convince Jesse it didn't matter. The kids were still outside tobogganing on the south hill near the field on Jesse's place. We had taken turns with the boys on a dozen or so runs, and in the meanwhile, Meike and I glided down on a cushy inner tube. When Jesse and I announced we were cold and finished, Sam chased me with a mitten of snow meant for my face. It took a promise of hot chocolate, if and when they decided to join us, to end any more harassment.

"You seem worried," Jesse said carefully, sipping her drink. "Frustrated."

"Yeah. It's the motion to change custody thing." With the end of my tongue, I touched a dab of whipped cream on my teaspoon and then slid the cream into my mug using a fingertip. "There's no reason for a change, really. Walt can ask all he wants. But consistency, that's what's best for Meike and Sam. That's what's important."

Jesse set her mug down and contemplated. "I'm convinced," she said after a moment. "And I think what Walt's doing is selfish."

We watched the kids from the kitchen window. Joel waited at the bottom of the hill until the toboggan came to a stop and the others rolled off. The boys picked themselves up and headed toward the house, Joel towing the toboggan with Meike on top.

I wasn't completely honest with Jesse. Some of the worry she had picked up on stemmed from my attempt to avoid the subject of Reverend Byker.

"The hill is starting to ice over," Joel told his mother when everyone had shed their boots and snowsuits.

"If we get the five inches predicted," Jesse said, "it'll be fresh again." While she poured the milk for hot chocolate, the kids took a place at the table.

Joel floated two marshmallows on top of his chocolate. "Mom, can Sam spend the night?"

"That would be fun," Jesse said. "But it's 'May Sam spend the night.' And of course he may. How does it sound to you, Sam?" she asked, her smile inviting. "Did you and Joel talk this over already?"

Sam nodded and they all looked at me.

"Sam could just borrow a shirt from Joel and you could pick him up at church tomorrow," Jesse said. "How perfect is that?"

I agreed and didn't take it as a set-up or anything. Jesse's my best friend.

~

On Tuesday morning, I headed out for some basics from the grocery. With a cloudless sky, the warmth of the sun felt luxurious though it couldn't have been more than 25 degrees. Inside the store, I paid for my few items and proceeded to the exit. Walking toward my car through the melting snow, I heard "Hey, there," and spotted Cindy making her way toward me.

Dressed in jeans and a quilted vest over her flannel shirt, she zipped her keys into a pocket. "Enjoying this weather?"

I switched my bag to the opposite arm. "Not bad for December."

"Glad I ran into you. I was thinking to give you a call. Keith plans to take the kids to the basketball game tonight but I'm not interested. Aren't Sam and Meike at Walt's on Tuesdays? You want some company?"

"Sure. Well, if you're not offended by a rather cheerless evening."

"No problem," she said, her smile reassuring me.

"About seven then?"

"That works." Cindy glanced around the parking lot. "Janie, do you know about Liz Speelhof's request?" Her expression had turned somber. "To the consistory last week?"

"You know I'm not in the loop."

"She claims Art Byker's . . . been . . . well . . . improper. She wants the issue addressed publicly. After the service on Sunday, there's going to be some sort of ad hoc congregational meeting. I guess Liz is asking others to step forward."

"Holy shit."

"I wondered if you knew."

I shook my head slowly and looked down at the melting slop over the asphalt. "I haven't talked with Jesse all week, or anyone from church for that matter."

"You think Liz is on to something?"

I met Cindy's gaze square on and shrugged. "Let's talk tonight."

It was into the afternoon before I made a decision to phone Richard, and I was lucky to catch him. I explained what Cindy said, relayed the incidents I had experienced with Reverend Byker—the bike trip, the time at the lake cottage, the by-no-means one armed hug and the proposed light-in-the-office signal.

"Poor Liz," I said. "I kind of feel responsible to speak up."

"Well, you're not," Richard said. "You're in the middle of a custody battle, Jane. Do not get involved in that mess."

We confirmed our next appointment and I hung the phone back on the wall.

Shortly before three, I watched through the front window as the school bus dropped the neighborhood kids at the corner. Meike and Sam splashed through the slush on the sidewalk. Once through the garage and into the den, they removed their hats, mittens and boots on the old orange shag.

They hung up their coats but didn't bother to unpack their school stuff. We ate a snack of peanuts and apples. When Walt arrived promptly at four, I hugged Sam and Meike goodbye.

"I love you. See you tomorrow," I said.

"Go ahead and bring your backpacks to the truck," Walt told them. "I'll be right there." He clipped the leash to Odie's collar. "You heard about Art Byker?" he asked me once the kids were through the door. "About Liz Speelhof and her accusations? And I guess some other women now, too. You talk to Jesse?"

"Oh, Cindy told me. I probably won't talk with Jesse until our movie night next week." I caught myself and frowned. "Wait. Why am I telling you this? Why are you asking? You sound like a gossip."

Walt shrugged and ran his hand over the top of his hair. "Well, people might be asking you. Just thought I'd give you a heads up."

More like he was fishing, seemed to me. "You have a strange way of taking care of me," I said as he left, my sarcasm bounding like Sam's one-inch super ball does in the hallway.

I heated up a bowl of pea soup for supper and, just before seven, built a fire in the fireplace. When Cindy arrived, a bottle of Napa Valley Pinot in hand, the room was glowing with warmth.

We were finishing up sipping our second glass of wine before Cindy brought up the subject. "Janie, what's your experience been like with Byker?"

I reached for the Pinot and helped myself to a generous splash, then poured as much into my guest's glass and set the empty bottle on the end table. Sitting back in my chair, I raised my glass as if making a toast and said to Cindy, "Ask me again in five years."

~

Jesse often razzes me about my fussy housekeeping. She removed her ankle boots on the rug in the hallway and handed me *Somersby.*

"Just released."

"Thought you were fed up with Richard Gere." I set the video on the counter and took her peacoat, wet from the heavy snowflakes melting on the wool.

"Those dimples do it every time," she said while studying the movie jacket. She ran a hand through her straight, dark-walnut hair and the slight gap between her front teeth showed in her smile.

"What'll it be? Tea? Hot chocolate? Something stronger?"

"Tea's good."

I filled the kettle and set it on the stove to heat.

"How are Sam and Meike? With Walt tonight?"

"The usual Tuesday. Sam caught a cold Sunday but otherwise they're fine."

She nodded slowly as her grin disappeared. "Hmmm. I get it. That must be why you weren't there Sunday."

"There? As in the church meeting?"

Her face darkened. I had never said or even hinted I would attend, but it is the kind of thing a friend might have assumed I would know to do.

"Oh, Jesse." My neck felt limp and I tilted my head. "I'm sorry. Richard insisted I not get involved. That I should stay away from the whole thing. I'm really sorry. I should have told you not to expect me."

Jesse's dark brown eyes caught mine, and I wondered if my best friend questioned my honesty. She stepped aside as I reached for the kettle.

"About the meeting. Tell me." I poured the hot water and let the tea steep. "How was it?"

"It was awful. Just awful."

I handed her a mug and picked up my own, sliding the video under my arm. "Let's get comfortable downstairs."

Jesse took the corner of the love seat and tucked her feet up on the cushions, under her legs. I took the couch, the end table between us holding our tea.

She told me three women had come forward. Three separate stories, each attesting their experiences with Reverend Byker.

"All exaggerations, I'm sure," Jesse said. "Making the worst out of good intentions."

"Could be right," I said.

She picked up her tea and blew it carefully, not sipping any after all and setting it back down. "Some of those women—unbelievable. Like they have nothing better to do." She shook her head. "Calling him too friendly and forward, even suggesting worse. And the rest of them just sitting there. The men just sitting there nodding." She stopped, tried her tea again, swallowed and cleared her throat. "You know how they are, Janie. How they can be." Her voice lifted in a question.

"I do know how they can be." And by saying they, I knew I was generalizing. But I wanted so much to have this understanding between Jesse and me. Besides, the two of us were right about people too close to other people's business. "I know how they are," I repeated.

She reached to set down her tea and looked at me as if begging. "You think it's a misrepresentation?"

My turn for a swallow. I took two.

"Jesse," I said in my best kind voice. "What would you say if I told you . . . I'm real uncomfortable with him . . . it seems to me . . . he *is* . . . —"

"I don't want to hear it." She tightened up and wrapped her arms around her knees, pulling them to her chest. Her slender fingers over her ears, she buried her head in her hands and repeated, "I don't want to hear it."

We never did watch the movie. Never watched any movie, ever again. We didn't say anything. I watched Jesse breathe deeply until finally, she lifted her head and announced to the ceiling, "I'm not feeling well. Think I'll go home."

Silent, I followed her up the steps and watched her don her coat, head down, avoiding my gaze even while she opened the door.

"Good night, Jesse."

She didn't turn around. "Good night, Janie," I heard. Not loud, not angry. Maybe disappointed. Sad. Like I was as I watched my best friend leave me.

~

Early Sunday morning, snowy ice-rain layered the grass, sidewalks and streets like frosty manna. I used it as an excuse to keep a distance from Reverend Byker.

"I know it's the first Sunday of Advent," I said to Sam and Meike at the breakfast table. "But let's just stay home this morning." Setting my coffee on the placemat, I lifted the wreath and candles and fresh evergreen from the center of the table to the counter and replaced it with milk, orange juice and warm cinnamon rolls. "After dark tonight, we'll light the first candle. The purple one."

The purple candle symbolized hope.

I lit that candle every week through Christmas.

Thirty

Although Sam was somewhat reluctant about going to St. John's, Meike had appreciated the pageantry, to the point of delight when we had returned for Christmas Day service. But since the holiday, I weighed my own discomfort against keeping their routine. I opted for a impervious attitude toward Byker and with hidden audacity, sat with Sam and Meike in our familiar pew last Sunday. Lo and behold, the youth pastor presided over the service that morning, so I didn't even see Byker.

Walt's attorney had submitted a request that Judge Holton meet before Christmas "with counsel for the parties to inform them of his recommendations as to a possible modification of the temporary custody order." Instead, the motion was scheduled for argument in the county courtroom on Friday, January 7.

On the fourth day of the new year, with a forecast of seven degrees for a high, I had Meike tie up the hood of her parka with her knitted cap underneath and cautioned Sam to keep his hat over his ears when they left for the bus stop. The sun was up, the winds were calm, and I had not insisted they let me drop them off at school.

Snowflakes floated carelessly outside the office window like they might never reach the ground. Richard and I sat at the mahogany table, reviewing an outline of the argument he had prepared.

"You don't get to go along this time," Richard said with a slight smile that seemed to indicate I should just go ahead and trust him. "My plan is to stress that you have been in the home with the children without Walt now for nineteen months. You've given Sam and Meike a consistent and loving environment." He paused as if practicing his address. "The children are healthy. In a routine. Their report cards are A's and B's. Teachers report they are doing well, they are getting along with peers. Put simply, there is no cause for this motion, no reason for a custody change."

"And Walt spells Meike's name wrong." I spoke in a meek voice, like I was desperate for more reassurance.

"Yes. Well, there's that, too." He sat up assuredly, tapped the copy of the argument on the tabletop and set it aside.

We spent some time making notes on Walt's financial statement and finished just short of an hour after I had arrived.

"Meike did well at the Christmas recital," Richard said as we stood to leave. He opened the office door his giant hand lingering on the brass knob.

"Yes. Thank you."

But the reference to her violin performance stabbed my conscience. I stayed put, unnerved for a moment. "You know . . . ," I began, embarrassed. "Meike and I really battle it out sometimes during music practice." I felt a guilty heat rise on my face. "I yell. Impatient. We fight. She must sincerely hate me those nights."

We walked, silent, into the hallway and entered the reception area. Richard brought my coat and helped me on with it. He took a step back, his expression resolute, and said, "All part of good parenting."

I gripped the hand he offered and shook it, grateful.

~

On the day before the 7th of January, the argument to amend the temporary custody was cancelled and rescheduled for Friday, January 21.

On the 20th of January, the argument for custody was again cancelled and this time rescheduled for the 28th.

"How is it they can keep doing this, forgodsakes?" I asked when Richard called to tell me.

"Welcome to the House of Law," he said, not in a mean way. "The case isn't a priority. Which we could interpret as Holton's intention to leave things as they are."

On the 27th, Richard phoned again. "Just checking in," he said.

"Well. We're on for tomorrow then?"

"We're on."

"Can you call me right away when it's finished?"

"We are scheduled in the courtroom for 10 o'clock. I'll be in contact with you by noon."

The following morning at breakfast, Sam told me, "Dad said he's coming a few minutes early this afternoon."

"I wish he wouldn't use you to communicate with me," I snapped.

For a few seconds we just starred at each other. He shrugged and said, "Just telling you."

I watched the kids board the bus at the corner, then took a shower, wishing I could soften and scrub away my remark to Sam. I dried my hair and took Odie around a few blocks for some fresh air. At ten o'clock, I pulled out the piano bench and tried to concentrate on a Rachmaninov concerto. I should have known better. After stumbling through for twenty minutes, I switched to Purcell. The phone rang at 11:15.

"Looks like Walt's going to have a turn," Richard said.

Thirty-One

There are ingredients in life deserving high consideration. Music. Russian Sage. Politics. God. Death. Yellow. Theology. Red Bud Trees. Literature. Birds. Dance. Justice. Hunger. Ingredients calling for reflection or deliberation or puzzlement or mystery or celebration. This is humanness. Stuff to make room for in one's life, worthy of regard and conversation.

Among mothers as well as anyone.

Many of these components Walt disregards—well, not God or hunger. It's possible Walt isn't able to appreciate these portions of living or has come to dismiss them. More accurately, dismisses their importance to me. It seems he fears solitude, reflection, deliberation, shade, mystery. All of which begins to explain his distorted idea—protecting the children from me.

They moved on Friday, January 29, 1994. Each with a few cardboard boxes. Meike's violin. Odie. Their backpacks. Walt said they would shop if anything came up short. He had caught on yesterday after his suggestion we transfer Meike's white bedroom set, the one with the dresser with the little roses painted on the ceramic knobs, to his apartment.

"No!" I had said and stomped my foot. "This is still her room. This will always be her room. You are not taking the furniture. This is their house. This will always be their house. You are not taking anything more."

So everything else stayed in place, as if keeping me company during the longest night in history. HoneyNut cereal, videos, books in the bookcase, nightstands, dressers.

Under quilts and flannel sheets, the empty beds.

Gerrit called on Sunday and insisted on coming over in the evening, since I wasn't up to going there. When they arrived, Laura wanted evidence that I had eaten, and though we laughed over it, I had to show her the dirty soup pan still on the stove. We shared a bottle of Cabernet Franc while listening to John Coltrane, and later I slept relatively well until daylight.

Three or four inches of snow fell overnight. While the neighbors were in church, I shoveled the driveway so no one, thinking to do me a favor, would take their snow blower to it in the afternoon. I played the piano for a couple of hours until I left the house to have tea with my parents. They would have finished their Sunday nap by three o'clock and I still had to let them know about the custody change.

During the daytime, the door was seldom locked. If I waited for one of them to answer the door, my father greets me with, "Since when can't my children come into their own house?" With a quick, single knock on the glass pane of the door that day, I let myself in. Simultaneously, my father came from the den to meet me, his theology journal still in one hand.

Their four-room and a bath dwelling—one bedroom, a small den with bookshelves, a kitchen/dining area and a decent-sized living room with a sliding door to a private cement patio before the back lawn opened to a common area—is minimal compared to the house on London Street where I grew up. But the condominium, located in a little community called Amsterdam Village, is a place that my parents hardly dared hope for on retiring. They like it there.

My mother put the teakettle on the stove. She had on a long-sleeved white polyester blouse under a black wool knitted vest, tied at the top with a yellow-gold chain sweater guard. Her gathered skirt came just below her calves, brushing her hosiery and nearly reaching her soft-blue slippers.

"Blue Jeans?" she greeted me, not as unkindly as it might sound to anyone else. "I'm surprised. *'Tis Zondag*, you know."

"From now on, don't be surprised, Mom." I pulled out a dining chair and took a seat. I watched her fill one of the fancy Blue Delft plates with homemade chocolate chip cookies and windmill bakery cookies.

"Where's the kids?" she asked.

"They're with Walt today," I answered.

On a weekday at my parents, we just drink coffee from mugs. But since it was Sunday, my father set three China cups on three saucers and brought them to the table before taking his place. The kettle whistled and my mother filled the Sunday teapot and set it on the table to steep.

"The kids are with Walt today you said?" My father like to verify his hearing.

My mother poured the tea and I nodded slowly. After we each took a sip, I smiled with one side of my mouth and faced them both. "They're with him today, tomorrow, every day except Tuesday nights and every other weekend until we go to court."

They stared at me, silent, not seeming to understand.

"Custody's been changed," I said, my voice shaking. My hand trembled as I set down my tea. "Sam and Meike moved to the apartment with Walt."

My mother could hardly ask fast enough. "How can that be? Since when? Who does he think he is, *de schmellop*?"

"Since Friday." I spoke with a quiet voice, like I was resigned to it. Yet they knew better and could easily guess what lay under my words.

My father hadn't spoken. I saw his eyes well up.

"Now what?" my mother asked.

I turned to her. "Now I wait. Richard Dekker says to think of it as Walt's turn. It's temporary. To be fair and all that. It's —"

"He doesn't need a turn," my mother interrupted. "What about those poor kids? Doesn't he think about them? What about you? What are you supposed to do?"

I answered half convincingly. "We'll go to court. I'll be okay. Richard Dekker—he's a good lawyer. And I can always call Dr. Jennings."

"That's another thing I don't get," my mother said. "What's the point of those people? I don't get that. How can you talk to them? How can you trust them?"

I shot my father a glance. His brow wrinkled. I took a sip of tea, set down my cup and sighed.

I met my mother's eyes and said the brave, desperate words carefully. "I have to trust someone."

My father nodded.

College interim was over and I drove to class midmorning on Monday.

The route took me past the elementary school. I could have detoured. I considered it. Some back road, secondary side streets. Just turn on the right blinker instead of the left. Keep going to M23 until I-75 south until west I-40. All the way to California.

As I went by the school, my stomach churned its oatmeal and milk. My daughter is in that building. We haven't seen each other today. I didn't say good morning. I didn't guide her arm through her coat sleeve, didn't button her up or trade a smooch goodbye.

I drove one-handed, wiping my eyes with the other.

She's in there. I don't know how she's supposed to read, do her math.

Hell, I don't even know what's in her lunch bag.

When I said the word "home" it meant our house, our home, the place on Sun Valley Court.

Sam and Meike came home every Tuesday after school through Wednesday morning and every other weekend from Friday after school through Sunday at 9 p.m. Sometimes they took the school bus back and forth. Sometimes I would take them or pick them up. I let them choose. On Sunday nights, Walt picked up the children at the house. With the exception of Monday evenings when I continued to take Meike to her violin lesson and then youth orchestra, my trips to "Dad's place" were as seldom as I could possibly make them.

"You'll need to transfer their things," I told Walt, "so they don't have to bring their stuff to school."

"I don't know why they can't," Walt said.

"Sam and Meike shouldn't have to deal with all that. And they don't need to call attention to their situation when they're at school. None of the other kids at school have that kind of thing going on."

"You mean that they're living with me," he said. "You might as well get used to it."

But he complied and on Friday brought the violin and baritone, Meike's American Girl doll, Sam's *Star Wars* movie and Odie on the leash.

That first weekend after school, Meike shed her coat and boots and pulled a plastic recorder from her backpack.

"Every fourth-grader got one today," she said. "It's like a flute, Mom." She held it to her lips and blew. Uncontrolled high pitches blasted the air. I covered my ears and Odie yelped.

"Not so hard," I shouted. A few more blasts and she let up. "It'll sound better if you blow softer. Is that how Mr. Walters showed you?"

With what seemed like a deliberate smile, she shook her head and lessened the force of her breath, randomly opening and closing the holes with her fingers.

When Matt came calling to play with Sam that afternoon, I invited him in, intent on having their weekends with me like any other time they lived here. I served our supper at six, reminded Sam to feed Odie beforehand, insisted Meike practice her violin lesson afterward. We made popcorn and watched Friday night television from 8 to 10, our usual routine.

As we watched television, Meike settled on the couch in front of me and let me brush the tangles in her hair. Attending to small sections at a time, I worked through the neglected snarls carefully for almost an hour while Meike, her attention on the screen, endured the process with only a few screams and yelps.

Just before bed, Meike started on the recorder again, stretching its register to the limit.

"You may mess with it for ten minutes," I said, "if you don't do the screech thing."

Sam and I packed away the popcorn dishes. When her time was over, I called from the kitchen. "Put it in the case now." Meike ignored me and ramped it up. I entered the den and stood a few feet in front of her. "Enough already. Time for bed."

"I don't wanna." She took a breath and began a set of long blaring notes. Odie jumped from the couch barking and Sam took a seat.

I stretched out my arm. "Hand it over, Meike." She smacked the instrument on my open hand. I opened the case and slid the recorder inside, rubbing my hand on my thigh. "In the morning we're all going to sleep in." I placed the recorder on the bookshelf. "Don't even think about playing it."

"Not fair!" Meike shouted, her eyes scrunched and determined. "I'm going to Dad's. And I'm never coming back!"

"Holy crap!" I yelled and rolled my eyes to look all around the room. "Here we go."

For a moment, we just stared at each other. I stepped over and cracked the sliding door. "Go out, Odie." The dog slipped through.

"Don't swear at me," Meike said, her voice muffled in her throat.

I pretended to straighten my sheet music on the piano bench.

"It wasn't at you and 'crap' isn't swearing," I said quietly, turning from the piano. I opened my arms as an invitation. Tears welled her eyes, but she glared at me and stood firm.

I left the room.

Snow flurries drifted outside the kitchen window as I held the curtain aside. Odie finished sniffing around the yard and scratched at the slider. "Sam, let Odie in, will you?"

The unexpected sting swelled. I leaned against the counter trying to swallow my hurt, telling myself to go to her. Be the charitable one, the grown-up.

Odie followed Sam up the stairs to bed.

I took the dish towel in my hand and wiped the counter, although it wasn't in need of wiping.

Slippers scuffed in the hallway, then on the kitchen linoleum. "Mom?"

Shame on me. My nine-year-old daughter initiated the hug.

We held each other, silent apologies in our arms.

~

A few hours into the morning, a clear but crisp February Saturday, Sam watched as Meike and I took turns stirring a cake batter. "I'm bored," he said from the other side of the counter. "I want to go back."

"You can't, Sam. You're supposed to be here this weekend." I handed Meike the spoon.

"Too boring," he huffed loudly.

"Sam, you've lived here for years and years. Now all of a sudden it's boring?"

"There's nothing to do."

I ignored his indignant tone. "You could work on your coins. You could bundle up and take Odie for a run. I'll play a game of Monopoly." I held the bowl while Meike scraped the ingredients into the pan. "We're going out for supper tonight. You wanna make your cinnamon bread when we're finished here?"

"I wanna go to Dad's." He dropped a fist on the counter and stepped back.

"Well, you can't." We opened the oven and placed the cake on the rack. "Okay, Meike. Set the timer for forty-five minutes."

"She doesn't know how to set the timer," Sam said. "What a dork. Who wants to eat your stupid ugly cake anyway?"

"Sam. Cut it out."

He kicked the dining chair, tumbling it to its side.

"Go to your room, Sam."

"Make me," he yelled. He stomped to the closet, grabbed his coat and slammed the door on the way out.

From the living room, I watched him run halfway down the cul-de-sac, then slow to a walk. Meike joined me at the window. I thought Sam might stop in front of Matt's or see if Jason was home, but he kept walking until he turned the corner out of sight.

I went to the phone to call Walt, give him a heads up and have him let me know if Sam arrived. Meike stayed at the window watching after her brother, then came up behind me.

"Sam walks in his sleep, Mom."

I stared at the phone, then at Meike, then back at the phone.

My mind went to that first day the kids had moved to their dad's. Sam and I were sitting on the floor fitting his tennis shoes into his backpack.

"Too bad Odie can't stay," Sam had said with a slow, sad voice. I believe he meant to offer me compensation.

I managed a weak smile. "He needs to be where you are."

We got to our feet and his face contorted. "I'm sorry, Mom." He hugged me that day, then when he let go, I saw tears in his eyes.

"You're not to worry," I had said.

But he was worrying.

And sleep walking.

Instead of calling Walt, I drew a chair from the table and simply sat down. With an uneasy look, Meike stroked her neck with the end of the braid in her hair.

Sleepwalking is common in kids and doesn't necessarily signal emotional cause or harm. But I envisioned Sam's apprehension, months and months of misgivings, carrying the whole damn mess on his shoulders as he walked asleep. He could run into something, fall down the stairs, open a window. For crying out loud, they live on the third floor.

"Meike, do you sleepwalk, too?"

She shook her head slowly and put the end of her braid in her mouth. I motioned her over and pulled her onto my lap. We sat quietly, her head resting on my chest.

Odie barked and I heard the door opening. Sam entered the hallway. He hesitated there for a moment.

"Welcome back," I quickly said, peering around Meike's head. I nudged her a bit and she let me up, taking the chair for herself. "Take off your coat and stay awhile."

I filled the kettle with tap water and set it on the stove. Sam unzipped his jacket but left it on. He stepped a little closer, searching my face. "I was mad," he said.

I nodded a few times. "I know." The igniter clicked before flaring. I switched the gas to medium-high, then turned back to my son. "I'm usually the one dodging out for a walk when I need to think. That was actually very mature of you. Taking a walk to cool down."

Sam didn't reply but while I took three mugs from the cupboard and spooned instant cocoa powder into them, he took off his coat.

When the kettle whistled, I shut it off without pouring the boiling water. "I need to say something first." I placed a hand on Sam's arm and he let me lead him around to the other side of the counter. Meike sat in the chair all this time, not making a peep. Fine with me. She could hear this, too.

With both my hands on Sam's shoulders, I crooked my neck slightly showing the seriousness I felt. "I want you to stay, Sam," I said earnestly. "I miss you when you're at Dad's . . . . It's . . . " I choked up and tears stung my eyes. "It's hard. I'm used to taking care of you." I felt my anger rising but went ahead anyway. "This is hard for me . . .

and I'm so tired of it . . . . Where was your dad when you were little? I always took care of you." A deep breath and then another and then one more. I took my hands from Sam's shoulders, made a step backwards and softened my voice. "I'm not the bad guy."

"Who is?"

I faltered, but only a second or two. "No one."

~

Sunday morning went better.

Together, the three of us ate our cinnamon rolls around the table and then dressed for church. In the best interest of the children, I practiced an indifference toward the church. Keith and Cindy invited me over for a quick cup of coffee while the kids went to Catechism.

All earmarks of normal times.

In the early afternoon, we made a plan. Finish our homework first and then watch the video *Radio Flyer* we had rented.

Meike had taken to pestering us since lunch, snapping her fingers down on her thumb, imitating a jaw. "Hungry, hungry Hippo," she repeated every few minutes.

"Stop it, Meike," I kept telling her.

She stuck her clamping fingers, finally, in front of Sam's nose. "Hungry, hungry Hippo."

He punched her arm away. "Dork!" He reached across the table, grabbed her math sheet, crumpled it in a ball and whipped it at her head.

"Sam, you keep your hands off her," I said, coming to my feet.

"That's my homework!" Meike cried out.

I crossed my arms and jammed them hard against my chest like an old biddy on playground patrol. "Maybe we should forget about the movie."

"Good," Sam said. "I want to go to Dad's anyway."

With my fist on my hip, I narrowed my eyes and sent Sam a challenging stare. "No."

He went to the phone and called his father. Soon, on what must have been Walt's direction, Sam handed the phone to me. Walt and I agreed Sam should stay. Sam slouched down to the basement and I left him alone until a few minutes later when I heard him sobbing. I descended the stairs to help.

"It's okay, Sam," I said, approaching.

He shifted his body and lifted his head above the arm of the couch, his face reddened, tears running down it. "Leave me alone!"

As I turned to leave, Sam got up and stomped to the extension phone behind the bar. Again, he called Walt. Again, Walt and I agreed Sam should stay. I passed the phone back to Sam and heard his father tell him, "Hang in there, buddy," as if Sam were a P.O.W.

Within the next five minutes, Sam left anyway.

I called Walt again and he caught up to Sam in the pickup. Sam waited in the truck in the driveway while Walt came inside and collected Sam's things.

"You better do something different so the kids aren't like this," Walt told me on his way out.

I wanted to spit. I wanted to slap his pious face. I wanted to tell him to go to hell. But there was Meike sitting on the linoleum floor behind me, holding Odie by the collar. I pushed the door shut and locked it.

"Let's turn on some music," I said, marching to the stereo, not even trying to hide my anger.

I put on Meike's tape of her St. Cecilia orchestra, recorded when they performed last fall. It begins sweetly with a Bach piece, followed by Brahms' "Lullaby." We sat on the carpet, Meike stroking Odie's head, me lightly tracing my fist on her back. After a while, I loosened the stretch band on her braid and ran my fingers through the strands.

It's hard not to smile when Offenbach is playing. A minute into the "Infernal Galop," Meike took Odie's front paws in her hands and bounced them in the air. The Can-Can started and we stood up straight and carried on synchronized leg kicks.

When the tape ended, I switched to the Sunday evening jazz program.

"Can we watch *Radio Flyer*?"

I shook my head. "We better wait 'til next time."

We made some chips and cheese and ate vanilla ice cream after. At eight o'clock Meike said, "I want to go back." There was supposed to be an hour more. I nodded and helped her pack her bag. We drove to the apartment and I waited in the hall at the door with her until Walt answered and let her in.

Sam came to the door, rather sheepish.

"You okay?" I asked him.

"Yup," he answered.

"See you Tuesday then."

He turned and walked further into the apartment, so I left and went home.

I took my anthology of English Lit with me to the Barcalounger, but the book remained unopened on my lap.

I sank into a hole.

I saw the space of seventeen hours allotted me on Tuesdays a façade, and the place between Wednesdays and my weekends, barren gravel.

Thirty-Two

I dragged myself to Dutch class Monday morning after oatmeal and coffee. In our fourth semester, only ten students including myself remained of the first-semester group. Professor Leitsma insisted we set our desks in a circle when we met. I hadn't pulled out of my gloomy state, yet when we opened our texts, my mind welcomed the distraction, and I found myself structuring sentences without much struggle and reading aloud without stumbling. In my Survey of English Literature class, some forty students attended at a time. I took a seat toward the back, where I could take notes without being called on.

On Tuesday, Sam and Meike brought their report cards home, covering the two months before the holidays and the month of January. Meike received a B+ in Math and a B+ in Phys Ed. All the rest were A's, and she had earned checks in either the Satisfactory or the Exceeding Satisfactory columns. Sam's grades were A's or A-'s with checks "above average" in the columns. His teachers in the junior high building had made notes—"Good Work." "Really a fine semester's work, Sam." "Keep it up, pal, you have gifts." Sam and Meike had plenty to be proud of.

Ever since our past weekend, I had deliberated whether some kind of professional counseling might benefit Sam and Meike. Now, given their good reports, I wondered if professional help might be over-reaction.

I decided to ask Dr. Jennings for his input when we met that week.

"That the kids are testing you is to be expected," Jennings said after I told him how Friday, Saturday and Sunday had gone with Sam and Meike. "Not that it makes it any easier."

He sat with one leg crossed over the other, in a pressed white shirt with sleeves rolled to just below the elbow. He wore a tie, one of several I've seen him wear, always in good taste. We faced each other, his chair a straight-back with an upholstered seat, and mine a more cushiony one with arms, placed where I can view the garden through the window on the right.

Only currently, it was snowing.

"It's unnerving to see someone sleepwalking," Jennings said. "Or to imagine your child doing so." He lowered his foot to the floor, his hands folded on his lap. "Jane, I encourage you to have Sam and Meike meet with someone."

Although I had asked for his opinion, my resistance flashed. "I sure don't want their teachers interfering. Fricking amateurs who think they're psychologists."

"That's rather strong."

"Well," I shrugged, "they're always *krabben*, poking around asking questions. And one of Sam's teachers, Mr. Palmer—I wonder if some emotional manipulation goes on there." I had no proof of such a thing, only a gut-feeling based on my conversations with the man.

"I would recommend a professional."

"Yeah . . . well . . . any suggestions?" I asked. "Certainly not PCS."

Jennings flinched. "No. No question on that." In slow motion, he shook his head. "In fact, I'm insulted . . . more accurately, I'm hurt you would even think I might suggest PCS."

"Seriously?"

His brows knit together, and quietly he formed a question of his own. "Don't you think I *listen* when you talk?"

The genuine disappointment I heard caught me off guard. "Sorry," I said, bowing my head toward the floor, ashamed and then ashamed for being ashamed because I knew shame was not his intention. Feeling him watch me, I sighed a short, loud sigh, and by way of acknowledging his concern, softly said, "Damn."

We sat silently for a few moments, something I felt fairly comfortable with after all these many, many sessions together, knowing his eyes were on me as I stared at the familiar pattern in the area rug under our feet.

I breathed deeply, shifted in my chair, and finally looked at him. "Can you make a suggestion who the kids might see?"

Dr. Jennings pulled up his leg and held his ankle on the opposite knee. "Didn't Sam and Meike see Tony Werkema once, originally when Walt first talked about leaving home?"

"They did. A few times. But his advice was to tell Sam and Meike that *we* decided a separation was best, a mutual agreement he called it, which is a flat-out lie. I finally gave in, like in the best interest of the children and all that, but I'm sorry I did. I believe eventually the kids need to know the truth. And Werkema's direction seemed to leave too much to the kids' imagination."

"Did the kids take to him?"

"They balked at seeing anyone initially, but Walt and I persisted. They met with Werkema, the two of them together and then one-to-one, all in the same appointment. Walt made a separate appointment for each of them afterward and that was that.

"So, Sam and Meike know him. Never said anything against him. And Walt would think him a fair choice."

I noticed my thumb fidgeting with the wedding ring on my left hand, turning it, spinning it on my finger. "I blame Walt, but I don't tell Sam and Meike that. I mean, sure, marriage takes two, but Judas. His moving out wasn't my idea, and it didn't help a damn thing."

"Nothing?"

"Well . . . except maybe for me to realize what a complete total jerk he is. I raise the kids for ten years while he makes himself successful. It's what I wanted to do—raise the kids—and I'm damned good at it. But what does Walt make of it? A *harmful* Motion? And then a second Motion to put me out on the street?"

Jennings blinked hard several times. "And you want to stay married to someone like that?"

Still thumbing my ring in circles, I took a minute to answer. "I thought it was my duty,"

"You just used past tense."

Frowning, I turned my eyes in the direction of the garden where all kinds of possibilities lay under the snow. "He could still change his mind. That's not a totally unreasonable expectation."

"Seriously? Is that what you want?" Jennings asked.

The unconscious slipped to conscious. With the garden again in my direct view, I spoke out loud. "Five weeks from now, March twenty-three to be exact, is our twenty-second wedding anniversary."

Slowly raising my left hand out in front of me, I examined the half-carat diamond a full arm's length away, then drew it in closer to my face and inspected it at different angles, along with the soldered yellow-gold band. I twisted the ring slightly and with a dilatory and ceremonious tug, removed it from my finger.

The ring in my right hand, I studied it for a moment longer and then pushed it into the pocket of my jeans.

"I needed somebody to witness that," I explained.

"Yes. You did," Jennings answered.

We sat silent for a moment.

"Our time's up today, Jane."

Dr. Jennings doesn't scribble notes during our sessions, which I appreciate. Instead, we meet for fifty minutes, he walks me back down to the lobby where we schedule the next appointment, and then, he tells me, he returns to his office to make any necessary comments in the record.

I found my car in the stone parking lot. On the drive home I realized a significance in having someone witness the official removal of my wedding ring.

There's no liturgy for that.

My thumb found my finger and felt nothing smooth or round or solid. How scary and strange and empty it felt.

Not as scary and strange and empty as the house without Sam and Meike, I thought while pulling into the driveway.

~

The night before his twelfth birthday, Sam phoned and said he couldn't wait to tell me the news. Walt had arranged for him to take flying lessons.

I had to fake enthusiasm. I didn't even know a child could take flying lessons at the age of twelve. Ridiculous.

When we hung up, I mixed a dark chocolate glaze to spread over Sam's birthday cake.

I had to hand it to Walt. He chalked up points with Sam and, given my own reluctance to fly, managed to rub my nose in my inferiority at the same time. I went to the basement to wrap the birthday present I'd hidden there—an unassembled pitcher's net in a long rectangular box.

I've never liked competition. Actually, I hate it. An ideal morality wouldn't even allow competition. That might make a good research paper in a theology class someday, but when it comes to custody decisions, competition has no place.

On a Sunday night when he came to pick up the kids a few days after Sam's birthday, Walt lingered on the rug in the hallway while Meike and Sam took their backpacks to the truck. Walt politely announced he was pulling the kids out of school at the end of February for a six-day vacation in Florida.

"Now hold it," I said. "No way."

"It's fine," Walt said.

"You can't do that without my consent."

"Their teachers are assigning them homework to take along."

"As if you're going?"

"Sure."

"Walt. We've never done anything like that before—let the kids miss school."

"The kids can use a vacation," he said, "and I won't be around for spring break. I'm going to Iowa to see my folks."

"So you got it all worked out. Without even saying anything. Well, too bad because I'm saying 'no.'"

"Sam and Meike are hoping to go."

"You told them?"

"I said I'd check with you today."

"Stop pulling that kind of crap, Walt! You can't do that. Not to me and not to them."

Of course, good mothers don't interfere with a Disney trip. And I remembered the year before and Meike's broken leg. Of course, I wasn't going to disappoint Meike and Sam. Of course Walt knew that.

"I'll be sure to let Richard know," I said. "Now get out of here."

I locked the door, wondering when it is that children get just plain jaded.

Thirty-Three

At Walt's request, the afternoon before their trip I brought an extra suitcase to the apartment. The suitcase we used on our honeymoon when we drove to Daytona Beach, the same suitcase we used when we flew to Seattle, and when we went to Hawaii for our fifth wedding anniversary, and when we flew to the Diamond Blade Coring and Drilling Association in Las Vegas.

Sam opened the door, pumped and blinking, pumped and blinking, pumped and blinking. He gladly took the piece of luggage from my hand.

"Our plane leaves at 11:20 in the morning, Mom," he said, blinking wildly. He could hardly hold still. He let me hold him in a quick hug.

Meike and I squeezed our arms around each other while she promised to call as soon as they reached their hotel.

At home in the morning, I shoveled snow off the deck with Odie at exactly 11:20 just in case they were looking down to wave, but then I decided that was crazy and quickly went back inside in case they were looking and saw me and began to feel sorry or guilty.

Three days in Disney World with Father Superior and the rest of the time at some gated resort on the beach in Naples.

I don't keep score. I don't do competition.

That night, with Odie lying at my feet under the piano bench, I played through Jules Massenet's "Meditation." The piece is not difficult for me since it's in D Major and is to be played *Andante*, "walking slowly." *Poco a poco*, Massenet noted, "gradually more and more passionate." It's not long, yet very beautiful, and in the last few measures I had to wipe tears from my face with my sleeve.

~

It occurred to me that Walt might have arranged the trip to Florida purposely to put me in serious despair. He could use my distress as evidence that my health made a bad environment for Sam and Meike. Yet, soon I realized such an invention on his part was unlikely, given how Walt still considered bipolar as a one-size-fits-all Patty Duke model, and given that he assumed any court decision would favor him.

At that point instead of focusing on Walt, I needed to pay attention to my immediate frame of mind.

Because what I saw was shadow. A shadow, so identifiable during times when November offered nothing but cold and darkness and a long winter, now sneaking into February territory. A shadow now threatening spring sun and warmth and my vision of hope.

If I hadn't remembered my standing appointment in the morning with Jennings, that shadow would have kept me awake all night. And lack of sleep attracts mania like our corncrib in Moline had attracted mice.

Dr. Jennings was proud of me. Not only had I recognized the depression intensifying, but I acknowledged it first thing when I sat down in his office, tears running on my face.

"So, here's the picture," Jennings said. "Fun with Dad. Not so fun with Mom."

I nodded my agreement, a tissue pressed to one eye, then the other.

"The lack of routine might be fun for a while, Jane, but later, children miss that comfort," he continued. "Or it might be years before they realize it."

Always more bad news. Always fucking more tears.

"In the meantime, Jane, you're reaching out."

"Don't say that." I kept my voice low and most of my anger out of it. "Reaching out? Puke. I hate psycho-jargon." Lifting my shoulder, I wiped my face with the top of my arm. "Besides . . . it sounds so very frickin' needy."

"But you can be needy here," he said quietly. "No embarrassment. No shame."

A minute or two passed while we sat, wordless, and I wiped my face over and over.

"What I need is more tissue," I said finally, holding out the empty box. I pressed my lips together and formed a determined smile.

Jennings retrieved more tissues from the bottom drawer of his desk and set the box on the end table next to me. He sat down again, his expression serious.

"In the past, I agreed with you when you said you didn't need to give Walt the satisfaction of your tears, and I still agree with that," he said. "And Jane. When you're at their school, at the kid's music concerts, at their programs, I hope you hold your head up."

My only answer was nodding a few times as I dabbed my eyes.

"Before our time is up," Jennings said, "I want to check if you've talked with your brother Gerrit lately. He's been such a helpful resource for you."

I took a moment, like I had to catch my breath after running around the block. "Yes. You'll be pleased to know I had dinner there Sunday."

"And what else have you done while Sam and Meike are in Florida? For you, I mean. Something special."

"Well, the snow's melted and I have been jogging a couple times. So Sunday, I made myself a chocolate soda with vanilla ice cream for supper. Potato chips on the side."

Jennings eyes were shining in delight. "No shame in that."

I hadn't brought up Jesse lately. "And I had Cindy over one evening."

"Good for you. Gold star. End of session." His brows knit together, and his voice took a concerned tone. "And of course, you know the number here."

Walt set the suitcase down on the linoleum next to the rug. "We'll need to cut her hair," he said, as if he and I were in this whole thing together. "There's too many tangles. No way can we get them all out."

Meike's hair was tied into a loose ponytail with an elastic band, her face tanned, the skin on her nose peeling. Extra freckles had popped out while they were gone.

"I don't think I want to cut my hair, Mom."

I wrapped an arm around her shoulders and lifted her chin. "You can have a nice long warm bath. I'll wash your hair in the tub for you and use lots of conditioner." I winked at her like we were sharing secret girl-talk. "We'll see if the snarls come out."

Sam sat on the floor with his jacket unzipped and Odie between his legs. He nuzzled his face in the dog's neck. "I'm tired. I want to take a nap."

"I have your favorite—macaroni and cheese—in the oven and it's almost ready. You can tell me all about your trip while we eat and after supper you can go to bed for the whole night if you want."

"You should go to boys' club, Sam," Walt said.

"Oh, come on, Walt. Just because it's at church doesn't make it mandatory. Maybe Sam needs a rest."

What I didn't say was that needing R&R after a vacation with Walt wasn't hard to imagine. I shouldn't be squabbling in front of the kids. I wanted a smooth transition as Sam and Meike came back.

Bring the kids home, Walt. Then leave us alone.

"I put underwear and dirty t-shirts and so on in a plastic bag in the suitcase," Walt said. "A lot of stuff is still clean. Judy said she'd wash the stuff if you don't want to."

"What? Are you kidding? I can wash my own kid's clothes, thank you very much. Judy Lynch? She does your laundry?"

"Never mind. I just thought it was nice of her to offer."

"Mrs. Lynch brings Dad cookies," Meike said.

I rolled my eyes at Walt. Sometimes I get wacko when I think what Walt must tell these women, how he wins their sympathy or how they go about feeling sorry for him and bring him casseroles, maybe even clean his apartment. This afternoon, I was too happy Meike and Sam were home to want to think any more about the wonderful, kind ladies who lend their sweet, sympathetic hand to my damn husband.

"I need to talk to your mom alone," Walt said. "You guys go on and take your backpacks upstairs."

"We won't be long," I said, watching Odie follow Sam and Meike up the steps. "Supper's almost ready."

Walt scowled, kicked at the rug, hands in his coat pocket. "I'll need you to sign for a second mortgage on the house."

"What are you talking about? There's less than two years left on the loan."

"Well, as collateral I mean. I've found the house I want."

"A house?"

"For Sam and Meike and me. It's just a small one, one story over on Judson."

"Why do you assume these ideas of your make sense? Or that I'd co-operate with you? Don't you get it? I don't want you to buy another house. This is Sam and Meike's house."

"But you won't give it up."

"Of course not. It isn't that I won't. It's because I don't want to and I don't have to and I shouldn't."

"But paying rent is throwing money away. What am I supposed to do?"

"I don't care. Go sell a truck."

Thirty-Four

Sam needed a ride home from school because it was Friday and he had to practice his baritone over the weekend. We made a stop at the elementary building where Meike stood near the turn-around waiting for us. Walt had dropped off Odie in the morning, and we heard his bark from upstairs first before he scooted down to greet us.

"Why so gloomy?" I asked Meike after we had each gobbled up a granola bar and Sam took off to call for Matt.

"I don't want to go to the face-painting party tonight," she said, pulling a frown.

"I thought you were looking forward to it. Aren't Sarah and Becky going?"

Meike nodded once, slowly working her head up and down.

"Looks like you need to draw one of those big white upside-down smiles, with droopy eyes and clown tears. Boo-hoo."

She broke into sobs. I reached to hug her and she grasped me around the hips.

"What's wrong, Meike?"

Her voice was muffled, buried in my sweatshirt. "I'm not going."

She was referring to a gathering of the girls' club from church, with soda and pizza, where the leaders would help the girls paint each other's faces. This was meant as fun and practice for the upcoming spring bazaar when the girls would paint faces of other children who held fifty-cent tickets.

"You don't have to go, Meike." I touched her shoulder. "Nobody's going to make you go." Her little body trembled.

I walked her over to the couch and we sat, her head on my chest. I curved her hair around her ear until the crying mostly dwindled and Meike lifted her face.

"They ask me questions, Mom."

"Who asks you questions?"

A long, convulsive sigh escaped her. "The ladies. Mrs. Deemter. Mrs. Hall. And Sarah's mom."

"What kind of questions?"

"About you." She whimpered and gripped my sweatshirt. "About Dad. About Sam." She burst into tears again. "About where I live."

We sat clutching each other as my own tears spilled.

Jennings said that in keeping with his policy, he would not testify in court. Disappointed and angry, I accused him of copping out. So when Richard had Jennings subpoenaed, I worried he would be angry with me instead.

"No, Jane. I'm not angry," Jennings had said. "Comes with the job."

Two weeks later, Walt's attorney informed us they would not accept Jennings' deposition as evidence.

"They will argue anything he says is biased," Richard explained from across the table. "Walt claims you have Jennings wrapped around your little finger."

"Right," I answered. "First Walt insists I need hospitalization. When Jennings says I don't, Walt won't accept it. When Jennings says I'm bipolar, Walt pushes the diagnosis to extreme. Later, Walt calls me weak because I'm 'still seeing that doctor.' What am I supposed to do?"

Looking away, I stared at the carpet, my elbow resting on the arm of the chair, the palm of my hand over my mouth. Richard let me seethe for a minute. When I turned back to face him, he pushed his chair a few inches away from the table and set his pen down on the yellow notepad.

He spoke carefully and, before he finished, I knew why. "Are you willing to call in a third party?" he asked. "Someone you have no history with? Someone Walt will agree to?"

My shoulders slumped and a long, fatigued sigh from somewhere deep slipped out. I breathed in hard as if to compensate. "I am so fed up with Walt telling me what I am and what I am not." My head whirled at the idea of another professional, someone else writing down my answers, another probing. And for what? To prove myself to some shrink? To Walt? A neighbor? A judge? Why do I need to answer to everyone?

I trusted my attorney. But I had to ask, more like quietly beg, to be let off this one. "You think I should?"

"Your bipolar isn't a textbook case. We know that. But a totally outside source can help. Since Walt's being such a jerk about it." He waved his hand at the air and raised his voice. "We can appease him forever if we have to."

I swallowed in attempt to loosen the tightness in my stomach. I folded my arms on the table in front of us. "Whatever."

He took my response as a signal to proceed. "We'll get a reference Walt agrees to, then subpoena whoever that doctor is. I'll argue that PCS is not an expert witness. Then we'll subpoena Riley." He paused as he thought further. "We can bill Walt for it."

One side of my mouth curved up for a few seconds. I shifted in my chair, re-crossed my legs and watched through the window as the early March wind played with old downtown paper debris and last autumn's leaves.

I remembered watching the same thing here a year ago.

Tomorrow Walt would leave for Iowa and Meike and Sam would be home with me for five days in a row.

I breathed a little easier.

Richard continued, his sauciness vanished. "We've got work ahead of us." He picked up his ballpoint and flipped to a new page. "Think about the trial. Witnesses. Not several. Three people who will give a strong testimony. Not relatives . . ." he shrugged, "preferably."

"Ruth will do it."

"Ruth?"

"My neighbor. Sam's best friend's mom. Three houses down. Ruth already volunteered."

Richard nodded. "Okay."

"She calls me the Kool-Aid Mom."

My attorney made a note.

I heard the wind at the window and looked out, considering names. A shame Cindy and Keith wouldn't participate.

And Jesse. Well, that wasn't going to happen.

My throat felt thick as I glanced around the office—high ceiling, wooden door, antique-gold wallpaper, the brass lamp on the end table in the corner—avoiding Richard, embarrassed I wasn't coming up with other possibilities.

"Wait a few days," Richard said. "Give it some thought."

He flipped to a new page and, pen still in hand, set folded hands on top of the yellow pad. "Jane, I'd like you to start writing things down. Nothing fancy, just notes. Sam and Meike's grades. Where Walt goes. Where he takes Sam and Meike. What he says in front of them." He opened his hands and laughed. "I mean, you know, not every single thing . . . ."

"You mean, like he's off to Iowa for five days?"

"Yes."

"Like how he picks up the kids from school and brings them to the shop where they do their homework and he finishes up his phone calls?"

"Uh-huh."

"Like how he leaves Meike home alone for an hour or more?"

"Yup."

"Sam says that I'm over-protective. I asked him what over-protective means. He doesn't know. Guess where Sam got that from."

"That kind of thing. Fill up lots of pages. Let me filter through what's important and what isn't."

In capital letters I could read upside down, Richard printed "Financial" on the notepad and underlined it. He checked his wristwatch and thought a moment. "Let's set up a time on Tuesday to discuss finances."

I shook my head. "I have classes Tuesday and Thursday mornings."

"We'll check with Gina on the way out. Maybe early Wednesday afternoon."

Richard escorted me to the lobby. I rode the elevator down, noted the balminess in the wind as I crossed the street to the parking lot, and drove the Town Car up Fulton Street to the expressway. Walt was leaving in the morning, and Sam and Meike were coming directly home from school this afternoon. I'd have to make a stop at the grocery on the way home.

The school bus dropped Sam and Meike off at the corner, and a few minutes later Walt brought Odie and the kids' things to the house. Shortly after he left, a thundershower popped up, and we watched through the sliding door as the grass turned greener right before our eyes.

"It's the nitrogen in the lightning," Sam said.

We finished dinner and when she loitered at the table, I reminded Meike to practice her violin. "Go ahead and get started with your warm-ups. I'll pack the dishwasher and then we'll work on your recital piece together."

Meike's solos had grown in complexity, and I had found it necessary to practice the piano accompaniment separately. Before the trip to Florida, Meike and I played through the third movement of Seitz's Concerto no. 2 for Mrs. Dekker during lesson time. Mrs. Dekker admired the rendition and praised Meike for her "innate interpretation of dynamics." We were now to concentrate on smoother phrasing and consistent tempo.

I could tell that Meike had not practiced regularly. "Let's start again," I said after the first few measures. Following two more starts and stops, we played into the second page. "Okay. Hold it. Remember what Mrs. Dekker said about eighth and sixteenth notes here. It goes one and two and three-and-ah four-and-ah-one and two . . ." I clapped the rhythm as I counted.

Meike sighed heavily, re-positioned her chin on the chin rest, lifted her bow and nodded to me.

"Here we go. One and two and three-and-ah . . . . Nope. Try again. One and two and . . . you got it . . . . Nice." By the end of the line, we had to stop again.

"Aaaagh!" Meike said, her bow at her side.

"I know. It's hard. Okay. Measure forty-nine. Three-and-ah four-and-ah one . . . . Try it again." I had folded the corner of the page, but when I reached and turned it, I stumbled. "My fault. Keep going, I'll find you . . . ." I slipped in and recovered. "Slow it down here now. You're rushing . . . still rushing . . . . Stop, Meike. You're rushing."

"I hate this. I don't want to do this." She stomped her foot.

"We're just out of practice, is all. Let's try again. You want to start at the beginning?"

"No! I hate the violin. I hate you." She stomped again but set her chin in position and lifted her bow.

"From the top then. One and two . . . ." I tried to ignore her level dynamics, her flat E's, even her rushing—until a whole note received only one beat and a rest was ignored entirely. "Stop."

I slowly turned on the piano bench, reached, and pushed the music stand to its lowest position so my daughter and I could talk face-to-face. "Meike," I said, "the recital is in two weeks."

She didn't blink an eye. "I want Dad to accompany me at the recital."

I looked at her straight on, rolled my eyes and left the room.

While Meike packed her violin in its case, I started my list for Richard. "Does not schedule, encourage or enforce practice of music lessons."

She entered the kitchen, her heavy steps pounding on the linoleum. "What time is it?" she asked. "I want to watch *Home Improvement* with Sam."

"It's only six-thirty." I closed the rolled-top with my notes inside. Our leftovers had cooled, and I opened the refrigerator, setting them on the top shelf. "Are you remembering we have a lesson with Mrs. Dekker tomorrow night?"

"Not on Thursdays."

I shut the refrigerator door harder than intended and the glass jars with the condiments rattled. "It's a make-up lesson," I said. "Because we missed one when you were in Florida."

"Well, I'm not going on Thursday," she shouted. "You're mean!"

"Listen, lady." I banged the salt and pepper shakers down and slammed the cupboard door. "No more!" I slammed another cupboard door, opened two more and slammed them too. I stood in front of Meike, shrieking. "I'm sick of your sass! It's not my fault your dad tromps you all over hell's creation!"

She shrank back, crushed. "It's not my fault either," she whimpered.

"I know that." Lowering my voice only slightly, I pointed upstairs. "Now go to your room."

She turned and fled.

I winced in guilt and called after her. "I'll come get you for *Home Improvement*."

~

"Is it a trick?" Ruth asked, walking up the driveway where Sam and Matt were setting up the pitching net.

"Fine with me," I said. "If Mother Nature wants to give us a few balmy days the first week of March, I say, take 'em while we can get 'em."

I held Odie on the leash, and Ruth leaned over to pet him. We stepped into the front lawn where Meike snapped the straps on her roller blades in place. She wore her knee pads. I offered Meike a hand and pulled her up from the grass. She steadied herself a moment on the cement before accepting the leash. Then off she rolled, with Odie pulling her down the sidewalk.

"Are you going to the Mothers' Club meeting Wednesday night?"

"I didn't know Mothers' Club was this week."

"It's been in the newsletter," Ruth said. "I'll pick you up if you want."

My reflex said to turn down her offer, just like I would anyone. Preference would have me arrive alone at the last minute and leave as soon as the meeting adjourned. Yet, I realized, here was a friend offering a small invitation. "Sure," I answered, secretly proud of myself.

I stayed in that more amiable attitude for a while—even waved to Judy next door as she backed their van down the driveway an hour later.

~

My sister-in-law called on Saturday morning to say she and Jerry were having the Berendses over for pizza at seven and that the kids and I should join them. "I haven't seen Case and Denise since summer."

With all the kids there and my reluctance to dwell on it, we pretty much avoided the subject of Walt. Instead, we spent the evening enjoying pizza, soda and beer, several rounds of Trivial Pursuit, old jokes, each other.

Even though when the evening finished we promised we would stay in touch, I was surprised when Denise phoned so soon on Sunday afternoon.

"I kept thinking about it through the whole church service this morning. The fun we've had," Denise said. "All the times the kids played together. All the time we spent camping. And in the winter, we'd go sliding at Charlie's Dump."

"Yeah, great stuff," I said. "Last night was a blast. We should make a camping reservation again for summer."

"So, I wanted to tell you." Denise paused a moment. "I'll vouch for you. I'll be one of your witnesses in court."

I hadn't asked her. We hadn't discussed the custody arrangement. We hadn't talked about the pending trial. But she and Lynn must have.

"Thank you, Denise . . . thank you so much."

~

After the unseasonably warm weekend, a cold front moved through late Sunday night, and on Monday morning a light rain began to fall as we readied for school. "I can drop you off," I told Sam and Meike, both happy at the suggestion.

First was Meike's building. Next, the middle school. "I have to stop at the office," I said.

Sam directed me to a parking spot he saw. He waited for me to take my purse. We walked together to the front entry where he said, "Bye, Mom," before he headed down the north hall to homeroom.

I passed through the glass door of the school office. Doris stood behind the counter, Luanne beside her. Two students were in line ahead of me. I waited my turn, thinking how only three years ago, when I was president of Mothers' Club, I often spent an afternoon here using the computer, printer, copy machine or meeting with Dwight Sytsma, the principal.

"Hi, Jody. Hi, Terra," I greeted the girls as they finished their business and turned to go.

"Hi, Mrs. Weber."

I jacked my bag up on my shoulder and stepped to the counter. "Hi, Doris."

"Hello, Jane. What can I do for you?"

"I realized this weekend I'm not getting the newsletter."

"Hmmm." She walked over to the computer near the opposite wall and clicked on the screen. With her back toward me, she sat down, straightened her skirt, and clicked again. She scrolled through a list for a moment. "Oh . . . they're going to Walt's address," she announced from across the room and I winced—Doris doesn't grasp *discreet*.

I set my bag on the counter and folded my arms on top. "Well," I sighed. Doris approached the counter once more. "From now on, please send one to me as well."

"The computer won't do that."

I dropped my voice almost to a whisper and squinted. "Excuse me?"

"The computer is programmed for only one address per family."

"Well, fix it." I picked up my bag, lifted my chin and waltzed out.

Thirty-Five

"And what can I get you lovely ladies this evening?" the waitress asked.

"I want double chocolate cake," Meike said, pointing to the glossy photo on the menu.

"Good choice, honey. And for you?"

I raised my eyebrows in anticipation. "French Chantilly, please."

With the violin recital behind us that Friday night, Meike and I stopped on the way home to celebrate with dessert. Sam had been ornery all through dinner and at the last minute refused to attend the program. Walt agreed to slip out and go home to check on him once Meike finished her solo.

"I'm really proud of you, Meike," I said as we waited for our cake. "You did so well tonight."

All smiles, she touched the headband holding back her crimped hair, a strip of wide elastic we covered with a remnant matching her dress. "Once we got started, I wasn't even nervous, Mom," she beamed. "It was kind of fun."

"You're a natural. And you looked like a natural."

The waitress brought me a cup of coffee. When she served our cake slices, she produced two large, cloth dinner napkins. "No offense, hon," she told Meike. "Don't want chocolate on that pretty dress of yours."

We spread our napkins on our laps, tasted our cake and traded a bite. "Yum," Meike said retracing her spoon with her tongue.

I set my spoon on the edge of my plate and sipped some coffee. "You know, Meike . . . I'm sorry I get impatient sometimes when you practice—all that yelling . . . I shouldn't . . . I'm sorry . . . you're so talented."

Apparently, she didn't know what to say to my meager apology. The shrug she returned told me she at least heard what I said. I dipped the end of a finger in my butter cream icing and sucked on it. Meike eyed her chocolate frosting and imitated me. We looked at each other and giggled, reached over at the same time and swiped more sweet goop from each other's plate.

When we returned home, I told Sam to turn off the television and come upstairs. I didn't know what conversation had passed between Sam and Walt earlier that evening. But Sam and I had some talking to do. He made no pretense, entering the den still belligerent.

"I had chocolate cake," Meike said, setting her violin in the corner. Sam picked up a pillow from the couch and whacked her across the back with it. She screamed and covered her head with her arms as he hit her again.

"Sam!" I yelled, stepping between them. "None of that!"

He whipped the pillow at me and collapsed into the Barcalounger, yanking up the foot rest that banged against my leg.

"I'm tired of Sam hurting me and my stuff," Meike cried and buried her face in the front of my sweater.

I glared at Sam. I kept my voice firm without shouting. "Go to your room. Now. I'll be up shortly. Be prepared to talk."

"No. It's 10:30. I don't want to talk anymore tonight." He shimmied out of the chair, stomped to the main-floor bathroom, slammed the door and locked it.

"We're going upstairs to get ready for bed," I said through the door. "I'll meet you up there." We left him to sulk.

Thirty minutes passed while Meike and I brushed through her hair, hung up her dress, and with Odie on the bed next to her, read a chapter from *Grandma's Attic.* I went downstairs and knocked lightly on the bathroom door.

"You going to stay in there all night?" I heard a low grumble, indiscernible. I waited at the door. "Want a blanket?" No answer. After a moment, I tried again. "Come out, Sam. Get yourself to bed. Odie will wonder where you are."

The locked clicked as the doorknob turned. I backed away a few steps and Sam entered the hallway. He cast a quick, dirty look my way and, without another word, headed upstairs.

I considered emptying the dishwasher so Sam would hear it and know I wasn't closing in on him. Instead, I listened at the bottom of the stairway. Quite likely, Meike's door remained only slightly ajar as I'd left it. No words passed between them. Soon, I heard Sam rummaging in his closet. He had gone to his room.

I went up to brush my teeth.

His door was open and Sam stood, still dressed, with his back to me, searching through a dresser drawer. Clearing my throat first as a heads-up, I entered his room. He turned and eyed me for a moment. I searched his distraught face and yearned to throw my arms around him, soothe his forehead, rock him until his fever broke.

He stepped in my direction and I moved to meet him.

"Get out!"

I stopped, dropped my arms to my side. "Sam," I said, pleading.

He raised both hands and pushed me on the shoulders. For a second, I swayed and stumbled backward. Straightening, I stood and met his challenging glare.

"Very well," I said quietly. I left the room, carefully pulling the door nearly closed.

I heard what must have been a kick, the sound of wood cracking as the door slammed shut. Odie barked. Sam's room went quiet.

Gathering my thoughts in the hallway, I heard a weak call. "Mom?"

Meike sat up in her bed, clutching her *koosie*, one arm around Odie. I went in, kissed her head, smoothed her hair. "It's okay," I said when she began to whimper.

"I'm scared."

"I know. Do you want to sleep in my bed? It'll be all right."

We crossed the hall, Meike holding her *koosie* against her face. She put her thumb in her mouth but immediately yanked it out again. I drew the spread to the foot of the queen-sized bed and held the sheet and blanket open while Meike climbed in. She patted the blanket and Odie jumped on and curled next to her.

I changed into pajamas, slipped on my robe, and got to brushing my teeth. When finished, I kissed Meike goodnight, entered the hallway and tapped on Sam's door. His light glowed under the door but he didn't answer. I opened the door.

"I'm coming in."

The room felt overly warm. Stretched over the bed, Sam lay on his stomach, face buried in the pillow. I stood there next to the bed and then knelt.

"Sam?" I asked quietly.

He answered, the word muffled in the pillow. "What."

Encouraged he had spoken at all, I took a long breath and held it for a moment choosing my words carefully.

"We expected you to go to the recital. You knew that . . . . Meike's feelings are hurt." Again, I paused, thinking what to say next. "This is serious. Hitting and hurting your sister. Pushing me. You deliberately disobey." My voice softened. "Sam." Tears welled in my eyes. "This isn't like you."

He turned on his side, facing the wall. I reached for my son, but hesitated, pulling away before touching him. A tremor in his shoulders was soon evident as he allowed sobs to escape. I rested my hand on his back.

"There's a hole in the door," he choked out.

"I saw that." I held my tongue.

He kept his face to the wall. "I'm sorry."

He couldn't see my tears and I let them run. "Okay. I know."

In slow motion, I moved my hand back and forth, two or three inches at a time, and slowly his sobs loosened and diminished. A convulsive sigh escaped him.

"Go to sleep, hon," I whispered, moving my hand gently across his back. If it took hours, I'd continue the movement until he settled, until he fell asleep, while he slept. I am his mother. I could do this all night if need be.

"Here's what's serious, Sam," Dan Miller said. "You can't grow up thinking you can hit your sister or push your mother."

Sitting straight and attentive a few feet across from Miller, Sam nodded. On Sam's left, my chair faced Miller as well.

After Walt and I discussed the possibility, Sam agreed to a little outside guidance. "Not a teacher or a minister," I had told Sam. "Not the guy you and Meike talked with before. Someone private. A professional—he counsels teenagers for a living. He has a degree in counseling. Teaches children about anger and what to do with it. Like a coach. You can talk to him as much as you want and there are laws that protect your privacy. Sometimes, we'll be meeting with you and him. He'll be like a referee."

Miller's office was small, yet without a cramped feel. His bicycle leaned on its kickstand in the corner. Walls painted a light yellow-gold were left bare except for a framed, large colored photograph of Tiger Stadium with a shelf below it, displaying Jim Abbott's autograph on a baseball and a navy blue cap with a white embroidered *D*.

Dressed in blue jeans and a R.E.M. t-shirt, Miller came off unintimidating. He sat with his fingers intertwined on his lap, palms up, thumbs out. "Your mom tells me you've been rather belligerent." His voice lacked accusation, came across as a statement, a plain fact, yet mellow and concerned. "Disobeying, throwing things, hitting, well . . . not your usual self." Miller paused and his brows creased. "Something is wrong."

Sam nodded, this time slowly, looking away afterward.

Miller set a foot on his knee, exposing a black high-top tennis shoe, and settled back in his seat. "Why question authority, Sam? Somehow you seem to have the idea you don't need your mom or need to listen to her."

I leaned back in my chair and crossed my legs, trying to imitate Miller's non-threatening appearance.

"I can't answer," Sam said.

A long pause followed, during part of which I looked Sam's way. He was watching me. I sent him a quick smile and we locked eyes for a moment. Perhaps conscious of Miller's observation, Sam faced him, gave him the once-over, glanced around the room a few times and then studied the floor.

"I guess I blame Mom."

His honesty struck hard. I said nothing.

"For the divorce?" Miller asked.

"Mmm-hmm," Sam said quietly.

The three of us stayed mute for a time, maybe a minute. I considered the courage it took Sam to speak so frankly and wondered if he was waiting for some kind of defense or explanation from me. I had no intention of offering either.

Sam spoke again. "Dad blames Mom and I do, too."

Miller nodded a few times. He framed his response with empathy. "Because you see the same things, or because Dad says?"

From my perspective, Miller delivered the question straight across the plate—in there for the strike—and Sam saw it. But there was no ump and no one called it. No competition here and we weren't counting.

"Have you ever had it, Sam," Miller asked, "when you're enjoying your lunch, drinking your milk, eating your sandwich, and the guy next to you says, 'This milk is sour.' You pick up the carton and sniff. Three minutes ago, the milk was fine. Or not? You take a careful swallow and pull a face. 'I ain't drinking this,' you say."

Sam tipped his head from one side to another.

"The power of suggestion is very strong."

"Yeah." He seemed to give this a good amount of consideration and Miller waited before going on.

"For example," Miller said. "I wonder why you have such a bad attitude when you go to the Lutheran Church with your mom. She says you're pretty hostile about it and wouldn't go on Easter, even though she told you a week in advance that was the plan and you promised to cooperate.

"I don't like it there," Sam told him.

"I'd like you to think about if your attitude might have to do with the time your dad threw the prayer book across the kitchen," Miller said. I winced, questioning his appropriateness, what's confidential and what isn't. I straightened my back, ready to speak up. Miller noticed and with his hand, signaled me to stop. "Hold on for a minute, Jane."

When it became obvious Sam wasn't going to comment, Miller addressed me. "The Lutheran thing, Jane. Is it compromise-able or a 'here is where it goes as I say?'"

"As I say."

"Good." Miller glanced out into the room. "You know, I've seen too many choices left to children. Too many wrong ones. Families end in chaos that way." He planted both feet on the floor and looked at Sam. "You don't get to override this one, Sam. I suggest you sit in church with your mom and sister—and not with your finger in your ear."

"Okay," Sam said, still quietly.

The three of us relaxed some, Sam and I each exhaling a short sigh. Miller placed a foot across his knee again and watched Sam eye the baseball. "Go ahead. You can pick it up."

Without hesitation, Sam stood and walked to the display. He placed the ball in his palm first, studying the signature, before grasping it between his fingers. My mind swirled to his fantastic pitches in Little League.

Sam returned the ball to its stand and returned to his seat.

Miller wrapped his hands around the bottom of his leg. "You know what else, Sam," he said, his tone like a man confiding in another man. "Your mom, she's slow to tell you and Meike things sometimes. I admire her for that. Just because she doesn't explain to you doesn't mean there isn't more to the story. What goes on between her and your dad might be adult stuff."

I felt like someone eavesdropping.

Miller released the hold and pressed his hands against his thighs. "Who's to blame may not matter, Sam—as long as you know you're not to blame. It's not so important who's at fault. What's important is that it's not your fault."

It appeared Sam needed to hear this. He lower his head and covered his face with both hands. Leaning forward, he rested his elbows on his knees. I saw his shoulders rise as he breathed deeply. He dropped his hands and blinking fast, looked at the ceiling. I watched him, my face set tight.

"Sometimes," Sam told Miller, "Dad will say stuff like, 'Don't tell your mom, but . . . '"

"Can you give me an example?"

"Like, 'Don't tell your mom 'cause she'll tell her lawyer, but I bought a motorhome.'"

"That's a huge secret for you to have to keep," Miller said.

Sam shrugged. "Or later, 'I don't want you to hate your mom or anything, but I sold the motorhome since your mom wouldn't sign for the house.'"

"Uh-huh," Miller said flatly. The look on my face told Miller I hadn't had a clue Walt bought a motorhome in the first place.

"Dad told me he tried and tried to work things out, but couldn't do it anymore and had to leave."

This isn't Walt's warped perception, I realized. This is lying. This is Walt's guilty conscience coming forward. This is when I want to tell Sam his father's a liar, when I want to say his father is a weak, intolerant coward. This is when I have to swallow the bile raising in my throat. This is when I look at Sam and only my tears speak.

Thirty-Six

Walt liked to watch *NBC Nightly News with Tom Brokaw* so I waited until just after seven to call the apartment.

"Hello?" Meike answered.

"Hi, Meike. It's Mom. How are you? How was school today?"

"Click," I heard her say.

Her cutting frankness isn't as hard to swallow if I pause to appreciate her wit. "Is that your way of saying you don't want to talk right now?"

"Click."

"All right. I need to talk with your dad. Will you put him on, please?"

I heard a murmur and some shuffling as she passed the phone to Walt.

"Ja?"

"Sam and I have an appointment with Miller this Thursday at 5 o'clock."

"You'll have to pick them up at Karl and Nancy's," Walt said. "The kids are staying there overnight. I'm going out of town."

"What do you mean, you're going out of town? Why aren't Sam and Meike staying here then?"

"I'm going with the guys to the basketball playoffs. I thought it would be nice for the kids to stay with their uncle and aunt."

"Walt, after last time you said you would ask me when you needed a sitter."

"I don't think so."

I stomped my foot on the kitchen linoleum. "You did," I insisted. "I was upset with you and asked you and you said you would."

"I never said that."

With a hard sigh, an attempt at patience, I kept my voice composed and said what I had to say. "You did. I know you did. You promised. Stop trying to coerce me. You got someone else to watch the kids, and that makes me angry."

"You should have thought of that a year or two ago."

In exactly one second, patience went to hell. "Oh my god!" I shrieked. "Goodbye."

I slammed the phone down and stared at it as if the wires themselves were guilty of twisting reality, and I had to hold myself back from tearing the thing off the wall and throwing it out the kitchen window. Then it rang.

"Mom?"

I struggled an answer out. "Hi, Sam."

"Got a joke for you."

"Okay."

"Why are gorillas' nostrils so big?"

"I don't know."

"So his finger fits when he picks his nose."

"Oh, Sam." I laughed a laugh that spewed like a faucet after the main waterline's turned back on. "That's the funniest gross joke I ever heard."

"Night, Mom."

"Night, Sam. I love you." I held the phone to my chest and caressed it for a moment before placing it gently on the receiver.

~

By the following day, I considered it might truly be healthy for Sam and Meike to spend the night at Karl and Nancy's, and though I didn't admit so to Walt, neither did I interfere any further.

Anticipating any awkwardness, I decided to avoid Karl and Nancy altogether that day. In the best interest of us all. I asked Sam if he would be waiting and watching for me at quarter to five. I had called Meike Wednesday night and wished her a good time. I knew full well when the time came, I'd have to deal with the sharp, shoving ache that rises when she's so close and I have to let her be.

The kids' aunt and uncle live only a few blocks away. As soon as I pulled into their driveway, Sam stepped outside and onto the sidewalk.

"You ready for this?" I asked as he fastened his seatbelt.

"Uh-huh, I guess," he said. "Does it have to take a whole hour though?"

"Maybe not." I slid into reverse and out onto the street. "We can play it by ear."

Instead of seeing us individually first like he did for our initial appointment, Dan Miller began the session with Sam and me jointly. He summarized our last discussion and asked Sam how things had gone for him Sunday at St. John's.

"It went okay," Sam said.

"Jane? Your version?"

"It was fine," I said. "Sam was dressed and ready on time and didn't give me any lip about it. He came along, no problem. Sat respectfully through the service. Wasn't mean to his sister."

"Good work, Sam," Miller said. He waited a moment. "You okay with that for now?"

Sam shrugged. "Sure."

"Jane? Any more about it today?"

"Well, actually, I am concerned. The problem is . . . I don't know . . ." I turned to my son, a twelve-year-old jumble of unassuming childhood, fresh adolescence and an awakening maturity he hadn't asked for.

"The whole thing last time, Sam . . . ." I said. "It seems like tattling when I told Dan about Dad throwing the prayer book."

"But I was there when he did it," Sam said immediately.

"Yes. But you don't feel like I betrayed you?"

"No," Sam said. "I brought it up before you came in the room."

Miller nodded and looked my way. "Better?"

I thought it over for a moment. "Better."

Steering the session back to Sam, Miller went on. "And Sam, you've had a week to chew on things. Any more you want to say about last time?"

Sam shifted in his chair and unzipped his windbreaker, as if stalling or, more likely, cautious. He cleared his throat and spoke to the carpet. "I think I hurt Mom's feelings."

The three of us sat with that momentarily until Miller made a suggestion. "You could ask her."

Sam nodded at Miller with a good-sport smile. Addressing me, his expression turned more bothersome. "Saying that I blame you," he looked away, his eyes traveling to the window. "I hurt your feelings."

"Sam, it was a relief. I was so relieved to hear what's troubling you, what's been on your mind."

He slowly turned my way again and I watched some of the apprehension on his face disappear.

"And your honesty," I said. "Being able to tell me. Thank you."

Miller studied both of us, held back comment and rested his foot on his knee while tightening the lace of his high-top tennis shoe. It seemed a good time to let our openness sink in, and we sat quietly awhile, until Miller brought us back around.

"When families are broken up," Miller said, "I often find the children are under an impression they need to protect their mother or their father." He bent forward slightly in Sam's direction and searched his face. "You know, Sam, that's difficult. Way too hard for any child or any teenager. It's not a good idea. And not expected of you. Remember that what goes on between Mom and Dad might be adult stuff."

We had used up forty minutes and I suggested that perhaps we should finish for the day. Miller agreed, but first reviewed the sour milk illustration he offered Sam the week before, suggesting that maybe Sam could just tell his father "Stop" whenever Sam thought Walt might be using those same tactics.

Sam agreed. "I'll try."

I didn't say so, but Miller's suggestion seemed beyond a twelve-year-old's maturity. Even Sam's.

As we stood to leave, we shook hands all around. I mentioned that Meike might eventually want to be included in one of Sam's appointments. We made no plan for her to attend next time, although Miller said the idea made sense. Sam acknowledged he actually look forward to her participation.

~

I believed in God. I had to.

The only way I could forgive myself—for slamming doors, yelling at Sam, the time I surprised him with a hard slap across his sassy mouth, the time I slapped Meike across the face in her room last fall—the only way was to have God forgive me. I didn't know for sure if Sam and Meike forgave me. Maybe they eventually would. I don't take it lightly. And I believe that God verified his forgiveness when I took communion offered at St. John's on Sunday.

Besides, I was a theology major. Not just earning credits for learning all that history, all those heresies and reforms, all those articles, creeds and confessions, so many systematics I already knew. But also making certain what I believed made sense.

It had to.

Even more important, if God is that than which nothing greater can be conceived, he is able to care for Sam and Meike when I wasn't allowed. I worried about my children when they were away, but I didn't go totally crazy, not completely nuts.

I believed in God. I had to.

~

A note I added one day to Richard's list grew from the short "Walt stole a weekend" into an extra-long paragraph. Walt had closed on the house he was buying and earlier asked Meike and Sam if they wanted to join in the moving adventure on Friday. They both wanted to help. Both wanted to spend those first days with their dad in that damn new house.

Putting up a barricade would look heartless on my part. Swapping a weekend now and then was understandable, and Walt and I would need to learn to cooperate on such matters. But I resented his talking to the kids beforehand, his assumptions, his audacity in general. Drawing a star in the margin, I scribbled under the paragraph "also example of why joint custody isn't pursued" and underlined the note several times.

On Saturday morning during my second cup of coffee, I heard Walt's diesel truck outside. I went to the window and watched Walt back the pickup into the driveway next door. He cut the engine and Meike and Sam jumped out. With Odie on the leash, they hustled across the lawn while I met them at the door and held it open.

"This is a nice surprise," I said. A morning frost was vanishing in the April sun and the kids had switched out their winter coats for sweatshirts. I tugged the lace and drew Meike's hood back, running my fingers through her hair. They caught in her tangles as we hugged.

"Dad's picking up some shelves from Mrs. Lynch," Sam said, fidgeting with Odie's leash. "For the laundry room."

Meike pulled away and looked up at me, her eyes joyful as an Easter morning. "We slept at the new house."

"Well, I'll be. How'd it go?"

"You need to come see inside, Mom," she said. "The carpet's brand new and Mrs. Lynch did wallpaper."

"She did?"

"Dad had her pick it out. And a bed and dresser and desk and night stand for me."

"Wow."

"She can't hang the curtains 'til next week, but meanwhile, there's shades."

I stepped back, nodding slowly. "I see."

"I got the bunk beds from the cottage and the old desk," Sam said, "but Dad's buying me a new computer game." He held the bottom front of his sweatshirt with one hand and with the other, ran the zipper up and down. "We can't stay. Dad said to just say hi."

"When can you come see, Mom?"

I bent and squatted next to Odie, my head down, arm around his middle. I buried my face and resentment in his soft, curly fur for now.

"Sorry, Mom," Sam said.

I lifted my head. "I know," I said with a crooked smile. "I know."

He stopped toying with his sweatshirt and said with a sad, worried face. "And I'm sorry we're taking Odie."

I stood up and put my hands on Sam's shoulders, smoothing the navy-blue fleece as if rubbing away his needless feelings of guilt. He pressed against me and we squeezed each other for a moment. Meike nudged her way under my elbow and Odie began to bark. "It'll be okay," I told them. "It's okay."

We stepped apart at the sound of the pickup's engine through the screen door.

"How about both of you give me a tour when I pick Meike up for violin Monday night?" I asked while searching Meike's face. If the suggestion disappointed her, I would find a way to take the dreaded expedition earlier, tough it out sooner rather than later. "I'll come a few minutes early. Okay, Sam?"

"Can you bring me a different pillow?" Meike asked with innocence that could melt a puddingstone. "The one Mrs. Lynch bought is mushy."

~

Late that afternoon, as daylight faded, I backed the Town Car out of the driveway on my way to dinner at Gerrit's. Apparently, I interrupted a conversation out on the sidewalk between Judy Lynch, Loraine, and Loraine's husband. The three of them turned and waved as I shifted out of reverse and on to Sun Valley Court. I acknowledged the greeting, fanning my hand back and forth a few times without lowering the window, without shooting Judy the finger.

I was her next door neighbor, had to look at her nearly daily. I couldn't think of a worse affront than helping Walt decorate the yellow house. It implied a certain *affinity.* I drove to Gerrit's wondering what pitiful tales Walt told to trigger Judy's cruel insensitivity and how Walt could continue to deceive what I now considered this whole sucking community.

When I brought up the new house with Jennings in our session the next week, he shook his head. "Walt doesn't know the meaning of 'wait.'"

I sat fuming, my arms folded tightly against me. "My next door neighbor wallpapered Meike's room, bought her new furniture, painted the whole damn place." My eyes darted sideways. "Bitch."

"I can see that makes you angry."

I rolled my eyes at Jennings and turned toward the window and the garden below. The daffodils had opened since last week, and tulips were sprouting again in scattered clumps that Dorothy had thoughtfully placed.

I didn't doubt the wisdom of having a professional monitor my bipolar, or of giving an account to Jennings on the lithium and Wellbutrin prescribed me. Jennings said he didn't underestimate that how I appeared to be doing was important to the custody decision, yet with over ten years between episodes, he thought I didn't need to sweat the bipolar issue much.

"And your concern of an episode recurring," he said, "also shows it's not likely."

For those reasons, I no longer considered Jennings an overseer as much as a counselor or confidant. Our sessions were a reality check in a way, but more important, my opportunity to speak without the leaden cloud that otherwise loomed. Without the impairing forecast that whatever I did or said could and would come raining down and held against me.

"The neighbor ladies pump Meike." I faced Jennings, my arms still wrapped in front of me. "Her leaders from girls' club at church, too. And I know some of the teachers set Sam up, dropping questions here and there." I smiled over Sam's prowess. He had finally told the teacher not to worry because he had a "real" counselor if he needed one.

"Everybody's probing," I told Jennings. "I get so fed up. Neighbors watching. Well, not Ruth. But people ask her, believe it or not."

Jennings nodded a few times. "So you feel like you live in a glass house."

I sighed, impatient. "You make it sound like paranoia or something. It really is the neighborhood's 'excessive weaving of lives too tightly.' I read that phrase somewhere."

Jennings moved his head very slightly back and forth a few times in slow motion and after that measly acknowledgment, we were both quiet for a minute or two.

"When is the trial, Jane?"

"Two weeks from tomorrow. I thought you knew that."

"You might say something about it."

"Yeah, well . . ." My eyes dropped and I studied my bouncing foot. When I swallow hurt, my throat thickens until the ache reaches my gut. When I swallow anger, the effect begins in the stomach and stretches up into my esophagus, leaking what feels like acid rain in my throat.

I swallowed hard and looked back at Jennings.

"You've been to the court before, right?" he asked. "You know what the room looks like?"

"Twice. The times we met with Judge Holton."

"So, what concerns you most about the trial?" Jennings asked, sitting back in his chair as if giving me all the time in the world to respond. Yet, sitting here in the least vulnerable place I could think of other than my mother and father's kitchen, I found it difficult to sort through all my feelings and misgivings.

There are more yellow daffodils than white, I noticed. There'll be more red tulips than yellow.

"Don't filter. Start with anything."

I rummaged through my thoughts, the garden still in view. If I remembered right, those hyacinths are purple, not pink.

"Walt has made such a big issue of the bipolar thing," I said. "Even before he moved out, if you remember. Whenever he didn't like something, when we'd disagree, he would question my judgment. Try to convince me I had things out of perspective. Time and time again. Over and over. All that kind of fricking shit." I looked at Jennings.

"It's called gas-lighting."

"Yeah." My arms loosened and my hands relaxed. "And it seems he's convinced everyone else. When, really, the whole thing is about his intolerance."

"Walt makes bipolar the issue," Jennings said. "Convenient, yes, but actually reinforces his intolerance."

I hadn't expected such quick affirmation and I choked up.

"Thank you," I whispered.

Even during our silences, the unbroken attention Jennings gives can still make me uncomfortable and I had to turn away again and gather myself.

"I've been reading," I said after a time, "that families where children only experience harmony aren't so very healthy. They grow into adults shocked at confrontation. Afraid of conflict."

"This concerns you."

"Because I have this reputation of shouting. But so? That's what I'm used to. That's what we did. I just want to know, why is yelling worse than sulking? Or moping. Or turning on the television instead."

"Are you still feeling guilty about the slapping?"

"I suppose some. Sure." I crouched a bit in my chair. "I slam cupboard doors, too." I sat up again and shrugged. "Big deal. But stuff gets taken out of context, you know?"

Jennings nodded.

"When the judge interviewed the kids, Sam said, 'Mom shouts a lot. Dad is easier to get along with.' But in the PCS report, Meike says, 'Dad yells more.'" I leaned against the back of my chair and slouched. "Walt does his version and counters this or that—because I won't tell."

"Jane," Jennings paused, folded his hands and placed them firmly on his lap as if in conclusion. "You are to be commended on not backbiting him to Sam and Meike."

I answered with a dubious smile. "Well, I hardly have the stomach for it anymore."

"I have a recommendation," he said. "Don't beat yourself up. Sam and Meike have a good foundation. They're good kids. They have two good parents."

"Two good parents? I don't think so."

Thirty-Seven

"They're not here, Sam."

"But I need them for the game this morning."

"Hang on a minute; I'll look in your room." I set the phone on the counter, ran upstairs, and checked his dresser and closet for the gray sweats. I picked up the extension in my room. "No luck, hon. But your caps are all hanging on the pegs. Braves, Tigers, Little League."

"Will you bring the right one, the Little League one, Mom?"

"Got it. See you about quarter to."

When I arrived at the township park, each of the four diamonds was occupied with teams alternating warm-ups. From the gravel lot, I spotted construction yellow t-shirts, Sam's team. I crossed onto the grass carrying my plaid car blanket. Meike ran from the direction of the playground to meet me. Stacy followed her, not far behind.

"I'm sitting with you when the game starts," Meike said as we hugged. Then they skipped off toward their friends jumping rope on the tennis court.

Near the chain-link fence behind the catcher's box, Walt stood with a few other dads, his hands pocketed in a navy windbreaker bearing the cement-company logo. I ignored him and headed in the direction of the first base line where Sam had gathered with his teammates. Seeing me, he jogged over. Like the other players, he wore a long-sleeved sweatshirt under the yellow t-shirt. And he had on his lost gray sweatpants.

Grinning, Sam planted the cap I brought on his head and pulled it down to shield his eyes. "Thanks."

I mouthed the words, "Kick butt." His grin stretched wider and with a yelp, he raised his mitt in the air and jogged back to his teammates.

Ruth patted the spot next to her in the second row. I dropped my blanket there, still folded, and sat on it.

"Hi," I said quietly.

"Good morning."

I turned my head to the far left and with a nod, acknowledged the only other folks already seated. Typically, attendance on Saturday mornings was sparse until the third inning. The aluminum bleachers faced east and I lifted my face toward the sun and closed my eyes. Stretching out my legs, I rested my feet on the vacant bench in front of us.

"One of these days I'm going to remember a thermos of coffee," Ruth said.

Soon, the girls trotted over. I reached and grabbed the bottom of Meike's coat, pulling her toward me. She fell on my lap giggling. When I let go, she squirmed off and wiggled in between Stacy and me on the bleacher.

The end of the fifth inning. Yellow ahead 10 to 3. The girls meandered back to the playground.

"Richard's going to call you next week. Go over some of the questions he'll ask."

"Good," Ruth said. "I was hoping so." Although she leaned closer, we both kept watch on the game and our sons. "Who else do you have? Will Walt's partner speak up?"

"My friend, Denise, and my sister-in-law, Jerry's wife. Michael won't do it, Richard says. Wants to stay out of the whole thing."

I felt her glance. "Walt's been telling people he's ninety-five percent sure he'll win," she said.

My eyes stayed pinned on the playing field. "He's such an asshole."

~

A mom wakes and gets up before her children, even when they're not under the same roof. When the phone rang at 7:20 Monday morning, I'd been up for an hour.

"Mom," Sam said. "I need clean blue jeans and a sweatshirt."

I lay the phone on the counter, checked his room and reported on the extension. "There are two sweatshirts here. No jeans."

No sobbing, no anger, no demand in Sam's tone. Just a slow, squashed voice. "All my jeans and shirts are in the wash pile." He was crushed.

On the way, I imagined Walt accusing me of spoiling the kids, not letting Sam grow up. He's twelve years old, I would remind Walt. He has other things on his mind. Heck, I'll drive all the way to Sears and Roebuck this morning for a pair of jeans if that's what he needs.

Sam answered the door in a pair of blue jeans and a t-shirt. Before I even asked, he explained. "I found these in the laundry basket." He rubbed his hand up and down the seam along one leg.

"They look fine," I said inside the entryway, handing him the sweatshirts. Walt was nowhere to be seen.

"Mom!" Meike called. She waved her bright orange t-shirt in front of me. The one with "Young Authors" written in bold white letters across the front. "You can wear it for school tomorrow."

The next day, I did indeed wear Meike's favorite t-shirt to classes and still had it on when Sam and Meike came home from school. "Shall I wear it tonight to the game?" I asked.

"No," Meike said. "I want to."

We had an early supper of macaroni and cheese and arrived at the ballpark a few minutes before six under a dark, threatening sky. Walt needed to attend his Builder's Association meeting and wasn't coming.

During the second inning, Sam hit a stand-up double. He slid in to home plate when Matt drove a hard liner over the shortstop and the centerfielder fumbled. Distant thunder could be heard by then and before the end of the third, the thunder rolled closer. Someone said a tornado watch had been issued. The ump called the game.

Pea-sized hail pinged the windshield as we drove in the pouring rain, lightning all around. Not more than five minutes after we arrived home, the siren sounded a tornado warning. Sam gathered Odie up and followed Meike to the basement. I bothered to grab a couple extra blankets first and, in the basement, found the portable radio under the bar and the flashlight in the closet of the half-bath.

Kent County plus a dozen more counties surrounding us ribboned across the bottom of the television screen. Our local meteorologist stood at his map, pointing a few miles northwest of the city where a funnel cloud had been sighted. He explained the potential of others.

"I'm scared." Meike cuddled near me on the couch.

"It's not really that close," I said just as a sudden deafening thunderclap split the air. Odie barked and crawled under Sam's chair.

Within half an hour, the meteorologist announced an all clear, although the watch remained in effect until midnight. We stayed put for *Home Improvement.* Meike wanted curlers, so I rolled her hair while we watched.

"I want to sleep down here tonight," she said when the program finished.

"Let's," Sam said, nodding quickly several times. He looked at me, eyebrows raised.

I shook my head. "There's school tomorrow."

"So what?" he asked, still eager.

I thought of how few times he agreed with his sister lately. "All right. But lights out at nine-thirty. No screwing around."

The storm moved on, thunder died away. Sam phoned Walt's place but didn't get an answer. He let Odie outside while I brought pajamas, toothbrushes and the pillows down. We crawled into our sleeping bags. Nine-thirty-five.

I love the Big Ben, ticking loudly, rhythm of a lullaby. We were all four asleep before his large fluorescent hands reached ten.

~

The alarm jangled from the bar, and I thought the clock would dance across the counter like in Saturday morning cartoons. I could see daylight through the egress windows. Bright daylight.

Sam and Meike had wanted their bikes over at Walt's, so that morning after breakfast, they rode them over. Several puddles stood in the curbs like miniature fishponds, and the sidewalks on Sun Valley Court were still dark with moisture. I followed them in the Town Car as they pedaled to the yellow house.

Walt had left for work earlier but Sam and Meike each had a key. We put the bikes in the garage. After adding a math worksheet to his backpack, Sam brought his baritone to the car and we drove to the middle school, arriving half-an-hour early.

"That's okay," Sam said. "I'll go in and finish my worksheet."

At the elementary school a few minutes later, Meike and I waited together in the parking lot. Clear sky. Sun warm through the glass. I cracked the window a couple inches.

"Can you find my shorts, Mom?"

I smiled at her optimism. "I know right where they are."

Meike yawned. Mr. Walters, the music teacher, parked his car and we waved as he walked by.

"Your hair turned out cool." I reached over and wrapped a section behind her ear.

"I want to get it cut. Dad'll take me to Mrs. DeLeuwe."

I didn't respond, and for a moment we sat quietly until I asked, "You doing okay living with your dad?"

Meike opened her backpack. She pulled a banana out of her lunch bag, inspected it and put it back inside. "I'm doing okay. If I would change, I'll let you know." She spoke in a matter-of-fact way. "I know about next Thursday, Mom."

"Yeah. That'll be weird, huh?"

"I would like to talk to the judge again." She looked at me and I saw sadness, so much sadness in her face. "I want to tell him I don't want to say."

"Don't want to say what?"

"Who to live with. I don't . . . " Her voice broke. "I don't want to hurt anybody's feelings."

"Meike." I held out my hand and she took it. "Please don't worry." I brought her hand to my face and placed it on my cheek. The schoolbus pulled in and Meike turned away from the window. My throat felt like it held an entire peeled banana.

"You can love both of us, you know," I said.

She blinked, saying nothing.

I lifted her chin and tapped the end of her nose. "You can love both of us at the same time."

It took a minute before she smiled. "Will you walk me to my room?"

She let me hold her hand through the hallway.

"We have Jennings' deposition. If we submit Groenholt's, they'll submit Riley's."

"Even though Walt agreed to have Groenholt as a third party?"

In his tall leather chair, the tenth-story window behind him, Richard explained. "Walt agreed on his attorney's recommendation. They thought Groenholt would affirm Walt."

"So, good for us."

"Yes. And no. Of Groenholt's three observations, two of them explicitly favor us. 'Who is the other woman?' and 'Regarding parenting, Walt's personality loses.'" Richard read the document upside down, pointing the words to me with his slender ballpoint. "But the third observation, 'Why not joint custody?' leans strongly for Walt."

"Strongly?"

Richard nodded, his thick eyebrows furrowed. "Unfortunately. Possibly trumps the other two for more than one reason."

"Such as?"

"Sam and Meike currently live with Walt."

"So that Walt could have a turn."

"Originally. But we do need to be careful. Judge Holton loves that the father is involved. Which so seldom happens." Placing his pen on the legal pad, Richard counted two fingers and gripped them with his opposite hand. "Joint custody is certainly the trend." He added a third finger. "Judges look for cooperation. Your hesitation on joint custody gives Walt an advantage."

"But joint custody is not in Sam and Meike's best interest." I knew I had already said this to Richard, but I continued. "Joint custody can cause more harm than good. Research shows no clear conclusions and no guarantee it's in the best interest of the children." I knew Richard knew this. I nudged my hair behind my ears. "I see it with Sam and Meike, the continual flux . . . 'Oh, time to go to Dad's. Oh, time to go to Mom's. Where's my tennis shoes? Where's my jeans?' No matter how many pairs they're at the wrong place at the wrong time." Only a quick breath slowed me. "Then there's Father Superior. Walt's authority issue won't ever change. Think about it. He's got thirteen employees he's used to bossing around."

Richard jotted a note and looked back to me. "We both know what you're saying is true. But your . . . near insistent opposition to joint custody . . . you can't let that come through." Again, he paused. "Jane, the idea is for you to look cooperative."

I threw even more challenge into my voice. "Yet, somehow, Judge Holton needs to know Walt lied in that PCS report. He said *I* wouldn't agree to joint custody, after we had both talked about it and we both agreed we didn't want it. It would be too difficult and wouldn't work for us."

After a nod, Richard pulled his mouth straight, his neck tightening. "But Walt does have the health advantage."

"What if I had diabetes instead? Would they worry about that? Screw cooperation."

And then, whatever thin lines exist between cooperation and stubbornness didn't matter to me anymore. Maybe because of the proficient office here in general. Maybe the suit and tie, or the gold wristwatch. Or the violin lessons. Or the old neighborhood. I didn't know.

Whatever the reason, I dared to ask. "After a husband outright rejects his wife, can she really be expected to cooperate?"

Richard blinked slowly, his hands folded on the top of the mahogany desk.

He spoke slowly as well. "I need to know that you are mindful of all elements pertaining to this case." Pushing his chair a few inches away from the desk, he cleared his throat. "That being said . . . the PCS report is only a recommendation. Also, remember, the report does not say 'bad'—this is Walt's word—it says 'equal.' Therefore they used only the children's preference. I can argue that the preference is swayed. Not just the material bribery, but what's said to the kids or in front of the kids or in Walt's network, which includes the community."

"I told Riley off three times. And that fatso accused me of stashing records in my purse."

"Riley's backed off on that. Riley hinted to something like Walt just wants to be sure the kids are okay living with you."

"Pffft. What an insult. I doubt that motivation ever existed. Walt wants to save face. His conscience wants relief."

"Hofstra recognizes Riley's bias." He reached for the document. "Nevertheless, their objection claiming Groenholt's deposition 'unqualified.'"

"As if Walt is," I sneered.

Richard nodded with a tight smile. "I hear you."

My eyes wandered across the high plastered ceiling, the brass chandelier. The fixture reflected on the window glass. I released a sigh and gave my full attention back to Richard.

He laid the document on the desk and folded his large hands on top of it, his face turned earnest. "If we submit Jennings' and Groenholt's depositions, they will submit Riley's."

My mind went to the last time I met with Richard. His considerate manner when he asked, "So, tell me about your mom." His tactful questioning. "Tell me about the adoption agency." His calming patience that pumped up my confidence. All of which helped me decide here, today.

"I say we go for it."

He set the document aside. "Agreed." He placed the legal pad in front of him. "All right. Thursday will finalize the arguments. Meaning, that will be that. But Judge Holton may not decide, likely will not decide, on the spot."

I acknowledged the information by nodding, my mouth pulled to one side.

Checking his wristwatch, Richard took the pen and smiled like he was up for the battle. "Okay. Any surprises?"

"No," I laughed. "No surprises." I took my purse from the arm of the chair, dug around inside it and produced a scrap of paper. "More things for the list. Don't know if they're relevant."

"I'll sort them out."

"Walt missed an appointment for Sam with Miller. When I called the kids after school, which I often do, I learned Walt rescheduled the same day and Meike was home alone for almost two hours." I read while Richard took notes. "Let's see. Kids are gaining weight. Sam's twitch has returned. Walt complains Meike still carries her *koosie* around."

"Her what?"

"*Koosie denken.* It's like a security blanket.

"Another thing. Walt bragged to me Sam never cries around him. And, oh yeah, the school report." I slipped the note into my sweater pocket. "Meike's reading is down. Her teacher says Meike's just not quite as much into it. Her teacher's concerned she holds back too much, is closed, plays tough." Richard looked up. "The students write journals in fourth grade. Ugh. Poor Meike. People do prod her for information. So, well, for what it's worth."

I hesitated before speaking again, resting the purse strap on my shoulder. "Richard. Some of the stuff I've told you, like how Walt tells the kids I'm no fun, or that he prefaces things with 'I don't want you to hate your mom or anything but . . .' that kind of stuff . . . . I feel I've betrayed Sam telling you. And besides, if you mention it in court, what if Sam gets in trouble with Walt for talking?"

"I respect your concern. I'll be very careful."

We stood. Shook hands.

"I'll phone you on Wednesday," Richard said before opening the door and escorting me to the lobby. "If anything comes up in the meanwhile, let me know."

~

Having spent a good hour with Dutch exercises that Saturday afternoon and another two and a half hours with Edmund Spencer's "The Fairie Queen" in the evening, I put Butch Thompson playing Jelly Roll Morton on the stereo. I poured myself a glass of Cabernet Franc from a half-empty bottle Gerrit and Laura left behind the night before.

Soon, I found myself rehashing the advice from Richard.

I imagined the husband I once loved and since chose not to, standing courteous at my door, running a hand over his wiry hair. That unassuming gesture I once held so fondly. For a moment, I envisioned cooperation. Not any old cooperation, not all cooperation, not toward any form of marital reconciliation since that was way too late, but at least toward peace-making.

Then I remembered Meike's doleful cast, the twitch of Sam's face, and I welcomed my anger and its utility, calling a spade a spade, the offender a criminal, the animal a beast.

You hurt my children, I'll claw your face.

With new determination, I picked up my glass and literally danced in the den to the "Shreveport Stomps." I put on Mussorgsky's *Pictures at an Exhibition,* which I advanced to "The Gates of Kiev." When the piece finished, I shut the player off and eyed the piano. A collection of Franz Schubert's compositions rested open to Impromptu in E-flat Major.

I practiced several measures of the right hand before adding the treble clef. The piece begins with a lively scale-based melody set in E-flat Major. The middle section, *sempre legato*— an altogether smooth, even style with no breaks between notes—moves to E-flat Minor, naturally darker but still lyrical. The E-flat Major beginning is repeated and again, the ascending scale leads to E-flat Minor, the key in which the work ends.

It is one of few pieces that begin in a major key and end in the parallel minor.

~

The week unfolded in a zigzag. Richard called Monday morning to inform me the judge had bumped the trial from Thursday to Friday. Another county court issue took priority.

On Tuesday, Walt's attorney contacted Richard to inquire if we might yet settle without the trial.

"What's he proposing?" I asked when Richard phoned.

"Only that you grant Walt custody."

"Is this protocol? Etiquette?"

"No. No. I suppose it could be seen as a courtesy. Doubtful, though." With a short titter, Richard offered his version. "I think they're worried."

A few hours later, Walt called me.

"Can we somehow avoid Friday?" he asked.

Can you somehow rewind the last three years? I pulled my chair away from the kitchen table and took a seat. "If you give up this absurd custody idea of yours."

"Jane, I'm going to win. I've got the PCS report—"

"We're talking about our children, not some proof for a scoring system." I let my fist drop to the table audibly. I stood and paced as far as the phone cord would allow. "After all is said and done, Walt, you only got 'a slight nod.'"

". . . You stay there alone in that house . . . Don't go to church half the time—"

"Funny what a good mom I was while you were out making your million."

"That was for you and the kids."

"No. That was for you."

I heard him take in and let out a long breath.

"The kids want to be here," he said.

"I see you bought Sam new baseball shoes."

"The judge will want to keep things as they are. He'll go with preference."

"I'm going by what should be, not by what I think the judge might say."

He hung up on me. Anger breeds so much easier when you're not the one calling the shots, a reality Walt may have just undergone for the first time.

A little past noon on Wednesday, Richard phoned with a question.

"Will your parents be in the courtroom on Friday?"

"Yes. My sisters are picking them up. Gerrit and Laura will be there, too. And of course, Lynn. That's okay, isn't it?"

"Walt wants your father to testify."

"What the *hell* is he talking about?"

"I told Hofstra no way. But Walt claims he had a conversation with your father back before Walt filed for divorce. Claims your father said divorce might be best."

"My father would never say that."

"Walt told Hofstra your father said it's been hard . . . married to your mother."

"It's hard being married to my father, too. It's hard being married to anyone. But they would never do that. Get a divorce."

"It seems," Richard said, "Walt's getting desperate."

"You know my father and his type, Richard. He would never endorse divorce."

"That's what I thought. Thought I should warn you, just in case."

"Jesus," I said, my voice nearly a whisper. "My father's eighty-two years old. Can't they just let it be?"

"I'll see what I can do."

I threw on my running shoes. The way my morale see-sawed that week had nothing to do with bipolar. I left the house and ran, stride even, footfall, footfall, drumming up down, up down, for five and a half miles, without effort, without interruption, without stretching first.

Thirty-Eight

Gerrit and Laura suggested they pick me up Friday morning, but instead I asked them to meet me inside the courthouse. With the intent to hang on to my resolve and keep up my confidence, I thought any independence would help. And not knowing what to expect of the day or my response to it, I would likely want some privacy. So I rationalized, even though a good part of me felt scared to death and to some extent ashamed, like a little girl lost in a deep forest she was told never to enter in the first place.

I drove myself to the courthouse, parked, went through security and entered the lobby where Gerrit and Laura were already waiting for me.

"I need a bathroom," I said.

Laura went with me to find the Ladies. While we were gone, Marge and Betty arrived with my parents. I hugged my mother and father quickly. My sisters directed them to the folding chairs set along the wall on the east side of the lobby. The four of them sat, alert and quiet as church.

Gerrit wore a sport coat, white shirt and khakis, like my father but without a tie, and Laura, a navy business suit, sheer hosiery and pumps. I had dressed in a pastel floral print skirt that fell just below my knees. Meike called it my second grade teacher skirt. Choosing beige flats, an ecru blouse, soft and open at the collar paired with a light coral cardigan, I had aimed for a fresh, yet motherly look.

Jerry, Lynn and Denise joined us, and soon after, Ruth. I touched Ruth's hand for a few seconds. "Thanks for coming," I said in a hushed voice.

In the area to the right of the lobby entrance, Walt and his band were gathering, their voices less subdued than our side. With no intention of acknowledgment, I soon looked away after recognizing Karl and Nancy, Daryl and Lois from church, and Candice, Walt's receptionist.

With Gerrit next to me, we stood in a half-circle facing the windows that reached from floor to ceiling, offering a view to the sidewalk and street beyond. I kept my eye out for Richard.

"Peppermint?" Gerrit asked, gently nudging me with an elbow.

My hand surprisingly steady, I picked up the white disk from his open palm and put it in my mouth. I spotted Richard in a dark charcoal-grey suit trekking along the sidewalk perpendicular to us. He had one hand in the pocket of his suit jacket. With the other hand he pulled a small two-wheeled dolly. Two cardboard file boxes and a briefcase were stacked and strapped onto the cart.

"My gosh." I looked at Gerrit and stifled a nervous giggle.

Gerrit raised his brows with a slight snicker. "The guy means business, all right."

My father stood as Richard approached. We shook hands all around while I introduced everyone. I slipped a tissue into the pocket in the seam of my skirt and asked Laura to carry my purse for the day.

A city deputy opened the courtroom door and people made an orderly entrance. Escorting me, Richard held the gate as I crossed the bar into the well. I glanced at Walt and Hofstra, his attorney, already stationed at the Plaintiff's table, their backs toward us. With an outstretched hand, Richard indicated the table opposite. I took my place, straightened my skirt and, to steady myself, rested my arms on the table in front of us, Richard to my left.

As we waited for Judge Holton, my thoughts leapt back to over twenty years ago. Walt to one side, me to the other. Vows taken in front of a different official in a black robe. My father had escorted me then, past family and friends who were now seated behind us in the gallery instead of church pews.

"All rise."

If only this was an afternoon soap opera. If only this was Monday night Perry Mason. If only Judge Holton would immediately declare the trial over, already deciding in my favor. If only Walt would stand and announce the whole thing off—he had made a mistake.

Hofstra called Walt's receptionist, Candice, to the witness stand first.

After vouching for Walt's character, Candice stated she had nothing against the Defendant. She offered nothing of great importance other than her admiration for Walt consistently leaving work each day to meet the children after school.

Daryl and Lois, Walt's second and third witness, had known us for about ten years. Each spoke highly of Walt. Daryl owned a small business, something he and Walt had in common. Daryl admired Walt's reputation in the community, his work ethic and the success of his business.

"We're members of the same church," Lois said in her turn. "Our kids go to the same school, we had dinner together several times. Walt and the kids still come sometimes for supper."

Lois stated how impressive Walt's interaction with Sam and Meike is. "He cares deeply for them," she said, flushed, her voice quivering. "I can tell that the children are fond of their father." Her voice continued to quiver when she spoke and, for a second I felt bad for her. "Yes. Jane is a good mother. Very involved at school. President of Mothers' Club a few years ago," she volunteered. When she left the witness stand, Lois stared straight ahead, hard, her eyes fixed on the back of the courtroom. I had never seen her so obviously shaken. Somehow, I found that calming.

After a short recess, it was our turn. Richard called on Ruth. Last week Ruth admitted having butterflies just thinking about the trial. A few days ago, she had gone so far as to have her husband drive her the ten miles into town in order to get the route down, the parking lot chosen, the courthouse clear in her mind.

Richard guided her from point to point. Muscles in my neck and back began to loosen, hearing my neighbor hold forth under oath.

"Sam's my son's best friend. They're together nearly every day—eight years—at school, after school. Well, except now Sam is at Walt's." Her eyes shot poison lasers in Walt's direction. "My daughter is a year younger than Meike. We live three houses from each other."

Having established her unparalleled expertise given the close proximity of our lives, Ruth continued. "While other women chat on the phone, catch up on their housework, indulge in their arts and crafts, whatever, Janie pays attention to the kids. Turning the end of a jump rope. Perpetual catcher for cul-de-sac baseball." Ruth lifted her hand and flipped it over. "She's the Kool-Aid mom."

Richard let the statement suspend in the air several seconds before he steered her a trifle aside. "Some might call that hovering."

"No, no. *I* might hover. Janie doesn't hover."

He nodded and I sent mute praises to God.

"Janie doesn't interfere . . . or solve their problems . . . that sort of thing." Ruth allowed herself a smile. "I remember when the boys were in first grade. Janie had played the Beach Boys for them. *Endless Summer* all afternoon. Matt came home dancing and singing 'Little Deuce Coupe.' I have nothing against dancing," Ruth chuckled, "but we *just don't do that* at our house."

Ruth looked toward the ceiling for a moment, her expression thoughtful. "That's how Matt learned to play Crazy Eights, Rummy. No one else would have taught him that . . . . These days they have Monopoly championships when Sam's home."

A brief gap followed, the time it took Richard to take a few steps in the direction of the Plaintiff's table, turn and address Ruth once more. "Do you think Walt is a good father?"

"He thinks a lot of himself."

A pause. "Do you think Walt is a good father?"

"Sam and Meike are healthy, smart, good kids. That doesn't happen when the dad's working a lot, making a lot of money, running two or three businesses—unless Mom's doing double time."

Another pause. "Do you think Walt is a good father?" Richard kindly repeated.

Judge Holton couldn't notice Ruth roll her eyes, but everyone else in the courtroom could. "I understand there are worse."

Ruth stepped down from the witness stand with a look of satisfaction on her face. Catching her gaze, I smiled in appreciation. God, how could I thank her?

Richard pinched his earlobe, shuffled through a few papers on our table and called our next witness.

Our people are so much better at this than Walt's people, I thought, as Denise placed her hand on the Bible and took the oath.

Denise sounded like she had rehearsed. Herself a mother, she said. She spoke of my devotion to Sam and Meike. Loving. Nurturing. Caring. Not only a good mother, but surpassing most. "We go camping together with the kids every summer. You learn quite a bit about someone when your tents are pitched next to each other in the sand for a week." During the course of her testimony, Denise recalled our tenure, before the children were born, as live-in-house parents. "Janie was the stay-at-home mom for twelve special needs residents." Then she mentioned Sam and Meike's musical talent and my dedication to cultivate those abilities. "Something Walt doesn't seem to appreciate," she said. Denise even managed to slip in how I was to be commended for not disparaging Walt in front of the kids.

Every now and then, I stole a glance toward the Plaintiff table. For the most part, Hofstra blocked my view, although I had noticed Walt stir in his seat. Squirming, perhaps.

Almost three hours had passed since we started. Although Holton had given us a short recess I supposed most folks were shifting in their chairs, growing uncomfortable by now.

While Denise returned to the gallery, I heard my father cough and imagined my mother passing him a lozenge.

Once sworn in, Lynn answered the customary questions—name, age, occupation.

"Please tell the court your relationship to the defendant," Richard said.

"Janie is my sister-in-law, my husband's sister." In what seemed like the same breath, Lynn added, "And Janie is the designated legal guardian for our three boys."

"The sole legal guardian?"

"That's right. Just Janie."

"So, you trust Jane to be the responsible, caring substitute if something would happen to yourself and Jerry. Is that correct?"

"Absolutely."

At that point, Lynn volunteered she agreed with Ruth and Denise's testimony, although Richard hadn't asked. "Janie is a devoted mother," she stated. "First-rate. Very supportive of Sam and Meike."

His next question helped smooth out her eagerness. "Can you give an example?"

"Walt seems to have a hard time with negative feelings. With Janie, Meike and Sam are free to express emotions without worrying about consequences. They aren't afraid to be angry or cry when they're with Janie."

"And why is that, do you think?"

"Because Janie loves them unconditionally and Meike and Sam know that."

Her implication being there are strings attached to Walt's affection. I wished Lynn had somehow spelled that out.

"Do you think Walt's a good father?"

"I think Walt is angry because the doctor told Janie hospitalization wasn't necessary. Walt says the children have problems because they live with Janie, not because he moved out. A good father would take responsibility." She took a breath and added, "Then he had the nerve to want her out of the house."

Richard pulled his earlobe and cleared his throat. I caught him breaking into a smile. He quickly checked himself and the smile disappeared. "Thank you, Ms. Jansen. No further questions, your Honor."

Judge Holton made a show of checking his watch, holding out his arm and pulling the sleeve of his robe up nearly to his elbow. I leaned toward liking him. A hefty but not overweight late-middle-aged man with not much hair left on his head, he had a round face that held a soft rosy flush from cheek to jaw bone. He spoke with intelligence in the manner of one addressing others of intelligence. And though he allowed the kids to temporarily live with Walt, I nevertheless respected him.

Yet, I wondered what in the world he was thinking when, following Lynn's testimony, Holton adjourned the trial until Monday morning.

~

Meike and Sam were home with me for the weekend, diluting some of the agony in the postponement of the trial. Warm weather for the first of May drew us outside Friday after school. Meike put on her rollerblades and hooked Odie to the leash. He pulled her down the sidewalk, around the cul-de-sac, while I jogged along.

On Saturday morning, Sam and I came up with the idea to attend the minor league Whitecaps game later that afternoon.

"I don't want to go." Meike stomped her foot. "I want to play with Stacy."

"It's a beautiful day," I said. "A good day to spend at the ballpark. It'll be fun."

"Baseball is boring. I want to play with Stacy."

"I'm afraid you don't have a choice this time, Meike."

She continued to brood all through lunch. In the parking lot at the stadium, Meike lingered in the back seat of the Town Car, pouting.

"Come on. Come on," Sam said, standing on the pavement.

We found our seats, only a half a dozen rows from the infield. Enthusiasm from the crowd, the playful organ tune, a whiff of popcorn in the air, all seemed to contribute to the change in Meike's mood. Then the jumbo, yellow, feathery mascot jumped on the roof of the dugout not fifty feet from us and performed the chicken dance.

Including Sam, most of the fans joined in the ridiculous maneuvers and Meike began to giggle. We laughed out loud together. She leaned in, resting her arm on my leg, her hand clinging to my thigh, though only minutes ago she hated my guts.

I realized how my torture that weekend was likely nothing compared to Meike's and Sam's.

The game progressed. We watched and cheered and ate hot dogs and ice cream. I breathed deeply and soaked in the pleasant warming rays, as if the sun were a herald to summer and the time when the trial would long be over and the divorce settled and the children back home with me.

Thirty-Nine

On Monday morning, I left a brief message for each of my professors. "Absent today—trial extended." Final exams were less than two weeks away. Reviewing grammar and Dutch vocabulary on my own wouldn't be difficult for me, but I would miss the final lecture in Lit class.

Although I would be on the witness stand today, my anxiety was half of what it had been Friday. We started promptly at nine. City Deputy, Court Reporter, Judge Holton. The same friends and family supporting me, seated in the gallery behind us. Richard on my left.

Walt laid his hand on the Bible and swore to tell the truth, the whole truth, and nothing but the truth, "so help me, God."

Finishing the preliminaries, Sy Hofstra asked Walt, "How long have you and Jane been married?"

"Twenty years."

Twenty-one years and two months, to be exact. But I guessed Walt had stopped counting.

"And you have two children—Sam, your son, who is twelve years old, and your daughter, Meike."

Walt wore khaki pants and a knit burgundy-gold shirt. I would at least have put on a sports coat if I were a father under these circumstances. He exhibited his usual self-assurance, an easy posture nearly cocky, hands open on his lap, voice composed. "Yes. Meike will be eleven on July 7."

"Tell us about you and Jane becoming parents. You were working with an adoption agency at one point?"

"We tried to have a baby but after a few years learned we probably never could."

"So both you and Jane wanted to adopt a child?"

"That's right."

"And how did that go?"

"Well, it's a long process . . . ." Walt pulled a sad face. "There's a lot of waiting, and it was hard for her." He paused before adding, "Eventually, Jane had a nervous breakdown."

What the . . . do people even use that word anymore?

Way to go, Walt. Tell us more about how you don't know what you're talking about when it comes to me. Richard scribbled something on the legal pad in front of him.

"A nervous breakdown?"

"She was in the hospital for more than six weeks."

"I see." Hofstra cleared his throat and took a few steps to the side, as if making certain to include all of us while he spoke to Walt. "But there's a happy ending to the story."

"Jane came home on the weekends a couple of times, toward the end," Walt said. "They taught her relaxation skills. A month or so after her release, we learned she was pregnant."

Relaxation. Alleged neurosis. The hell. Never mind my failure to reveal intimate information I consider nobody's business. Never mind the test that indicated your low sperm count.

Why do I yet continue this cockeyed supposed duty to cover for my husband?

You shoot mostly blanks.

His attorney summarized. "The adoption was canceled, and Sam was born that winter?"

"That's right. February 18." A grin appeared on Walt's face, and a short staccato laugh followed. "I'll never forget. It was quite a day, that's for sure."

After a moment during which Hofstra turned and nodded slowly, his smile apparent to Judge Holton, Richard, and those seated in the gallery, he asked, "And Meike?"

"Born the next year," Walt said. "Another wonderful surprise."

"Your perfect family."

"Good way to put it."

Collecting what looked like about a half dozen papers from their table, Hofstra tapped them together in a neat pile, licked his finger, pulled out the bottom sheet and set it on top. He scanned it for a moment, the courtroom quietly waiting. "Yet, during, let's say the next few years, things became more troublesome?"

"I had started a small business . . . . Core drilling and cement-cutting using blades with diamond bits. One of only two in the area at the time. It grew quickly."

We had started a small business.

"You made a fairly decent living?" Hofstra asked. "Provided well for your family?"

"I would say so, yes. There were chances for us to travel. Vacations. Conferences. Conventions."

"You and Jane took advantage of these opportunities?"

"No. No we didn't. Jane doesn't fly."

Appearing to reflect, Hofstra waited before asking. "And they were too far to drive?"

"Usually. But the thing is, Jane didn't want to leave the kids."

"A sort of . . . unhealthy attachment?"

"Objection." Richard remained calmly seated as he stated, "The Plaintiff is not qualified to answer."

"Sustained."

Hofstra kept his eyes on the floor while rephrasing his question. "Do you know of any particular reason why Jane would not want to leave Sam and Meike for the night?"

"Not really. Just that she's overprotective."

Obvious speculation, I thought. My face flushed another ten degrees warmer. I swallowed the slam, my anger right then directed more toward Walt's attorney than Walt.

"Are there other reasons you consider Jane overprotective?"

I rolled my eyes, surprised Hofstra didn't just ask all of us in the room to say the word "overprotective" again just for effect.

"No riding bikes without a helmet. Umm . . . public bathrooms—a hang up with public bathrooms. Every single time, Jane makes Sam *promise* to wash his hands, like she's obsessed with germs or something."

Walt lifted his hand and rubbed his face like when he checked if he needed a shave. "The year Sam started kindergarten, on a trip to Florida with the kids, we rented a motel room for the night. Jane grew uncomfortable after the four of us took a walk on the beach for the sunset because a panhandler stopped us in front of the motel and asked where we were from. I told him Grand Rapids. After I gave him a few dollars, he walked on. Jane was angry with me. She said not only did I tell the panhandler where we lived, but worse, which motel was ours."

By quietly inhaling a few long breaths, I kept my body stationary.

Huh. He didn't even mention the tears on my face after I asked him on the way down if we could pull off the road instead of continuing on through the thick fog in the Smoky Mountains.

"I told her she was overreacting. Believe it or not," and here Walt gave a quiet, quick laugh. "Jane wanted to check out then and there, pack up everything and find a room in the next town. She worried the guy might break in and kidnap the kids or something, I don't know."

"Did you get another place that night?"

"No way. I refused. Jane was being paranoid. Turns out she actually made a long-distance call to her doctor before she agreed to stay."

Walt spoke as if that pretty much wrapped it up. His attorney, of course, knew better and invited him to continue the story.

"Things were okay for a few years. But Jane became less social, restless, uptight. She lost interest in the new house we were building. She wanted to go back to school. She wanted to join a different church. By that fall—that would have been '92—Jane was spending all her free time re-reading her old theology books, writing, playing the piano. She grew irritable easily and worried an awful lot."

"Anxious?" Hofstra asked.

I glanced at Richard, thinking he might object, and watched him scratch on his notepad instead.

"She'd cry over little things. One night, she got up at two in the morning, worried about the laundry."

I tilted my head toward the ceiling wanting to shout the difference between not sleeping because I'm doing the laundry or doing the laundry because I can't sleep.

"After that, I think she went a couple of days without any sleep at all. Finally, I talked her into calling her doctor."

"And that's when Jane went into the hospital again?"

"No. She didn't want to. So the doctor told Jane to stay in bed. Jane's girlfriend and my sister-in-law took turns coming in every day for over a week to stay with her and watch the kids after school. It was all very hard on us."

"And then Jane agreed to hospitalization?"

"Only one of those week-day out-patient programs where you come home every night. It's supposed to be six or eight weeks. She only did two."

I sat still while my heart pumped as if I had just performed military maneuvers.

Hofstra finished for now.

Richard stood, pushed in his chair, buttoned his suit jacket and began the cross-examination.

"When you applied for adoption, Walt," Richard began, "approximately how long, according to the agency, would it be before a baby would be placed in your home?"

"Two years," Walt answered.

"And how long had you been waiting when Jane was hospitalized?"

"Four years."

Richard let Walt's answer hang in the air for a moment and then continued. "Isn't it true that Jane volunteered to enter the hospital, but your solution was to take a vacation in the South instead?"

"It was just a suggestion."

"It was Jane's idea to be hospitalized, but you didn't want her to go. Is that correct?"

"I suppose."

Taking a few steps to the right of the witness stand, Richard stood in front of the judge's bench, between the American flag and the Michigan flag. He fumbled in one of his pockets and looked at Walt.

"As you said earlier, the pregnancy with Sam, his birth, and then when Meike was born—they were wonderful surprises. Your business and your life in general continued along pretty well," Richard said. "You enjoyed being a father?"

"I certainly did."

My attorney pulled his earlobe. "Did you ever get up during the middle of the night and attend to Sam or Meike?"

"Well, no. Jane nursed the kids."

Richard lifted his chin and nodded. "Let's see," he said. "Sam was eighteen months when Meike was born." He paused as if still forming his next question. "Did you change diapers?"

Walt perked up and answered, smiling with pride. "Oh, yes."

"You cared for both Sam and Meike while Jane went out running errands or . . . visiting a friend, let's say?"

"Sometimes."

"Sometimes?"

Walt shifted in his seat. "Not usually."

"Not usually," Richard repeated. "As a matter of fact, if Jane wanted to attend church on Sunday evening, for example, you would insist she leave only one child home with you and bring the other child to the church nursery. Isn't that correct?"

Telling Richard this information had entirely slipped my mind, and I silently cheered him for remembering.

"Well, Meike could get really colicky," Walt said.

Allowing the answer to rest at that, Richard waited momentarily. "Do you consider yourself a tolerant person, Walt?"

"Yes."

"Do you try to teach your children tolerance?"

"I do, yes."

"Do you know what *The Book of Common Prayer* is?"

"Yes."

"Could you tell us, please?"

"It's a Christian devotional book of some kind—not our church's or from our denomination, though."

"A tolerant person," Richard said. "And yet a month or so before you left the marital home, when you arrived late for dinner one night and found Jane reading with Sam and Meike at the table from *The Book of Common Prayer* for devotions, did you or did you not yank it from her hand and throw the prayer book across the room?"

"That's maybe an exaggeration."

"The prayer book crashed against the wall and landed on the floor. In front of the children. Which part is exaggerated?"

Walt said nothing.

"Which part is exaggerated?"

Walt shook his head just slightly several times.

Glancing toward the clerk, my attorney said, "Let the record show, 'Plaintiff shook his head.'"

As he approached the defense table, I thought Richard might just end the cross-examination then and there. He stopped at my left and again stood silent for a moment before turning around. He touched his necktie and faced Walt again.

"Several years before Sam and Meike were born, you and Jane lived in a group home as house parents for twelve mentally impaired adults. Is that correct?"

"Correct."

"About half way through that tenure, the two of you took a vacation. To Seattle, Washington, I believe."

"That's right," Walt answered.

"You drove all that way?"

Bracing himself with one arm, Walt leaned far to one side and took a deep breath. He crossed his legs and sat back again. "No. We flew, but Jane really hated the flight."

"Is it true that to celebrate your fifth wedding anniversary, Jane surprised you with an all-expenses-paid vacation?"

"Yes, that's true. She worked for a travel agency at the time."

"Hawaii."

Walt ran a hand over his wiry hair.

"Via what transportation?"

"We flew."

Richard hardly paused. "Where was the National Diamond Blade Cutters Convention in the fall of 1981?"

"I think it was . . . Las Vegas. Yes. Las Vegas."

"Did Jane fly to Las Vegas with you for the convention that year?"

I caught Richard's sarcastic tone, and all of us could see him raise his brow.

"Only one-way," Walt quickly replied. "She refused to get back on the plane. We had to take the Greyhound bus back. Three days on the bus."

Appearing to calculate, Richard's expression turned sober and his voice weighty. "That was November, 1981 . . . Jane was, what . . . six months pregnant with Sam at the time?"

Walt shrugged before answering. "Something like that."

Richard lingered briefly at the witness stand, observing Walt.

"No further questions, your Honor."

My attorney pulled back his chair, unbuttoned his suit jacket and sat down.

I could have kissed him.

~

Here's the distortion: Imagine having to defend taking a breath. Or that I am a woman. Or that I use two legs to walk, or that I put ice in my drinking water.

I am a mother. When anything threatens my children, intuition sharpens. Instincts peak. Claws flex.

I raised my hand to swear the oath and took my seat on the witness stand. I have never doubted that Sam and Meike need their father. It's important that Walt participates in their lives.

Walt might be ambitious, a hard worker, a faithful provider. But he knows little of nurture, or comfort, of tender caresses on a feverish forehead or all-night vigils. He knows nothing of lullabies or rocking chairs. He doesn't do music. He doesn't do tangles and snarls.

Only Richard kept me from pouncing.

My attorney addressed Walt's most petty aspersions first. In two sentences, I put the story of that first night in Florida into perspective. "The door to our room was outside on the first floor, direct access to the beach," I said. "The place was a dive and would give anyone the heebie-jeebies."

"And public restrooms?"

A short, audible sigh escaped me, and I sent Walt a challenging glare. "There is no issue with public bathrooms. The kids and I go camping for a week *in a tent, for crying out loud.*"

I took a less obvious breath, already struggling to bridle both tongue and tone in acquiescence to Richard's advice.

Given the weight Walt put on it and the likelihood judgment bent in his favor in that regard, of course we had to address my health.

Richard brought it up sooner rather than later, consistent with his wise strategy.

"Do you take your prescribed medication?" Richard asked forthrightly.

"Yes. I take 150 milligrams of Wellbutrin a day and the lowest therapeutic dose of lithium, with my doctor's permission." The record of Jennings' deposition had already been submitted to Judge Holton. "Doctor Thomas Jennings."

"The lowest therapeutic dose?"

I wrestled for the right words. "Doctor Jennings doesn't see the lithium as paramount. More as precautionary. I maintain a very low level so in the unlikely event more would be needed, lithium's effect kicks in more rapidly."

"Dr. Jennings—he's the same doctor that said you didn't need to be hospitalized?"

"Yes. He wrote it on the discharge slip." God bless him.

Richard lifted his chin and rubbed the side of his Adam's apple a few times. I glanced to the gallery and saw my father's solemn face attentive to Richard's every move. Gerrit caught my eye. He nodded once while flashing a closed smile.

As if amazed, Richard dropped his voice, enough for all to hear but just above a whisper. "Walt thought he knew better than Doctor Jennings?"

"Objection," Hofstra called immediately.

Richard lowered his head, and I saw the corners of his mouth curl up for a second or two. I suppressed my grin.

"Jane, I gather Walt wanted you to stay in the program?"

"Yes. He was disappointed Jennings didn't require it." I pushed my hair behind my ear. "I think Walt was angry and disappointed because the hospital proved unnecessary—there went his excuse for the divorce."

Richard shot a look to Judge Holton. He took a few steps sideways, standing between the Plaintiff's table and myself. Walt sat with his arms crossed firmly on his chest.

"Walt initiated the divorce proceedings," my attorney stated. "Did you want this divorce, Jane?"

"No."

"And now?"

"At first I thought things could be worked out," I answered. "But I was reminded time and again that Walt's idea of resolving issues is "Okay, you can have one more chance to do things my way."" I stared at the empty jury box for a moment and the rail separating the bar from gallery. "Walt told the kids . . ." and here I added a coat of sarcasm to my voice, "that 'he tried and tried to fix the marriage, then had to leave.' The reality is, he agreed to marriage counseling but actually quit after two sessions."

While Richard waited for me to continue, I debated whether to say more. Just below my cooperative façade, old anger stirred. I sought an answer to how, after twenty years of marriage, a man can choose to leave home, his wife and his children, live separately, gather a community of support around him, file for divorce, attempt to remove his wife from the marital residence, then falsely accuse that she is "harmful" and sue for custody of their children. At what point does this descend into absurdity?

I took a deep breath and studied my lap.

Apparently understanding I had finished, Richard changed focus. "Jane, do you view Walt as a tolerant person?"

"No. I don't."

"Would you give us a reason, some examples of what you consider Walt's intolerance?"

"You mean besides throwing the prayer book?"

"In addition to his throwing the prayer book," Richard said with a smirk that people behind him couldn't see but sure as heck encouraged me.

"Well, I'm not clear on why, maybe because God's Kitchen is in the inner city, or he thinks they don't deserve it—kinda one of those 'pull yourself up by the bootstrap' people—whatever, Walt disapproves that the kids and I bake a cake once a month and bring it to God's Kitchen."

"Maybe you can skip the why," Richard said kindly, "and just tell us the occasion."

"Sure . . . for instance, Meike and Sam and I sponsor a child in Guatemala through the Christian Foundation for Children and Aging. Each month, Meike and Sam send a one-page letter in their own handwriting. They often get a letter back from—Hernandez is his name. Walt doesn't like it. He claims we might as well throw the money out the window. He said he doesn't trust the organization because it's Catholic."

I paused shortly and then went on without prompting.

"When they were younger, I took Sam and Meike with me and my parents to visit my brother in Milwaukee. We called Walt from out of town to say hello. Given all the family visiting we'd done, during our conversation on the phone, I slipped out of English. 'Don't talk Dutch to me,' Walt said and then hung up on me.

"He doesn't want me to speak Dutch. He doesn't want me voting for Clinton. He doesn't want me to spend time writing. He doesn't want me to go to college. He doesn't want me going to the Lutheran Church . . . "

I waited long enough for Richard to indicate if I should continue. He must have been satisfied and approached another angle.

"Music is important to you and your children. Is that correct?"

"That's true. Well, music is important to me and it's important *for* Sam and Meike. They don't like to practice, of course, but then . . ." I slowed down, "children don't always know what's best for them. I believe the kids are coming to see the importance of music. They're good at it. And because of their lessons, they're growing to appreciate music more and more."

It seemed wise to stop before reminding the judge how Walt doesn't encourage their music, or before asking if anybody recognized the benefit in Sam using music as an outlet someday. All that pent-up frustration he's carried since his dad left. Or that Meike may *need* some musical expression for those intense emotions of hers PCS didn't like.

Instead, I just said, "They have excellent musical intuition."

Richard picked up on my concern. "Do you think the children are free to show their emotion . . . express their feelings when they're with Walt?"

"Not really. He tries to manage them. Walt's always wanting to fix feelings rather than just letting Sam or Meike have them." A careful listener would hear a quiver in my voice. "Walt's afraid of feelings. Mine and his own."

"Objection," Hofstra called. "The witness is conjecturing."

"My client, having lived with the Plaintiff for twenty years, is describing her experience."

"Overruled," Judge Holton granted.

After allowing everyone a moment to absorb the remarks, Richard spoke again.

"Your children, Meike and Sam, are healthy . . . talented . . . they get A's in school. They are good children."

"Yes. Yes, they are, thank you."

"Jane, do you consider it in Sam and Meike's best interest to live with you?"

"Absolutely."

Richard remained silent, and I wondered if his silence was an invitation to rail against Walt some more. I thought of how Walt always considered childcare women's work. I thought of how bad mothers don't raise good children. I thought how I wished I had served Walt that jar with bean botulism years ago.

It all seemed relevant but I said nothing and waited for my attorney.

"In your opinion, Jane, when is the most important time to be with your children?"

My answer started easily, no quivering. "First thing in the morning . . . at meal time . . . when the kids arrive home from school . . . in the evening . . . at bedtime . . ." I cleared my throat. There are homes where two people have to work to make ends meet. I went on anyway. "You don't wait for the lamb to tangle in the briers before you come around. You support and guide them on the way. You don't hover but you hang near. Hear what the children have to say to you about things as they come up."

Richard ran his hand over his tie. When he raised his brow, I took it as a call for any final word.

While I spoke, I watched my attorney closely. "When a child comes home from school bursting with excitement or news, that child will be greatly disappointed if no one's there to listen."

I checked my hands, now open and relaxed on my lap. "I'm only saying, you can't just designate a certain time, like after a meeting, after a television program, for children's—for Sam and

Meike's—disappointments or questions or hurts or wonders or jokes or whatever. Being available then and there. That's in the best interest of the children."

On returning to the defense table, Richard sat and calmly folded his large hands on top of the notepad in front of him, ballpoint set to the side. We exchanged a look. His expression carried a serious weight, but I drew encouragement from his nod.

A slight stir took place in the courtroom while people fixed a new position in their seats. Hofstra rose and stepped in front of the Plaintiff table, standing closer to Walt than to me. Walt squared his shoulders and crossed his arms with his head tilted a bit, expectant.

A patronizing smile came and went across Hofstra's face while he stepped forward, still a good distance from the witness stand. He waited a moment, looked at me with the smile returning, and began his questions.

"Jane, how often do you visit St. John's Lutheran Church?"

I thought it very odd Hofstra would bring up any church preference, given the emphasis on Walt's intolerance. And besides, Walt had been taking Meike and Sam to one of those new mega places, which was not our home church either.

"I attend services there on Sunday when the children are with Walt and from time to time with Sam and Meike."

"Do you spend time at St. John's during the week?" Hofstra asked.

"No. Well, I might hear a concert there once or twice a year."

"I see. But before you and Walt were separated, how much time were you spending at St. John's?"

Now I sensed a trap and I hesitated. "I played the piano there . . . my piano at home is a cheap spinet . . . I enjoyed the release . . . they have a beautiful grand piano in the sanctuary they let me play . . . the pastor there knew our situation."

"How often were you there?"

"Three or four times a week."

"So, quite often —"

"Objection," Richard called in irritation.

"Sustained."

"How many hours a day would you say you were at St. John's?" Hofstra asked.

"After a few hours of playing the piano my shoulders ache. Can't practice much more than that at a time." I shrugged. Curtness felt appropriate at first. Hofstra deserved it. A defensive reflex kicked in. "I was always home before school got out."

"You were at the church at least two, three hours —"

"Objection." Richard rose to his feet without hurry. His hands remained flat on the table. "Irrelevant, your Honor," he said, leaning forward. "Where is this going? Prosecution needs to get to the point."

"Sustained."

I shifted in my chair and toyed with the folds of my skirt. Hofstra took his sweet time and stepped several feet to my right. He turned and stepped far to the left, this time stopping just in front of Walt.

Staring in the air, Hofstra rubbed the back of his head. "Help me out with some history here. Am I correct, Jane, that on more than one occasion when you were a young girl, your mother was hospitalized for mental illness?"

Do you even have a mother, you son of a bitch? She's sitting right here.

"It's called depression," I said.

I slipped a desperate look toward Richard. He nodded consent. I pushed my back against the chair and lifted my chin. I planted my eyes, squinted in loathing, on the rail of the galley away from Hofstra and off of Walt, until my face relaxed.

Whether or not Hofstra delayed for some sort of added affect, or if he truly needed to evaluate his next move, the silence in the courtroom stretched until I noticed that even Walt stirred impatiently.

When at last Hofstra spoke, he rendered another topic altogether. "What are your thoughts on joint custody?"

I realized an opportunity to clarify things, and cleared my throat. "Well, first of all, I need to say that even though Walt told PCS that I would not consider joint custody, Walt and I had actually already discussed it. We both agreed that joint custody would not be a good option for us. Walt deliberately lied about that." Remembering Walt's deception, I flashed my husband a raw, challenging glare.

He looked away.

Richard picked up his ballpoint and scribbled something on the notepad.

Ignoring what I had said, Hofstra asked, "Do you consider joint custody . . . a negative?"

I lowered my eyes and straightened the folds on my skirt some more. "I've done some homework," I said despite Richard's mantra of cooperation ringing in my head.

Surveying Hofstra's demeanor, I chose words carefully—words from documented sources I have written in my spiral notebook. Words I have repeated to people a half dozen times by now. "Several articles I found reviewed cases where joint custody proved to be a disadvantage for the Best Interest of the Children. Joint custody can be confusing for kids. Back and forth, back and forth. Different rules. Nothing consistent." I took a deep breath. "There's research that shows joint custody can be a strain for the children. And multiple studies document that instead of two parents, there's none. Each parent assumes the other has taken care of things, or worse, they just hope so."

"Therefore," Hofstra pushed, "no joint custody?"

My sigh was quick but obvious. "You need to understand my disadvantage . . . Walt has little use for my perspective. And he doesn't stick up for me. Like when I took Sam's television privilege away one Friday night and Sam called him to complain. Walt says, 'Hang in there, buddy,' as if the whole idea is for Sam to tolerate me."

My frustration flushed on my face, exposed for better or worse. After a moment where Hofstra said nothing, I tried a more succinct explanation and continued. "Walt doesn't see me as legitimate, let alone an equal." Walt's attorney only looked at me blankly, stupidly. He was either staging or a birdbrain. "I've no validity in Walt's mind." My voice increased a decibel or two. "Walt dismisses me . . . he's a chauvinist . . . a bully . . . ." I shut my mouth.

Hofstra sighed as if impatient. "I am wondering, Jane, if you would consider joint custody."

Resisting any glance at Walt, I answered quietly. Answered with the best I could do. "Maybe."

Hofstra waited, flipping his hand over a couple of times, examining his fingernails. Finally, he addressed me again, offering me that patronizing smile he likely thought he'd earned a right to offer. "No doubt, we would all agree, Jane, that you love your children very much."

"Of course I do." I had gathered myself.

"Just like we agree Walt loves Sam and Meike very much."

"Okay."

Hofstra stood in front of me now. He put his hands in his pocket, jingled some keys, erased the smile. "Jane, are you bipolar?"

"It's Bipolar II," I snapped.

My eyes roamed the floor. I didn't dare look at Richard.

"Please answer the question 'yes' or 'no,'" Hofstra said. "Jane, are you bipolar?"

I allowed a pause before answering, the pause my only power.

"Yes."

Forty

The suitcase set empty on a top shelf in the bedroom closet where I had stored the thing ever since Walt had left over two and a half years ago.

I would run from here. Just leave. Move to California.

Missing my children would be easier from far away. Instead of Sam and Meike coming home on Tuesday nights and every other weekend, I would leave. Go to California.

My sacrifice. My absence a favor.

I went so far as to convince myself it was in the "Best Interest of the Children." Sure, Meike and Sam would miss me. But they were children. Eleven and twelve, for Pete's sake. How would they know what was good for them?

So many nights in the Barcalounger I weighed the possibility of leaving.

And then I would remember one of those first times after the ruling. Sam and Meike were home with me. It was a late, chilly evening. Sam was taking a long hot shower. Too long. Just as I approached the bathroom to knock and say, "Let's call it quits," I heard Sam whimpering through the closed door.

No, he wasn't whimpering, he was sobbing. Crying louder than he thought his mother could hear over the ceiling fan and the water pouring down. Outside the bathroom door, I stood with his hurt and mine until his sobbing stopped and the faucet squeaked.

I stepped into the kitchen and waited. Hair still dripping, he appeared in his blue and gold Michigan sweats. He took one look at my opening arms, stepped forward and let me hold him a long time.

Or I would remember a ringing phone at 3:30 a.m.; I picked up before the second ring, a mother's sense still attuned.

"Mom." Meike's whisper was barely audible over the line. "I can't sleep," she said between choking sobs. "I tried to wake up Dad. He won't wake up."

Oh, good, she needs me to come get her . . . Oh, good, Walt can't do this . . . Oh, good, Walt's dead . . . . I pictured him sprawled on the couch, still in his boots, dark blue work pants, light blue shirt with "Walt" printed on the pocket.

I had the courage to leave. The question was if I had the courage to stay.

Some days, I mustered the attitude that anybody who thought they'd be rid of me that easily had another thought coming.

One Thursday in September, Sam called from school. "Please Mom, I need some shorts for gym class."

I brought him clean gym shorts. I stopped at the school office afterwards, since I still was not receiving school newsletters. The secretary gave me the same old song and dance about their computer program not accommodating two-home families. I asked for Dwight Sytsma.

We stood, the Christian school principal and I, with the counter between us.

"Dwight," I said, "it appears you need to mark your own calendar to make certain all communications are sent to me. As timely as everyone else's."

"I'll make a point of it, Jane," he said. "What is your address these days?"

"The same home address you've had in the records ever since Sam and Meike started kindergarten."

It is at my insistence our divorce agreement spells out I am responsible for one-half of the tuition until the children graduate from high school, which I had been paying promptly by mail all along.

"Since I'm not mailed a receipt of any sort, I'd like to look over our tuition account while I'm here." I drew my face into a full, sweet smile. "You know, just to make certain the record's in order and all."

"I can't give a second party access to that information. The account's in Walt's name."

I pointed my chin in his face. "Second party?"

The very next day, Richard mailed a letter to Sytsma. Though it did not address how the school's fossil ideas of family affect Sam and Meike, the letter did state that Walt and I have joint legal custody and further explained what that meant for the school—insinuating what a lawsuit might look like.

Eventually, it occurred to me if Walt omitted telling the school we had joint legal custody, certainly he never told anyone else. It was not until October before I realized Sam and Meike didn't know either.

For all my resolution, on other days I fought another side.

Not for power. Not for revenge. Just plain relief.

November was worse.

I called the emergency number Jennings had given me. Twice in November. Once sometime during January, deep, deep in the night.

Jennings would say strong things to me. "Don't give Walt the satisfaction." Or "Not on my watch." Or "It matters." Or "Sam and Meike need their mother."

Then I'd find my way through the dark again.

Walt insisted we use the financial settlement his accountant had worked out. He continued to argue that his statement is what we'd originally agreed to. As often happened when talking with Walt, I began to doubt myself and called Richard to verify my understanding.

"As usual, Walt's assumptions are way off. The accountants were hired to assess, not divide," Richard confirmed.

Potential of the cement-cutting business we had started was difficult to assess. After the trial, I once ran into Michael, Walt's original business partner, in the supermarket parking lot. "He divorced me, too, you know," Michael had said in anger. "Sucker's opening a branch in Lansing and another one in Indiana—"

"Hold the invectives . . . ." I had one hand raised in traffic-cop pose, since Meike was standing right there with me.

Richard reminded me to think long range. Way long range. As in down the road at retirement age. But other than drawing on Walt's annually topped-out social security payments when I reached sixty-five, my plan was to live independently. I would never ask Walt for a damn thing again.

Besides, I was done. Depleted. Tired of Walt overrating what he did all day, tired of him sanctifying his ambitions in the name of family, tired of him failing to see I had freed him up from other responsibilities like cooking, cleaning, shopping, sewing, shoveling, music lessons, Chutes and Ladders, Kool-Aid, cookies . . . .

I would do it all again—for Sam and Meike.

No charge. No charge.

"We have to sell our boat because Dad has to pay you money," Sam told me one day.

So much not to say.

Forty-One

We were married on March 23, 1973. The divorce was finalized on March 7, 1995.

Walt had won physical custody. "In the Best Interest of the Children."

But the child never wins.

Meike seldom practiced her violin but spent whole afternoons or evenings watching Disney movies. Sam stayed up too late, trying to keep up with schoolwork after hours of television or video games. He had incomplete assignments and Walt called school to excuse him. They couldn't find the magazine-sale money. They swayed from purchase to purchase, entertainment to entertainment. They gained weight. Fast food and snacks for comfort, or boredom, or guilt, or depression.

And there's that Honorable Judge.

Meike and Sam were made to choose between the one they love and the one they love.

Dear Sam. Dear Meike. You were required to sit down in that man's chamber. Again. What you say when you are eleven or twelve is not your burden. You are not accountable for your choice. Not then. Not now. Not when you are twenty or thirty or forty or one hundred years old.

Who can pry that clamp on their conscience loose?

I will stay around.

My heart breaks when I think how theirs did.

Forgiveness is inconceivable.

I think God is crying.

Yet, Sam and Meike are Walt as much as Sam and Meike are me. We are forever attached by that same love that connected Walt and me in the first place. As long ago as that may have been, it had been.

I could hardly imagine and didn't feel myself move there, but years later, a pity for Walt knocked my animosity from first place. And I could picture a time when I would muster short breaths of indifference toward him.

Maybe someday we would sit on the same bench in the airport and together greet Meike and the grandboys. Maybe on Sam's 40th birthday we'll meet to raise a glass.

~

For eight years, Walt would pay me "alimony in gross." Not "alimony," but some sort of definition the court used to spread his monetary debt to me and give him a better tax rate.

I took one-half of the cash settlement and put it in an IRA. With the other half, I paid my attorney fees and my college tuition and replaced the Lincoln Town Car with a 1996 Saturn wagon.

And I purchased a new beautiful mahogany full upright piano.

A person with bipolar should have two pianos. A Yamaha with acoustic voice crisply provocative and bright, *and* a Kawai with tones richly mellow and deep.

I chose the Kawai.

~

Gerrit and Laura continued to invite me for dinner. I usually accepted. Often on Thursday nights, we'd meet for jazz at a nightclub. Even though I might have already popped my head into Gerrit's office at the college earlier that day, sometimes they would invite themselves over here and we'd build a fire and listen to music. No need to feign lightheartedness.

On certain days, it comes to me. Assaults me when I'm reading a textbook, listening to music, taking a shower, making lunch. I feel the dark. Visit the sinkhole.

I can do that. Walt is afraid to.

I didn't know how to teach Sam and Meike these things. Except to be there. Not run to California. Staying would help them learn not to be afraid of sadness. Or joy either. Or darkness or radiance or anger or shouting or tenderness. Not to fear silence or questions or quiet pondering.

And hope of all hopes, not to fear love.

I will move back to the city once Sam and Meike have a driver's license. Meanwhile, I continued to live in our house, always home before school let out. One never knew if Sam would ride his bike over in quest for cookies. One never knew when Meike would call and ask me to braid her hair.

As years pass, the story continues on forever—like love mothers have for their children.

In spring, I played my piano with the windows open.

And the birds sang back.

Acknowledgments

To my readers, thank you for your interest. And for the many book clubs where I have been a guest, thank you. We've had multiple and varied discussions. I treasure each of them and look forward to more.

To Independent Book Stores near and far, in all directions. You are a refuge and power to communities everywhere. Thank you for your support and your shelves.

Thank you to folks at Wipf and Stock, with special thanks to Jonathan Hill and editor, Matt Wimer.

Thank you to Monthly Monday Writers for your comments on the Saint Nicholas pages. Hugs to my good friend, Sylvia Cooper.

A huge thanks to River City Writers' for your dependable honest critique and wisdom. Cheers to Albert Bell, Greg Dunn, Dan Johnson, Lisa McAllister, Rose Martin, Paul Robinson, Sheila Shotwell, Nathan TerMolen.

Thank you to Mary Risseeuw and Will Katerberg for the opportunity, following the publication of *London Street*, to write further on themes of secrets, silence, submission and mental health.

Thank you to the people at CRC Safe Church Ministry, whom I will keep anonymous, for your assistance and research.

To Professor James Vanden Bosch for your support in this, another project—including your most thorough copyediting and your friendship—thanks Jim.

To "Dr. Jennings," with respect and gratitude. For privacy purposes, the name is fictionalized. But the role is literal, authentic and true of a real person, as are the scenes and events involved.

Thank you to Peter Kladder.

To my brothers, Arie and Gerhard, and also Kris and Merv, dearest thanks. You are so much a part of these pages. Love and appreciation to all of you always.

Thank you, Tom, for your continuous encouragement and support. I give you tender affection and kisses, along with dances and meatloaf whenever you want.

To Mark and Kate, I know you know I love you. "Now let's go home and put our slippers on like how people do."

www.ingramcontent.com/pod-product-compliance
Lightning Source LLC
Chambersburg PA
CBHW071424150426
43191CB00008B/1033

* 9 7 9 8 3 8 5 2 4 9 3 2 9 *